divergent trajectories

divergent trajectories

interviews with innovative fiction writers

flore chevaillier

THE OHIO STATE UNIVERSITY PRESS · COLUMBUS

Copyright © 2017 by The Ohio State University.
All rights reserved.

Library of Congress Cataloging-in-Publication Data
Names: Chevaillier, Flore, 1979- author, interviewer.
Title: Divergent trajectories : interviews with innovative fiction writers / Flore Chevaillier.
Description: Columbus : The Ohio State University Press, [2017]
Identifiers: LCCN 2017013731 | ISBN 9780814213438 (cloth ; alk. paper) | ISBN 081421343X (cloth ; alk. paper)
Subjects: LCSH: Authors, American—20th century—Interviews. | Authors, American—21st century—Interviews. | American fiction—History and criticism—Theory, etc. | Fiction—Authorship. | Berry, R. M.—Interviews. | Di Blasi, Debra, 1957—Interviews. | Everett, Percival—Interviews. | Field, Thalia, 1966—Interviews. | Gladman, Renee—Interviews. | Rider, Bhanu Kapil—Interviews. | Martone, Michael—Interviews. | Maso, Carole—Interviews. | McElroy, Joseph—Interviews. | Milletti, Christina—Interviews. | Olsen, Lance, 1956—Interviews. | Singer, Alan, 1948—Interviews. | Tomasula, Steve—Interviews.
Classification: LCC PS135 .C47 2017 | DDC 813/.609—dc23
LC record available at https://lccn.loc.gov/2017013731

Cover design by Thao Thai
Text design by Juliet Williams
Type set in Adobe Minion Pro and Myriad Pro

∞ The paper used in this publication meets the minimum requirements of the American National Standard for Information Sciences—Permanence of Paper for Printed Library Materials. ANSI Z39.48-1992.

9 8 7 6 5 4 3 2 1

contents

Acknowledgments   *vii*

Introduction   1

   R. M. Berry 5

   Debra Di Blasi 23

   Percival Everett 41

   Thalia Field 56

   Renee Gladman 70

   Bhanu Kapil 80

   Michael Martone 96

   Carole Maso 114

   Joseph McElroy 130

   Christina Milletti 144

   Lance Olsen 160

   Alan Singer 182

   Steve Tomasula 197

Afterword   215

Index   *219*

acknowledgments

THIS BOOK WOULD not have been possible without the remarkable work and extraordinary generosity of the thirteen authors who agreed to participate in this collection. I am grateful for their time, commitment, patience, and fascinating writing. Meeting and corresponding with R. M. Berry, Debra Di Blasi, Percival Everett, Thalia Field, Renee Gladman, Bhanu Kapil, Lance Olsen, Michael Martone, Carole Maso, Joseph McElroy, Christina Milletti, Alan Singer, and Steve Tomasula was a wonderfully enriching journey, which, I hope, translates into an even more enriching reading. I could not ask for a more generous, understanding, and intelligent group of people to work with.

The idea for this book grew out of my monograph, *The Body of Writing: An Erotics of Contemporary American Fiction,* and began to take shape after I read the inspiring essays collected in *Fiction's Present: Situating Contemporary Narrative Innovation,* edited by R. M. Berry and Jeffrey Di Leo. I am thankful for R. M. Berry's encouragement to publish a collection of interviews during the conception stages of this project. His belief in my work has always been a profound source of support.

Many thanks to Lindsay Martin, who was always available, patient, and insightful as I revised my manuscript. I am very appreciative for her enthusiasm for this project from the start and for her precious help throughout the publishing process. The entire Ohio State University Press team had many astute and practical recommendations to make the book more reader friendly. They worked extremely hard in the service of a better project, and I am thankful for their time, expertise, and professionalism.

I am remarkably lucky to have received valuable feedback from two anonymous readers whose advice and guidance have greatly improved this book. Their meticulous comments, wise suggestions, and confidence in my work are much appreciated.

I am grateful for the permission to reproduce an earlier version of the interview with Lance Olsen, "Talking with Lance Olsen: Interview with Flore Chevaillier," which appeared in *Rampike* 20.1 in March 2011.

I would also like to express my deepest thanks to my friends and colleagues Amy Hobbs Harris, Kimberly Kendricks, and Jayson Iwen, who generously offered time and ample opportunities to discuss this project. Their loyalty, commitment, encouragement, and advice were crucial to the development of this volume.

My parents, Arlette and Bruno, and my siblings, Maud and Luc, have left an inestimable mark on this book—I have shared with them, from an early age, a deep interest in adventurous arts. They have been exceptionally supportive along the way.

Last but certainly not least, Fabien, Noah, and Jackson have lived with this book for many years. I am forever indebted to the time, kindness, support, and energy they continually, selflessly, and, at times, unknowingly offered. Their presence in my life has nourished me in more ways than I can express here.

introduction

THIS BOOK PROPOSES to examine the aesthetic, political, philosophical, and cultural dimensions of contemporary fiction through a series of interviews with some of today's most cutting-edge fiction writers. Formally innovative texts are often thought of as texts that disrupt the conventions according to which readers have understood what constitutes a work of literature—pagination, orthography, print, character, narrator, and plot structures. Recently, new relationships between literature, media culture, and hypertexts have added to modes of experimentation and reshaped the boundaries between literary and pop culture media; visual arts and literature; critical theory and fiction writing; and print and digital texts. This collection of interviews undertakes such experimentations through an intimate glance, allowing readers to learn about each writer's journey as well as their aesthetic, political, and personal choices.

While I insist on the personal and intimate qualities of the interview format, I am convinced that the interview genre has possibilities extending beyond literary gossip or small talk. Consequently, the main focus of *Divergent Trajectories* is not personality issues. Writers expand on their writing process, work habits, influences, and motivations, but they also explore the political, ethic, and aesthetic issues raised in their work. More specifically, R. M. Berry, Debra Di Blasi, Percival Everett, Thalia Field, Renee Gladman, Bhanu Kapil, Lance Olsen, Michael Martone, Carole Maso, Joseph McElroy,

Christina Milletti, Alan Singer, and Steve Tomasula consider which forms of innovation might be viable today, which narrative explorations might be exhausted, and what new areas of experimentation might now be discovered. I have focused on writers' commitment to such questions over their reputation, influence, and representation.

In addition, by focusing on writers who reflect on experiments with form and content, I have omitted authors with a more conservative writing agenda. This commitment to innovation implies that contributors to *Divergent Trajectories* (re)examine central narrative assumptions and decipher new aesthetic orientations; their opinions often call for a reflection on the central logics that has produced today's fiction. Of course, the authors interviewed here have different visions on such issues. For instance, in his interview, Olsen points out that the goals of innovative writing are commonly "seen through a pessimistic optic that emphasizes its destructive, nihilistic, depressing qualities," but, to him, such writing also enables "a joy taken in the destruction because of the possibility it creates for regeneration." Berry explains: "The aim of experimental writing is not to disrupt conventions. Its aim is to find out what writing is. [. . .] I write as I do, not because I want to disrupt anything, but because I want to discover the literary medium." For Everett, "the corruption of so-called convention, or the recognition of such corruption, exploitation alteration, whether motivated by aesthetic, political, or commercial (money's not the only currency) interests, is a commitment to generic rules more rigid than an adherence to the so-called accepted conventions" ("A Modality" 211). Such divergences in opinions provide, I hope, a comprehensive view of the state of today's literary expressions.

Therefore, the title of this volume, *Divergent Trajectories*, articulates differences between each writer's viewpoint on contemporary literature as well as their divergence in artistic choices and personal habits. It also expresses writers' common goal toward a literary research that diverges from traditional paths of storytelling. Hence, this project provides a framework that allows innovative authors to discuss in some depth their works, backgrounds, formal research, thematic preferences, genre treatment, aesthetic philosophies, dominant linguistic expressions, cultural trends, and the literary canon. Several writers were unavailable when this project was designed, but the writers interviewed here represent a wide range of literary practices and opinions in recent fiction writing.

Because the formal and thematic concerns of these authors are intimately related to other postmodern art forms, my discussion with each author involves interdisciplinary explorations of literature and philosophy, history, science, technology, visual arts, genetic art, and music. To cite a few examples,

Tomasula has researched and written about genetic arts, and this artistic form appears in his fictional treatment of texts and bodies in *VAS* and *The Book of Portraiture*. Olsen's work examines the question of representation from various angles, including the use of photography in *Girl Imagined,* one of his collaborations with visual artist Andi Olsen. Di Blasi's work has engaged in multimodal arenas, involving written, audio, and visual texts in interactive multimedia projects. These multidisciplinary explorations attempt to give justice to the complexity of today's literary production and reflect on its future.

In addition, a study of formally innovative writing cannot be fulfilled without an examination of the publishing trends that affect its dissemination. Many of the authors involved in this project have fundamental roles in nontraditional publishing arenas. Berry is the former chair of the board of directors of the Fiction Collective Two, the author-run, not-for-profit publisher of artistically adventurous fiction. Olsen now holds this position. Di Blasi, the founding publisher of the multimedia publishing company Jaded Ibis Productions, ran the press from 2008 to 2015. Renee Gladman has edited Leon Works, an experimental prose chapbook series, as well as the Leroy chapbook series. Our discussion of publishing trends gives readers insights on the pragmatics of the contemporary American publishing industry that are rarely addressed in literary criticism but that are central to the evolution of experimental writing.

In the context of literary innovation, the inherent spontaneity of the interview genre is particularly fitting because it allows a practice of and reflection on the kinds of experiences formally innovative writing attempts to provoke. In fact, interviews allow collaboration and improvisation, which are central to the modes of innovation also discussed in the interviews. Moreover, research in fictional experimentation often translates into an exploration of the very modes of expressions used by the authors interviewed here. Maso and Kapil, for instance, have used formal and thematic experiments that confront patriarchal modes of storytelling, while proposing alternative modes of writing. Olsen has written "critifictions" that blur the boundaries between fiction and theory. Tomasula has probed the relationship between commodities and literature in his art books and digital texts. A questioning of the interview genre during our discussions was thus the logical development of a debate about form, content, and medium.

While the medium of the interview was not always the focus of our discussions, the actual medium used to develop our exchange had an impact on them. Some interviews were conducted live, recorded, transcribed, and edited; others evolved as email discussions; finally, some involved various modes of dialogue and correspondence. The interview with Martone, for example, uses a different medium for each set of question and answer—letter, postcard, email, Twitter, etc. Because the question of medium and materiality is so important in the fictions of *Divergent Trajectories*'s authors, it seemed logical to invite writers to choose the medium that they found the most appropriate to discuss their work. Consequently, this choice, in addition to writers' literary research and temperament, shaped the final discussions published here. In that sense, my approach to this project allowed writers to re-shape and play with the interview mode in ways that respond to the many experiments presented in their fictions. I used this method both for the recorded interviews that were revised in collaboration with each author and for the other, less traditional interview forms—electronic or multimodal.

The following thirteen discussions feature explorations of the goals and roles of formally innovative literature as well as investigations of writers' personal choices and habits. The interviews also address central literary concepts, including textuality, materiality, and sensuality; defamiliarization, experimentation, invention, and avant-garde; authorship, collaboration, appropriation, collage, and originality; theory, philosophy, narrative, reality, and history; capitalism, publishing trends, and cultural movements; and technology and new media. Thus, beyond their appeal as individual interviews, these discussions form an assemblage that reflects recent literary developments in the United States.

The interviews compiled here were conducted over a fairly wide period of time, so several authors revisited their discussions later in the process; others worked in a more concentrated manner. Details on the parameters of each exchange are presented in the introduction to each interview. The introductory sections include bibliographical information that, I hope, will be a useful starting point for readers who wish to find out more about the writers showcased here. The listed works by and on these authors are, in many cases, not comprehensive, as they were selected based on the themes addressed in the interviews. In this context, they are meant to represent the major works by each author and a range of perspectives on them in relation to the matters discussed in the conversations that follow.

work cited

Everett, Percival. "A Modality." *Fiction's Present: Situating Contemporary Narrative Innovation*. Ed. R. M. Berry and Jeffery Di Leo. Albany: State U of New York P, 2007. 209–12. Print.

r. m. berry

R. M. BERRY IS A PROFESSOR OF ENGLISH AT FLORIDA STATE UNIVERSITY AND WAS PUBLISHER OF FICTION COLLECTIVE TWO (FC2) FROM 1999 TO 2007. HIS FIRST COLLECTION OF SHORT FICTIONS, *PLANE GEOMETRY AND OTHER AFFAIRS OF THE HEART*, WAS CHOSEN BY ROBERT COOVER AS WINNER OF THE 1985 FICTION COLLECTIVE PRIZE. HIS NOVEL, *LEONARDO'S HORSE*, WAS A NEW YORK TIMES "NOTABLE BOOK" IN 1998.

FOR YEARS NOW, I have been focused on the intrusion of the word *nowhere* in sentences. Sometimes, I e-mail copies of these intrusions as presents to R. M. Berry since my quest started after I read his essay "Is There a Language Problem?" published in 2004 in the *Electronic Book Review*. In the essay, Berry notes:

> I find for myself that I am easily tempted to pronounce 'nowhere' by analogy with 'novice' and 'nothing,' that is, by disregarding possibilities such as 'no' 'vice' and 'no' 'thing,' rather than by analogy with 'notate' and 'noblest,' and I only need gaze at the word for a few seconds for it to start behaving like the duck/rabbit, flashing convulsively back and forth before my eyes, now here one moment, no where the next.

For Berry, "the word 'nowhere' [...] has long been a source of wonder" because it expresses the "educational potential of [...] present-ness." ("Is There a Language Problem"). Like him, I have always been fascinated by words like *nowhere*, perhaps because, as a nonnative English speaker, I had to ask when learning English, "Why do we say this word this way?" In a Wittgensteinian and Cavellian tradition, Berry's interest in *nowhere* relies on the fact that "the obstacle to knowledge is no longer anything we don't know" but in "the conventions that make us what we are" (Berry, "What is a Narrative" 18).

Berry's own works include quite a few *nowheres*. In the middle of *Frank* (2005), an "unwriting" of Mary Shelley's *Frankenstein*, we find three pages on which the words *this, now,* and *here* appear. These pages are followed by "stink of mire spike of scum little light at the edge of wordswarming muck & bloodrustle, stay tuned, Maker! Hear nome spieling still to come" (85; 87). These words are the beginning of a monstrous creation that Frank Stein, cousin of Gertrude Stein, has written and rejects. Berry's parody of Shelley's epistolary mode and mannered formality collides with the contemporary frustrations of academic life. This collision asks questions about what it means to write and unwrite a novel, or, more broadly, what fiction is.

Frank's narrator explores "unwrit[ing]" (13), "undoing" (14), "unplot[ing]" (15), "unfolding" (19), and "unburden[ing]" (181) so that the novel becomes an exploration of the removal, release, and depravation of writings, doings, plots, folds, and burdens that cannot quite be reversed. While there is something monstrous about this removal or release, there is also much humor involved in the process. In the opening letter to his sister Marge, the narrator notes that he "attempted to read the whole Norton of Anthology of English Literature. Just like Gertrude Stein said she did, and [he] still [doesn't] believe she's telling the truth" (2). We find, in *Leonardo's Horse* (1997), similar witty situations when the narrator, R, attempts to clarify his marital status (or the lack of thereof): "Deidre and I were 'divorced.' I suppose I should speak less 'absolutely,' say we were still 'joined.' But if our 'life together' ever becomes 'contained' like that, 'I' 'dread' the 'unspeakable' 'deed' that will 'certainly' be 'necessary' to set 'us' """"""""""""""""free"""""""""""""""" (228). Berry's collections of fiction, *Plane Geometry and Other Affairs of the Heart* (1985) and *Dictionary of Modern Anguish* (2000) are also humorous in their absurd episodes, surprising juxtapositions, exaggerations, or impossible situations.

Yet, in their humorous extremeness, these strange texts are also uncomfortably plausible. The narrator of "Second Story," for example, concludes: "As far as I can tell, nothing remotely like 'Second Story' has ever been written. For this reason I call it a novel" (Berry, *Dictionary* 40). "Pretense" starts with "Cleo had always seemed wise beyond her years, for until she turned sixteen she'd never really lived. Or so she recalls" (*Dictionary* 41). These witty instances point out the gaps in language that make us smile but also reveal, more seriously, how we take linguistic expressions for granted. *Dictionary of Modern Anguish* stresses language's inadequacy through parodies of book reviews, prefaces to books, and ads; narratives of dictionary entries; and a series of amiss quests: a scholar's reconstruction of Beckett's legacy after the discovery of a thousand-page realist novel, an anthropologist's eager study of cruelty, a bitter scholar's suspicious telling of his failures. The collection's absurd situations, unreliable narrators, wordplays, and experimental pagination lead us to ask ourselves, after all, what *is* language?

We go through this line of inquiry when we read "Knott Unbound." The story mentions Knott's struggles with recollection in a pointedly absurd way:

> That the missing time should be missing from *his* life seemed, if you thought about it, the merest of accidents, like bad genes or rich parents, and the thought that Knott's well-being rested on nothing surer, nothing but the likelihood that his every second would follow the preceding with no break, all this struck him as fantastically irrational. How did humans abide it? (Berry, *Dictionary* 145–46)

Here, Knott's amusing and sinister situation questions our sense of time and timelessness. What is both frustrating and exhilarating about this questioning is that, instead of transcending our everyday sense of time or language, we examine the nature of our daily lives, what is right in front of us, what was just there throughout.

Thus, Berry reminds us that the "significance of a writer's work [is] not located in anything new it had to tell us," a point that comes up in the following electronic interview. The beginning of our discussion starts with his qualification of today's fiction in *Fiction's Present: Situating Contemporary Narrative Innovation* (2007), the collection of essays that also initiated this collection of interviews. In *Fiction's Present*, Berry and Jeffrey Di Leo invited fiction writers, theorists, and critics to explore "both the current state of literature and its criticism and connections between contemporary philosophy and contemporary fiction" (xi). More specifically, the writers of *Fiction's Present* ponder "whether fiction that continue[s] in the tradition of modernist innovation still ha[s] any reality for emergent political groups and cultures" and "whether the novel [can] react to the present demands of global capitalism without abandoning its formal distinctiveness" (xi). After reading writers' answers to such questions, I became interested in further exploring and requalifying some of the matters brought up in the essays, while also allowing readers to learn about contemporary authors' artistic choices. In the case of R. M. Berry's work, these choices involve matters of time, narration, philosophy, the physical qualities of writing, publishing, and politics. The following discussion is the result of a stimulating back-and-forth of e-mails from 2009 to 2010.

•

In the introduction to Fiction's Present *that you wrote with Jeffrey Di Leo, you point out that "recent military, economic, and environmental threats demand more direct forms of verbal intervention." What "forms of verbal intervention" have you developed in your own work in response to such threats?*

I believe there's a slight misreading in your question, one that really doesn't affect the sense but that, in order to avoid confusion, I need to correct. In Jeffrey's and my intro, we did not "point out that 'recent military, economic, and environmental threats demand more direct forms of verbal intervention.'" We merely noted that "many feel" these threats call for greater directness, that is, for forms of expression—that is, essays, journalism, documentaries—in which these threats are treated as explicit topics or represented content. Although I do believe that greater directness—in some form—is needed in fiction at present, Jeffrey's and my way of broaching this issue established a critical distance from those making such a demand: first, by suggesting that it has a vague or uncritical understanding of what "more direct forms of verbal intervention" would look like, and, second, by suggesting that its sense of an unprecedented level of threat is provincial and melodramatic. Where this leaves us is with an acknowledged demand for greater directness that cannot be satisfied in the terms in which it is being made.

Your question, of course, is itself quite candid and clear, obviating what the anonymous "many" may or may not feel and making my quibbles irrelevant. You ask: "What 'forms of verbal intervention' have you developed in your own work in response to such threats?" I can't myself provide any adequate account of how my attempts to develop "more direct forms of verbal intervention" may relate to the concrete threats people face today, and so I will just refer you to my introduction ("Writing in the Present") in the anthology *Forms at War* (U of Alabama: 2009). In those pages I try to make somewhat more concrete how I see formally innovative fiction, or the kind I care about, addressing the events leading up to and accompanying the Afghanistan and Iraq wars.

However, the larger question of verbal directness is, to my mind, the one on which I have been working as a fiction writer my whole life. I believe the key to answering it is to see that there are always two actions in a fiction, the action narrated and the action of narrating it. The significance of any story is a function of their relationship, which can be either very close or very distant but is, and I believe has always been, fundamental for our experience of novels. My own fiction is an attempt to come up with ways in which the closeness of these two actions is maximized, almost to the point of indistinguishability at times. This can occur in particular sentences or phrases: for example, "I couldn't tell what was happening," a remark that seems simultaneously to recount someone's past confusion in the midst of an event and also to repudiate the narrator's position as such. It can even occur in particular words (e.g., *account* or *relate*) or in material features of a book or page or font (e.g., the use of newspaper columns in my fiction "Second Story"). But I like best to come up with situations in which narrating is itself part of what has created the narrated situation, that is, the problem, crisis, conflict, or predicament. If you ask me why I believe that this tendency of narrated action to be overcome by the act of narration is necessarily a more direct form of verbal intervention, the answer is simple: actions speak louder than words.

While your work maximizes the closeness of the "action narrated" and the "action of narrating it," this relationship is, as you mention, "fundamental for our experience of novels." Then, is there a difference between contemporary explorations of this relationship and past explorations?

Yes, I believe there is a difference between present and past explorations of the relationship between the narrating and the narrated. Of course, here I feel the need to add a long and tedious qualifying paragraph, insisting that I don't mean that no one writing in 2009 writes as those in 1909 wrote, nor that everyone writing in 2009 or 1909 writes or wrote alike, nor even that the present difference I have in mind is missing from all or most fictions written in 1909, and so on. When I speak of a difference between present and past writing, I am speaking in both evaluative and descriptive terms. Evaluatively, I mean that the works that I believe to be of the present exhibit this difference, and descriptively, I mean that what makes these works different is their exhibition of the present. I don't think I'm ready to attempt a general statement about this difference yet, or not one to which I would want to be held, but I suspect that when or if I feel ready I will describe the difference in terms of the book, by which I mean the still dominant form of technology for literary texts. In other words, present explorations of the relation between the narrating and the narrated seem to me likely to approach the present through various discoveries of how narrating is done on paper. To my mind, this means disclosing the narrative significance of such commonplace facts as, for example, that print is displayed flat on a material field of limited size, requiring contrast between black figures and a white background, utilizing bound together leaves or folds, such that the story literally unfolds, with its development occurring left to right, in a series of equal-sized portions that are numbered sequentially, and so on. There's more to say here but I suspect that at present there is a much greater need than in, say, 1930 or 1950 to account for these seemingly accidental material conditions of our artistic medium, since they no longer have the status of nature for us. Electronic and visual media have put an end to that. In my writing I'm always looking for ways to show how what I am doing, or its significance, is a function of its being in a book.

Here you mention the "seemingly accidental material conditions of [the] artistic medium," an idea that you have also explored in previous essays. In "The Present of Fiction," you compare "fiction's bookishness" to "human's corporality": this "bookishness" "resemble[s] toothaches or migraines" that are "too close to us, too unstinting and inseparable from the fabric of experience itself." In "Writing in the Present," you remind us of Gerald Bruns's idea that "our words exist closer to us than representations, as 'close' as our skin." I can't help but trace the corporeal images that taint your depiction of language, of the fictional medium, and of artistic materials.

You are certainly correct that for me the comparison of my language to my body has become unavoidable. Part of what strikes me is the odd combination of closeness and alienness in my experience of both. I can forget my body in the same way that I can forget my words, by becoming absorbed in what I'm saying, for example, but if I'm recalled to material reality, I have the feeling of having known I was there all along, having never imagined I was anywhere else. It's like being caught in a self-deception. You always knew what you were doing, and yet somehow you didn't know, somehow you fooled yourself. And being recalled to my body or words usually takes the form of a mistake, accident, or misstep. It is often accompanied by pain or embarrassment. Although I don't think I can fail to know that I have a body or a language, I'm not sure that means I know I have either.

Dictionary of Modern Anguish deals with some of the comparisons you make here. The collection explores invasions, abrasions, cuts, reshapings, mishaps, and abortions of the body, language, and discourses. Could you say more about the relationship between the physical and linguistic in these stories?

Well, the most important thing I could say, which probably wouldn't be very helpful, is that the most successful of these stories manage to make the materiality of the book surprising. I have in mind the footnote in Samuel Beckett's *Middlemarch* that references itself or the typewriter typeface in "Mimesis," which provides the basis for one of the narrator's comparisons or the ambiguous reference of the word *this*, which begins "Abandoned Writing Projects." In all of these cases something that is normally accidental to literature, merely part of its physical vehicle or material support, turns out to be essential, part of its meaning or significance. I don't think that anyone can feel that the font in "Mimesis" is particularly significant in and of itself, although we're aware that the narrator is typing. But, for me, the one brief comparison of the soulless typing machine to the blind man has something eerie about it, as though in reading I abruptly feel blind to something, or perhaps mechanical, or as though material reality possessed a soul I'd failed to see. Of course, significance of this kind, if one recognizes it, will feel like a kind of mishap, as you say, since it is something to which the narrator is wholly oblivious. In general, *Dictionary of Modern Anguish* is full of stories in which mistakes (or abortions) are the means by which meaning is revealed—or created.

I was thinking of the physical not only in relation to the materiality of the book but also in relation to your previous comments on the body. Could you expand on that aspect of the physical in Dictionary of Modern Anguish?

Well, I probably can't say much without greater thought than I have patience for at this instant, but if I could, my comments would have to do with how deeply into our bodies (reflexes, kinesthetic responses, sensations, throat musculature, etc.) our language penetrates. Think of all of the involuntary bodily responses you have to certain words, everything from getting sexually aroused to cringing at a grammar mistake or squirming in your seat or tensing your muscles. If you're trying to think of the right word, do you ever actually try to feel for it, I mean with your body, even at times trying to feel "where" it's located "inside" you? I trust I won't sound mad if I acknowledge doing such things. I hoped that in *Dictionary* readers might sometimes feel themselves trying to get situated physically while reading it, as though they weren't sure just where they were relative to the text. I'm thinking of the way that you can find yourself physically trying to adjust your position as you look at a painting by Cézanne.

Do these material and physical aspects of reading and writing relate to your play with pagination in Frank, Plane Geometry, *and* Leonardo's Horse? *I am thinking specifically about the pages where NOWHERE and NOW HERE appear in* Frank *and the use of visual texts in* Plane Geometry *and* Leonardo's Horse.

I dream of making every part of a book expressive and significant. What would it be like for an author to *mean* the whiteness of the page? Any time that one of the conventions of printing is violated, the question arises why one ever does things in the conventional way. At that moment, the author is challenged to justify his or her decisions, to make them count. Or put another way, only when conventions cease to be conventions and become options does following them become a decision. When one *decides* to compose her novel on paper, rather than doing it because that's simply what composing a novel is, then the question of the significance or meaning of composing on paper, as opposed to composing on, for example, sand, a computer screen, film, canvas, wood, first arises. At that point, meaning the convention becomes possible. The test of whether one really means the whiteness of the page is whether or not there is now in one's writing a significance to the page being white, whether the whiteness carries an importance that other textures and hues and materials wouldn't. Anyway, the answer to your question above is that in the works you've mentioned above, I'm trying to figure out how to mean the book as a material object, one with such characteristics or properties as flatness, squareness, blankness, colorlessness—and whatever word you would use to describe the availability of some material objects for receiving figures that can be seen as such by the human eye.

Much like your fictions, your answers to my questions have affinities with Wittgenstein's work. Why and how is he an influence on your writing?

In many ways, Wittgenstein's *Philosophical Investigations* is the book that taught me how to write. Or how I wanted to write. Partly, this is because of the writing techniques Wittgenstein employs, especially techniques of literalization, materialization, and abstraction, and partly, it is because Wittgenstein shows the significance of these techniques, in particular within the context of a pervasive, all but universal, human alienation. In Wittgenstein's work, every subject discovers that she is herself at the source of life's problems. This discovery does not mean that material limits, bodily suffering, and social injustices are negligible, but it does mean that neither an individual nor a society can overcome any limitations, pains, or injustices that she/it feels compelled to misconceive. Wittgenstein's writing is aimed at a situation in which the representation of any problem is part of the problem, not primarily because one misrepresents every problem but because one lives as though one's relation to every problem were a matter of representing or misrepresenting it. The modernist turn in Wittgenstein's writing is its awareness of itself as a kind of action, an action that the agent doesn't understand and, at pain of absolute failure, must figure out, subject to experimentation, rediscover. It is a cliché to say that Wittgenstein subjects all language, including his own, to critique. It comes closer to the truth to say that Wittgenstein subjects all critique, including his own, to critique. The surprise is that the result of this severity is a human life.

My close friend Mark Cooper, the film critic at the University of South Carolina, once asked me to which of two ancient figures my writing and thinking conformed, chiasmus or litotes. The former occurs when a grammatical or narrative sequence is juxtaposed with its formal or logical opposite, as in "The more precise his language became, the further from the truth his meaning wandered." Some critics cite the plot of *King Lear* as an example of chiasmus, since the good and bad characters' fortunes seem to cross, as though in parallel descending and ascending lines. The second figure, litotes, occurs when a positive statement results from making a negative statement about a negation, as in "Language is far from a meaningless signifier." I was surprised by the quickness and confidence of my reply to Mark. I said my work took the form of litotes. My conviction arose, I believe, from my intuition that the goal of my writing and thinking is the recovery of nature, an experience or achievement that, if it is to occur at all, must occur immediately and beyond possibility of question. This can only be the case when every criticism, every doubt has been shown to be senseless, so that one no longer has any idea what he or she would be doing if she were to try to question, doubt, criticize. One of Wittgenstein's achievements was to show that doubting is as difficult as believing. That we imagine doubt to be what remains when our actions prove groundless reveals our modern naiveté. In a sentence, Wittgenstein showed me that intellectual work in the context of modernity is unrepression. It is our religion.

This is one of your longest answers, and I have been thinking about the conciseness of your answers so far, of what it might imply about who you are as a writer, thinker, and person.

I do regard the conciseness of my responses as something of an accomplishment. When my ideas are only half formed, I tend to go on much longer, which was characteristic of my way of speaking and writing when I was younger. I still fall back into it at times, when I'm caught off guard or am tired or think I know more than I do. In general, when I know what I'm talking about, I can hit the nail on the head. When I can't, I'd rather keep my mouth shut or, which amounts to the same thing, erase what I've written. There are too many people eager to spout off worthless opinions for me to feel comfortable when I sound like just one more. Every word should count.

Does the idea of "unrepression" you mention in the context of Wittgenstein's work relate to your "unwriting" of Mary Shelley's Frankenstein *in* Frank? *I'd like for you to expand on this practice of "unwriting," but I am also interested in it because, as a French speaker, I've played with translations of this word. As you* may know, there is no equivalent in French, and in trying to explain the unwriting process to my French colleagues, I struggled with the coining of a new term, flirting with Derrida's "sous-rature." Nothing quite fits, and this wrestling with "unwriting" became part of my understanding of it.

There are essentially two ways of viewing the putative groundlessness of modern or postmodern existence. One is that all action is historical, constituting a commentary or interpretation of past action. We live in the present by continuously reconceiving what we were doing when living in the past. The underlying idea is that the past is an unfulfilled promise that looks to the future for its realization. This is more or less Hegel's idea, and it inhabits Heidegger and hermeneutic philosophy. Joyce's mature writing derives from it. The other way of viewing groundlessness is that, at bottom, action is natural, a present venture about which nothing meaningful can be said. We are condemned to live in the past by trying to represent, verbally or otherwise, what we do in the present. The underlying idea is that the narrative of unfulfilled promise eliminates presentness, which exists only with the cancellation of indebtedness to past and future. This is more or less Kierkegaard's idea, and it inhabits Wittgenstein, at least on Stanley Cavell's reading of him. Gertrude Stein's work from *Melanctha* on derives from it, and Lyotard's aesthetics explicates it. Ultimately, I think these two accounts of ungrounded existence are the same, but the former appears by turns tragic and comic, whereas the latter oscillates between stoic and ecstatic.

My writing is formed by the second, so its goal is to eliminate the need for writing. The idea is that all narratives are naturalizations. We tell a story to explain how something we would not have anticipated, believed, or approved comes to be. The need for narrative is, therefore, our need to recover a nature from which we feel alienated. I think that this is true regardless of whether the narrative is fictional or historical, and it explains why we get such pleasure from narratives that end badly. Ultimately, the pleasure (or satisfaction, relief, peace) is in being able to see how a world that feels unsuited to me could have resulted from the same conditions I resulted from. Already, this description of narration inaugurates an unwriting, since it deprives narration itself of naturalness, making it a response to particular circumstances. The turn that at a point in my artistic development I began to make occurred when I recognized that narratives weren't just representations of actions; they were actions themselves. At that point the groundlessness of all action meant that either I was narrating to realize the unfulfilled promise of past narration or, assuming narrating wasn't just natural, I was narrating to displace what was presently happening to me. The goal in both cases was to stop narrating.

The problem of translating the word "unwriting" is that, while it is a negation, it is also active. The word "writing" is a verb in substantive drag, as though the present imperfect named an object. When I call *Frank* an unwriting, am I describing a thing or an event? *Sous-rature* seems, at least to my imperfectly French understanding, to lose the verb altogether. I want to say that "unwriting" is something one must do. But then I admit that it is also the result of one's undoing.

Here, in the twenty-first century, we cannot in good conscience say the word *nature*. Therefore, unrepression, unwriting is as close as we can get. Nature is what, in a traditional age or organic society, we would call action that in our own age can only be unrepressed, unwritten, uncontained, released—except that in the mythic past no one ever needed to because nothing needs saying, nothing said would help.

In "Second Story," you write, "nothing seems harder than to tell what isn't happening," which is part of the narrator's realizations or admissions about the "Second Story" (Dictionary 39). *The phrase itself, I think, also relates to what you've been explaining about your writing. When I came across it, this statement struck me both as serious and funny. The two negations and the fact that I had to slow down to figure out what the sentence was saying felt playful and witty, especially since, at this point, the story that I was reading was more and more out of control, exploding or dissolving, but in a way that was very humorous. At the same time, of course, the fact that "nothing seems harder than to tell what isn't happening" isn't really a joke.*

I have greatest confidence in my writing when it approaches an insane condition in a sober and unstrained manner. In general, I am inspired by circumstances that seem perfectly obvious, even ordinary, and at the same time puzzling or mad. Such predicaments frequently strike us as funny weird, approaching the sublime or profound, but sometimes also as funny haha.

One infinite source of such predicaments involves something consistently, habitually, or unnoticeably absent. For example, it rarely strikes us that we have five fingers, not four or six. Everyone knows that we don't have four or six, and so it feels impossible to be surprised by that fact, and yet, if you actually imagine a situation in which someone *discovers* that she has five fingers, not four or six, you experience a kind of giddiness, vertigo, or confusion. Such a situation might involve giving piano lessons to a child missing a finger on each hand or trying to grasp a handle designed for two opposable thumbs. In such cases we discover something that is always the case—that is, I am always using my hands in ways specific to beings with five, not four or six, fingers—

but that is hidden from notice by the absence of contrasting conditions that almost never occur.

The context that goes without saying is our ordinary human context, and I'm interested in situations that require that context to be made explicit. Whenever such situations occur, we're surprised to discover how hard it is to know what a human being is, how surprising is the knowledge of what we are at every minute.

Literature is essentially the self-knowledge of human beings, but such self-knowledge is always difficult and often painful because we acquire it only when our humanity is shaken. Tragedy is a literary genre about humans trying to be more than human, and satire is a genre about humans trying to be less than human. Both genres can have their sublime or ecstatic versions, and language always becomes very interesting under such extreme pressure.

Do you think that this approach to fiction writing has been consistent throughout your career or have you seen changes in your approach over the past twenty years?

This question, whether I've always written the same way or whether my way of writing has changed, has been one I've asked myself many times. Sometimes I think that I've always approached fiction writing the same way and that the only change has been my awareness of it. If I had to date my awareness, I'd say that it began in the late '80s, early '90s, and that by the time I'm writing the stories in *Dictionary of Modern Anguish*, roughly 1995 to 1998, I'm describing my practice in the same way that I'm describing it here. However, I tend to think that my way of writing itself changed. What changed it was my becoming aware of what I'd always been doing, or trying to, with the result that I started discarding material that a decade earlier I would've kept. Everything came to depend on my ability to bring to the surface, to make explicit, conditions that were always, but invisibly or unnoticeably, present. I realize that in the previous paragraph I spoke of conditions that were always (hence unnoticeably) absent, and now I'm speaking of their being always (hence unnoticeably) present, but I don't see much difference. The point is that my work focused on things that, being who we are, we couldn't just lack information about. The best examples involve pains to which we've become so accustomed that we don't feel them, or not as pains.

So, I think I write differently now, even though the best parts of what I was doing thirty years ago were already doing what I'm trying to do now, and I'm sure that I understand what I'm doing differently than I did thirty years ago. At the same time, I recall having once found in something I'd written decades earlier an idea I'd for the first time encountered only recently. That has left me with the disorienting suspicion that I've always been repeating myself, that my every idea has been from the beginning, that my sense of discovery is merely my endless forgetting who I've been.

Could you say more about your writing process itself? How do you "bring to the surface . . . make explicit, conditions that were always, but invisibly or unnoticeably, present"? Does this process come to you as a surprise? Do you have to work at it in some ways? Does it happen when you write or when you don't write? Is it a different process for each of your books? Perhaps you can't single out this process as a single moment of realization, but I'd like to know about it in more practical terms . . .

There's a story that is sometimes told by philosophers of science about the attempt to distinguish genetic disposition from environmental variables. You take the seeds of a plant and put them into every different type of soil in every different type of climate. In some places the plant grows to four feet high, while in others it grows to five feet or only grows to two, but nowhere does the plant ever grow taller than eight feet. So, even though the plant's height varies depending on the environment, its genetic disposition determines its maximum height of eight feet. Then one day someone sends a rocket to the moon and plants the seed there. It promptly grows to ten feet.

The interest of the story is that no one thinks of the planet earth as an environmental variable. That's because earth is our continuous frame of reference, the context in relation to which everything that makes sense makes sense. Like the experience of visiting a centuries-old house in which the doors and beds are scaled to shorter bodies than ours, stories of this kind bring to the surface of our awareness conditions that are always present, always stable, always constitutive of who we are. Such conditions comprise the form of our consciousness—for example, we see everything from the standpoint of creatures who stand our height—not its content, and so we know everything by means of them without actually knowing them. However, in particular circumstances, they can become the content of consciousness. Usually those circumstances involve a fundamental change of conditions or the discovery of a new world.

As I've described it, bringing the formative constituents of our experience to the surface of consciousness could occur in any story that imagines those forms to be different from what they normally are. All the storyteller must do is consistently and scrupulously describe all the ways in which our experience would be changed by this difference. If the storyteller imagines distance or sex or butterflies from the standpoint of a boy who *discovers* ice, the storyteller will be imagining experiences in which our modernity plays little part. It will be as though the form of our normal world had become an object, a variant or other we can discern against a contrasting background. So, for example, if Samuel Beckett wrote the novel that, in our world, George Eliot wrote, then that would mean the novels influenced directly and indirectly by Eliot would not have been written in the ways that, in our world, they have been, and so the writers that, in our world, influenced Beckett would not have written the works that influenced him. Our Beckett would become just one version of Beckett, contrasting with another Beckett who, for example, knew James Joyce only as a minor writer.

When Brian McHale describes the postmodern novel as ontological, he has in mind the process I've just described. By altering the formative conditions of knowledge or experience, a whole new world can be imaginatively projected, bringing the limits and conditions of our own world into sharp relief. However, my work since *Dictionary of Modern Anguish* has been trying to take a further step. That step begins with the question of what happens when the formative conditions that one alters are those of narrative, literature, language, or fiction itself? In other words (a commonplace phrase that, in this context, abruptly instances the process I'm describing), what if the formative conditions we wish to make into an object, a variant contrasting with new or changed conditions, are those that comprise what the reader and writer are presently doing? How can the form of one's *present* action or experience or consciousness become conscious?

What I'm describing is the process of reading in other words as though in other words. The words I have in mind are obviously nowhere to be found, not unless now here, but if asked what I have in mind, I can't tell. Narration seems to be approaching a limit, or consummation, as though once and for all arriving each instant at itself. To describe this writing as writing about writing describes it instead of writing. There's no end to all that's missing. Every present's a gift.

Are you working on a new project right now?

I'm always working on a new project, although I'm never sure which one or how many. My immediate attention is on a book I've almost finished about modernism and Wittgenstein, although I haven't written anything on it since early spring. In the meantime I've finished an essay and am right now working on a book review. I need to finish these projects before returning to fiction in the way I want, although I continue to fiddle with fiction in the idle moments between other activities. Lately I've considered the idea of another book of interrelated short fictions, and I've never finished my novel about a voice in a box, which is the project to which I'll return after finishing the Wittgenstein book. I also have made initial sketches for a book about nothing, or about Nothing, based on the form of consumer guides, which I hope to finish eventually, as well as a book about my final, unfinished work. I think that one's called *White*.

And, of course, I must finish this interview.

From 1999 to 2007, you were the publisher of Fiction Collective Two. Could you say something about your work with the press and the ways in which you think of today's publishing industry?

Basically, my goal at FC2 during those years was to create an intellectual community around the question of what fiction is. My belief is that this question is a concrete, practical question, more like the question of what will bridge a chasm or how to behave morally around a drug addict than like questions about the definition of art or beauty. Practical questions regularly draw people into discussion and collaboration, even people who, like engineers or social workers, may not think of themselves as intellectuals. Along with Brenda Mills, the managing editor of FC2 during those years, I felt that publishers should be more like community organizers than like proofreaders or promoters or writing contest judges, and the way to turn an aggregate into a community, or so I thought and think, is to engage the members in a shared effort or project. Our project was to discover literature, and to do that, literature can no longer be a given; it must be a question.

I felt that we made real progress during that period, bringing a number of intellectually engaged and curious writers to the press, establishing a custom of gathering for conference panels, of interacting with each other in serious aesthetic discussion and debate, and of contributing to forums and special issues of journals, and so forth, and I was proud that FC2 became known, not as a press that published good writing, which is, of course, what virtually every press does or believes it does, but rather as a press that published a distinctive kind of writing, a kind that could not just as well be published somewhere else. At the same time, I don't think we ever got to the point where Brenda's and my idea of a publishing house as an intellectual community could really survive very well on its own, and I regret that. Any independent, alternative artistic project needs to be as much a political reality as an artistic one, creating a dispersed and living vision of itself that does not depend on any particular individual or inner circle, and even though Brenda and I weren't necessary to the survival of FC2, which continues today just fine, we did remain necessary to our version of it. Or so it seems to me now.

The biggest difference between our version of FC2 and any other literary publisher, either trade or nonprofit, is that other publishers think of writers as individuals. That is, they see each one as a unique talent whose work derives from his or her own imaginative vision and personality, and they see the history of writing as a series of these unique productions, a succession of masterpieces created by geniuses. Needless to say, such a view can make no sense of the obvious fact that these individual geniuses produced works that appear to us sufficiently interrelated that we call them novels or fiction or poems or literature or whatever we call them. There is something Stein and Joyce have in common that differentiates them from Matisse and Stravinsky, however much they may have learned from Matisse and Stravinsky, and this thing they have in common is the reason we call them writers, not painters or musicians. I believe that the whole value of any publishing project, or of an avant-garde or literary alternative, is that they make the question of what writing, literature, fiction, poetry, texts, or language *is* into a real question. If it weren't for experimental writing today, that question would cease to be real and become academic.

To ask this question, the fictions published by Fiction Collective Two, or other avant-garde presses, often alter, corrupt, disrupt, or challenge traditional modes of storytelling and conventional language uses. Some readers and critics consider the need or wish to disturb conventions just as dogmatic and rigid as these conventions. Percival Everett's essay, "A Modality," in Fiction's Present *humorously hints at this paradox, for example (209–12). What do you think of this perception of formally innovative writing?*

I think that experimental writing will appear to be following a dogmatic requirement only if you do not recognize its aim. The aim of experimental writing is not to disrupt conventions. Its aim is to find out what writing is, and whenever it succeeds in doing this, it disrupts conventions. People who feel that radically innovative writing is formulaic are focusing exclusively on what it doesn't do. Their normal expectations are not being met; they feel annoyed; they decide it's a pointless defiance. It's like imagining that someone talking on a cell phone is deliberately ignoring you, not caught up in another conversation.

Part of this confusion results from the two senses of questioning. To question someone's authority is not the same as asking a question of someone authoritative. One difference is that only the second kind of questioning expects to get an answer. I think that experimental writing is more like this second kind of questioning. It isn't just a free-floating suspicion, an attitude of distrust or irony. It's an attempt to find something out. However, unlike asking a question of someone in authority, experimental writing has no one but itself to question, no one in a more authoritative position than its own to ask what it is. In this sense it's more like the young person who is discovering what sex is, how his or her own body responds, what certain experiences feel like. No one else can find out any of this for you. But the question you have is a real question, and the knowledge you seek is real, too.

I write as I do, not because I want to disrupt anything but because I want to discover the literary medium. The difference between myself and a more traditional writer is that I don't think the literary medium is known.

works cited

Berry, R. M. *Dictionary of Modern Anguish*. Tallahassee: Fiction Collective Two, 2000. Print.

———, and Jeffrey Di Leo, eds. *Fiction's Present: Situating Narrative Innovation*. Albany: State U of New York P, 2007. Print.

———, ed. *Forms at War: FC2 1999–2009*. Tuscaloosa: U of Alabama P, 2009. Print.

———. *Frank*. Portland: Chiasmus Press, 2005. Print.

———. "Is There a Language Problem?" *Electronic Book Review*. N.p., 21 Oct. 2004. Web. 3 April 2016.

———. "On Freeing Words." *NewPages*. N.p., 2005. Web. 3 Apr. 2016.

———. "The Present of Fiction." *Electronic Book Review*. N.p., 1 Sept. 2002. Web. 3 Apr. 2016.

———. "What is a Narrative Convention? (Wittgenstein, Stanley Cavell and Literary Criticism)." *Narrative* 3.1 (1995): 18–32. Print.

further works by and on r. m. berry

Berry, R. M. "Afterword." *Criticism after Critique: Aesthetics, Literature, and the Political*. Ed. Jeffrey Di Leo. New York: Palgrave, 2014. 209–15. Print.

———. "The Avant-Garde and the Question of Literature." *Soundings: An Interdisciplinary Journal* 88.1–2 (2005): 105–27. Print.

———. "Did The Novel Die? (And Would We Know?)." *Rain Taxi* 11.1 (2006): 24–27. Print.

———. "In which Henry James Strikes Bedrock." *Ordinary Language Criticism: Literary Thinking after Cavell after Wittgenstein*. Ed. Kenneth Dauber and Walter Jost. Evanston: Northwestern UP, 2003. 245–58. Print.

———. *Leonardo's Horse*. Normal: Fiction Collective Two, 1997. Print.

———. "Metafiction." *Routledge Companion to Experimental Literature*. Ed. Joe Bray, Alison Gibbon, and Brian McHale. New York: Routledge, 2012. 128–40. Print.

———. "Narrating Presentness in Nicholas Mosley's *Hopeful Monsters*." *Soundings: An Interdisciplinary Journal* 43.3–4 (2011): 201–12. Print.

———. *Plane Geometry and Other Affairs of the Heart*. New York: Fiction Collective Two, 1985. Print.

———. "The Question of Writing Now: FC2 Responds to Ben Marcus." *Symploke* 14.1–2 (2007): 316–19. Print.

———. "Steve Tomasula's *VAS*, or What if Novels Were Books?" *Steve Tomasula: The Art and Science of New Media Fiction*. Ed. David Banash. New York: Bloomsbury, 2015. 99–113. Print.

———. "Wittgenstein's Use." *New Literary History: A Journal of Theory and Interpretation* 44.4 (2013): 617–38. Print.

Parker, Joshua. "'Words Cant Never Be the Same as What It Was': R. M. Berry Maps the Struggle towards Mimesis." *Recent American Letters*. Paris: Institut d'Etudes Anglophones, Université Paris VII-Denis Diderot, 2005. 35–41. Print.

debra di blasi

DEBRA DI BLASI IS THE AUTHOR OF *THE JIRÍ CHRONICLES & OTHER FICTIONS* (2007) AND *PRAYERS OF AN ACCIDENTAL NATURE* (1999). FROM 2008 TO 2015, SHE WAS FOUNDING PUBLISHER OF JADED IBIS PRODUCTIONS, LLC. SHE RECEIVED THE 2009 &NOW AWARD, THE 2008 DIAGRAM INNOVATIVE FICTION AWARD, THE 1998 THORPE MENN BOOK AWARD, AND THE 1991 EYSTER PRIZE IN FICTION.

FOR THE PAST seven years, Debra Di Blasi was known as the founding publisher of Jaded Ibis Productions, a press that publishes adventurous multigenre narratives. While she no longer directs the press, the works published under her direction from 2008 to 2015, much like Di Blasi's own artistic research and production, explored modes of writing that respond to the complex world we live in. Many of Jaded Ibis's titles and Di Blasi's own works branch into various media creations and involve collaboration between artists working in the fields of literature, visual art, music, film, and publishing. Davis Schneiderman's two hundred-page novel, *Blank* (2011), for example, includes drawings by artist Susan White and is accompanied by an original soundtrack by DJ Spooky.

One can trace the evolution of her writing from the publication of her two novellas, *Drought & Say What You Like* (1997) (about the private moments of relationships, published in a traditional print format) to her latest project, *Skin of the Sun* (2017)—a mixed media interactive book. Indeed, Di Blasi's latest productions have been immersed in new technological platforms—her interest in and theorizing of technological advancements has led her to ponder the nature of the book, of storytelling, and of authorship. *Skin of the Sun*, in its mere physical existence as a new media text, asks questions about the nature of narratives. Her artistic explorations venture into the realm of technology and its relationship with our sensory and intellectual lives. These explorations invite us to think about originality and collaboration as well as embodiment and cognition. These themes recur in many of Di Blasi's texts (multimodal or not); when approaching *What the Body Requires* (2008), the reader's senses become engaged, as Di Blasi explores the symphonic form of novel writing.

The Jirí Chronicles & Other Fictions (2007) is another example of her play with the literary medium: the book includes works of prose, poetry, music, interviews, visual art, websites, and ads for consumer products surrounding the life of Jirí Cêch, the elusive protagonist whose presence has branched out of the book to invade the "real" world. Jirí himself has written book reviews, published poetry and visual art, composed music, and participated in interviews, thereby breaking down the boundaries between life and art. The existence of Jirí is telling of Di Blasi's consideration of the contours of writing and of her research on art's reshaping of them.

A common thread among Di Blasi's eclectic production might be its honest treatment of topics that society often chooses to hide or romanticize: *Prayers of an Accidental Nature* (1999) bluntly addresses issues of sexuality, insanity, immorality, and untrustworthiness. *Say Drought & What You Like* comments on the themes of love, relationships, and violence with tongue-in-cheek humor. Di Blasi's commitment to a blunt treatment of social and artistic matters, and her verve in addressing them, is showcased in the following interview. Because Di Blasi is invested in self-fictional experiments, the interview also plays with the modes of self-fiction that she has developed in other publications. As she notes below, "only eleven parts of the more than 500 parts of *The Jirí Chronicles* were written by Debra Di Blasi.... All of the rest— poetry, music, blogs, clothing, odors, videos—were produced by either Jirí or his associates—for example, the members of the death metal band Umlaut." While the following discussion comes from Di Blasi, the question of authorship and where its limits are (and should be?) erected comes into question. We sent each other Word documents from January to July 2012, and each of Di Blasi's contributions was fascinating both in form and content.

The exchange resulted in a beautiful overview of what she is passionate about and offers clarity about her art and writing process. Each answer to my questions functions as a whole—as a small experimental essay—while also weaving information about ideas significant to Di Blasi's artistic research: multimodal experiments, new technologies, politics, literary traditions, and the nature of art and innovation.

•

You are involved in different kinds of artistic media, and, as a writer, you have sometimes combined these media to create fictions. Does your commitment to various media require a different mode of writing, practically speaking?

Imagine a workshop with tables containing various tools. Over there, you have ink pens and graphite pencils, paint and crayons. Over here, you have video and digital photography. There, audio: spoken word, music, and found sounds. There, a nearly infinite number of objects, from airline ticket stubs to mud, iPads to lead type. And here, you have text. The Text Table, like the other tables, is multilayered: It contains not just words but different fonts; the small and expansive negative spaces between words, sentences, and sections; various colors and sizes and styles; double entendre and rhetoric and grammar; meaning and music and architecture; and far more than you or I now imagine, when we are allowed to imagine.

When a question arises to which I require an answer—which is how I begin any work of art, whether literary or visual—I start gravitating toward this table or that, and among the various elements within each table. Each question simultaneously requires deep and wide exploration, through dedicated research and careful witnessing. That is, my research is never limited to only the area whence the question arose. If, for example, I'm asking, *What is the manifestation of personal extinction as it collides with global extinction?* then my research will likely come from a wide variety of sciences, etymology, "thinking walks" along Puget Sound, witnessing interpersonal behaviors in urban and suburban environments, national and global politics, history, conversations with my spouse and siblings, the weather, memory, and the failure of memory, ad infinitum. This is the bundling phase wherein I collect language (often in single sentences) and images (often in various media) while accepting or rejecting information and tools for this peculiar project. I bring everything back to my workshop, so to speak, and spread the bundle out on a clean table. Then I begin building my narrative. Textual elements can be manipulated and moved in the same way as visual elements; I experiment. When good painters paint, they don't paint by number; they add and subtract, shift and layer. It's a process of discovery, not substantiation.

Whether I decide to use only text on the page or a combination of media doesn't affect my writing process. Narrative is narrative, whether textual, visual, or other forms like audio and odor. My novel-in-progress, *Anything Now Gone*, is thus far only text on the page because I'm interested in creating a kind of spoken-word (à la Patti Smith) architectural score about the history of the United States since World War II as manifested through the Freudian instincts, Thanatos and Eros. Yet, I consider every section, large and small, in this novel as a separate tool on the Text Table. I'm interested in how one tool reacts against and with the others to create meaning relevant to the concept(s) within the narrative.

When I taught mixed media and experimental writing at Kansas City Art Institute, one of the very first exercises was asking each student to write a single sentence and then blindly select an image to juxtapose with it. We discussed how text is changed by image and image changed by text, both conceptually and visually. I then had students write another sentence and pass it to their left. Now, we discussed the juxtaposition of text to text. We performed the same experiment with two abutting images. My point was to help them see that text and image are the same—each creates a picture and each creates a narrative. A fiction consisting only of text can function multidimensionally, too. By the end of that course, students could comfortably produce narratives far beyond the page; the most successful projects weighted text and other elements in a way that illuminated the narrative's concept.

Like Flannery O'Connor, I strongly believe everyone interested in becoming a "writer" should also study drawing, at the very least. The haptic process requires and allows greater understanding of the nuanced relationships between diverse literary elements.

As the teaching of creative writing has evolved into academic and commercial *industries,* categories and subcategories have been manufactured in the same way every discipline develops esoteric terminology to protect its [self-]interests and power position. As a publisher, I fully understand the function of marketing in our consumerist system, and I loathe it.[1] I'm acutely aware of how much pigeonholing damages the perception of art and the creation of art. I, and some of my authors, have "written" books that defy category; thus, every attempt to define reduces the originality of the project for potential readers. While functioning as a "writer" I've learned to separate the ugly business side from the beautiful art side and let each project develop organically, without labels restricting natural development. This is the only way to keep literary art evolving rather than stagnating.

You mention that you "collect language," then "build" and "manipulate" narratives. I can't help but note the physical aspect of that process, which you have previously alluded to in your interview with Marc Lowe, when you said that "skilled fiction writers sculpt words" and in your interview with David Hoenig-

---

1. Debra Di Blasi sold her publishing company, Jaded Ibis Productions, LLC, and its imprint, Jaded Ibis Press, in January 2016 and retired from publishing to return full-time to writing and visual art.

man, where you explained that you conceive of writing as "architectural." Would you care to say more about the physicality of writing and reading?

So interesting that you ask this today, as I was only yesterday discussing the physicality of writing with a long-time friend of mine who is a painter.

It's true: I use 'logos' like Legos®.

> Relevant aside: My grandmother kept a container of "American Plastic Bricks" by Elgo®, circa 1950s, and my siblings and I spent many hours of many years constructing houses and various architectural structures. On the farm where I grew up, we built our own small houses in the woods, using trees, branches, twine, silage plastic, and found objects. We built igloos out of the great snowdrifts that arose in those days. At the farm's creek, we built dams and castles out of sand, rocks, and twigs. My older brother went so far as to build an elaborate dugout in which to live after he reached his terrible teens and wanted nothing to do with the family. (That's an important scene in *Anything Now Gone*, by the way, because it exemplifies a critical milestone in the development of Thanatos.) The concept of building something of one's own, whether it be a nest or a palace or a novel, really is about delineation of territory, isn't it. The writer builds both an invitation to and a fortress from others, as do most mating creatures. By the way, I'm married to an architect.

Composition for me exists within an imagined three-dimensional space. Therefore, all compositional elements are three-dimensional objects within that space. More than this, each consists of other physical qualities that guide me in putting them together as a whole: for example, viscosity; a full spectrum of light that includes dim to bright, cold to hot; a complete color palette; and qualities that remain beyond my purview—unconscious—but that I suspect are quite active in one or all of my sense detectors.

My painter friend is reading about Luca Turin's vibrational theory of olfaction that contradicts the convenient idea of "lock and key" scent molecules. I liken the theory to cooking, building a recipe from scratch. When I'm at my creative peak, I can walk through grocery aisles and collect flavors/scents that I know will make the most original, aesthetically delicious combinations. I don't know *how* I know that coriander, pears, fresh fennel, a pinch of allspice, and so forth will make that cod delightfully palatable to me. I don't know *how* any more than I know that a peculiar combination of colors and, say, a fluid the consistency of warmed honey, can form the foundation of a narrative about a day of childhood when a girl discovers life's relationship to death. It's a form of synesthesia. It may be how most people create, but, for some reason, most people ignore the process. Me, I'm more interested in process than product, as I've said and continue to repeat ad nauseam.

When Storyspace® software came to be, way back in the 1990s, I quickly adopted it as a literary composition tool because the program can simulate the nonlinearity of "4-D space"—that is, space over time over space. (Now that we're entering virtual worlds, this narrative shape will become increasingly predominant until, I suspect, it will overtake the imposed linearity of the traditional book-form novel altogether.)

Note that I say I used Storyspace® as a *composition* tool and not as a *publishing* or *reading* tool. I never developed a predilection for reading creative hypertext, although I taught it as a way to inform young writers of current technologies and to untether them from linearity and their dull expectations of literature. I do respect inroads plowed by folks like Shelley Jackson and Michael Joyce, but I often wonder if the reason I don't enjoy reading hyperfiction is because it entered that architectural space with too many alliances to traditional print narratives—akin to shoving a square peg into a round hole. Whatever the case, I found composing with links and nodes incredibly liberating as it allowed me to build from one part to the next, digressively, affixing parts to parts to wholes to wholes, and to keep visual track of the many convolutions. When I thought I had reached an "end" to my narrative, I'd print out all nodes and arrange them for the printed page in a way that did not destroy what I felt was the inherent architecture of the piece. That's why you'll find in my story "Haunted," for example, chunks of text separated by negative space; indentation; and different fonts, sizes, and styles; and a repeating semiabstract image in various gradations.

> By the way, I do not believe one can create an effective 4-D experience on the printed page because, in my view, it requires one's physical body or avatar to be able to manipulate and travel through those narrative nodes in the same way a body can move through and around a museum. The new 360-degree treadmill developed by the military, when combined with the surround sound / surround video projection, immerses the player so deeply into the virtual space that the distinction between "real" and "fiction" blurs to overlap. Plus, the player *really* gets shot by guns abutting the circular treadmill and, though not fatal, the physical pain is enough to trick the brain and the nervous system into believing the virtual experience is absolutely real.

Thanks to my beloved husband, I've spent time studying architectural theory and design, which have influenced and supported my views about narrative. Architecture is *not* about where you're going to put the bathroom or how many bedrooms you'll add or interpreting "rooms" as boxes, hallways as rectangles. That's an archaic, Cartesian view of design that has so little to do with what we now know of nature in the micro and macro worlds. The best architectural design is, as I said, about *interrelationships* between parts and the whole and vice versa. It's about the way the narrative (yes, architecture creates narrative) unfolds as you move through the space, with patterns forming via aesthetic relationships. Aesthetic relationships are created through repetition, juxtaposition, transparency . . . exactly as in textual and multimedia narratives. Ideally, architectural design is also about the whole's relationship to other wholes, as in how a building is positioned on its site in relation to not only its immediate urban or suburban landscape but to the natural environment, not just the immediate environment but the *global* environment. These latter relationships exist in literature, too, though you won't find many contemporary writers thinking about them, caring about them, or conscious of them.

All of this research—combined with getting older and continuing to process experiences and information from fairly diverse intellectual interests—was bound to lead me to Systems Theory. *The Jirí Chronicles* arose from a massive experiment related to systems, an experiment whose "findings" I'm still sifting through and hope to report on within the next two or three years. I've always been interested in patterns and interrelationships, but the *Chronicles* was deliberate research that led me both deeper into and further away from the contemporary concept of "creative writing." I've moved so far beyond fiction as product that I've become more interested in the function and meaning of "writer" or "artist" as "it" exists within an intricate web built of multiple systems mutating over time, that is, history. Navigating the inherent contradictions is challenging and beautifully fascinating.

I believe that your fictions invite readers to reflect on the ways in which language "configures" us and the ways in which it can be "reconfigured." Your fictions also challenge traditional gender roles and the ways in which we tend to type or brand humans. I'm thinking of your manipulations of and plays with language in The Jirí Chronicles *and of your use "THE WOMAN," "BOYFRIEND-YOU-NEVER-LIKED," or "FRIEND-YOU-NO-LONGER-LIKE," for example.*

The Jirí Chronicles attempts to function in many ways; one is to thwart stereotypes and false or incomplete assumptions about people and situations—to spread wide the gray zone of ambiguity. As you know, only eleven parts of the more than five hundred parts of *The Jirí Chronicles* were written by Debra Di Blasi; they're published in the last section of the book, *The Jirí Chronicles and Other Fictions*. All of the rest—poetry, music, blogs, clothing, odors, videos— were produced by either Jirí or his associates—for example, the members of the death metal band Umlaut.

> Umlaut was managed by Jirí Cêch and had three band members: Hans, lead vocalist; Karl, lyricist and polymusician; and Kurt, drummer. Their album *Umlaut: ültimate über death metal*, released in 2005, is popular in Europe, especially places like Finland. Jaded Ibis Productions still receives royalty checks every year. Umlaut changed its name a few years ago to "Umlaut with 4 dots not 2" because there were too many metal bands with the name Umlaut. The boys were working on a second album, *Cowpie Heart: Songs from Hell's Kitchen*, when Jirí Cêch was killed by lions in Botswana.

Of course, none of these people exist. Jirí is my animus. The boys in Umlaut stumbled out of what I imagined to be Jirí's imagination. In creating Jirí and his "voice," I most enjoyed leading the reader toward one presumption about him—the incredibly handsome Czechoslovakian opium addict / experimental poet / real estate developer / capitalist / vampire—and then suddenly spinning the reader in the opposite direction. That detour, of course, was first directed at me. I'd catch myself constructing Jirí's character out of *stock* literary characters and expectations—women and men with unambiguous moral conditions and unambiguous motives and behaviors. So, I'd have to burrow deeper into the real Jirí Cêch™.

Life is not tidy. We are not tidy, not easily packaged. I would rather spend time with an asshole that admits to being an asshole than with a "nice" person who views himself or herself as righteous—because the latter is impossible, isn't it? The nice person cannot be righteous if he or she does not also acknowledge the asshole that exists in all of us. Even Mother Teresa, in her letters, admitted to being a hypocrite and that (probably as a result) her life was "darkness" and "torture." I am an asshole. I am nice. I am so many Debras in-between and beyond.

Jirí Cêch began as a lover based on a real person who became, in many ways, more complex and therefore likeable than real people I know who maintain a [transparent] pretense of "goodness." (I keep my bullshit detector well oiled and directed at myself as well as others—though sometimes I choose to give my bullshit free reign.) Jirí Cêch evolved over the years (1998–2011) into a character that could not be reduced to facile descriptors: good/bad; stupid/smart; conservative/liberal; heartless/compassionate. . . . Women fell in love with Jirí, and men admired him, perhaps fell in love with him, too. Because Jirí *insisted* on being real, *insisted* on not being agreeable for the sake of popularity, *insisted* on contradicting me and my own illusions and delusions, he grew large over the years, powerful—far more powerful than I. Thus, Jirí gave me self-awareness that infected all of my writing and my philosophy on life thereafter. The conundrum, of course, is that Jirí is me, so it is I who infected myself.

Because the stories were written with very tight constraints, I was allowed to enter the potentially hazardous space of acute self-examination that included scrutiny of every single word and phrase that arose from my consciousness and from my unconscious overstuffed with the flotsam and jetsam of the information deluge that engulfs my world.

> The first short story, "Czechoslovakian Rhapsody Sung to the Accompaniment of Piano," attempted to prove that the mind can—and does—(re)form the daily deluge of unrelated information into a narrative with cultural and emotional significance. (Recent studies have indeed located the region of the brain responsible for creating narrative out of unrelated data.) The result was a mixed-media fiction utilizing text and white space as visual elements and incorporating a specific quantity of randomly chosen illustrations, footnotes, and text appropriated from ad copy; news headlines; magazine articles and billboards; song lyrics; movie dialog; and genealogical, scientific, and historical facts.

In the case of characters in other stories, the generic labels say much, I hope, about the way we dehumanize not only through stereotyping but through "writing" someone out of our lives. Enmity results in discard: We put the unloved person in a container ("WOMAN") and throw them away. Even the WOMAN's VERY BEST FRIEND is expendable by reason of her generic label. Discard is a defense mechanism that allows us to stop caring without inconvenient guilt. Names make us realer, don't they? When we omit names (as does the daily news: "Today in Syria seventy people were killed in bombing attacks.") we can't—don't have to—see each person and the tender peculiarities of his or her life. Imagine if the BBC named all seventy people. Yes. Imagine . . .

Caring is hard, as I state in the *Chronicles*:

> (Let's have nothing here but white space. Let's have nothing but a cool plane of white for our tired tired eyes, our weary weary mind. My mind is weary, isn't yours? And perhaps also your heart? It's strenuous, this acute caring, this heavy penitence, this thing writers and readers do. Oh yes, we're in this together, you and I. Didn't you know? For godsake, don't you know that yet?)
> —from "Czechoslovakian Rhapsody Sung to the Accompaniment of Piano" (99)

The new group of multimedia writings I'm working on now, tentatively titled *Otherwise*, explore personal and global extinction through another mode of language "reconfiguration" by "corkscrewing" syntax and grammar in an attempt to express the ineffable grief that results from the death of sibling, of self, and of entire species. (Imagine drilling down to the core, the essence of language—that is, to the yearning for connection, whence language arose.) I began this collection after my sister, only two years older, died an unbelievably painful and protracted death from pancreatic cancer. Her death coincided with my husband's cancer and news reports about bee colony extinctions, declining fish and amphibian populations, and a host of other environmental disasters from which I (and most scientists) do not see a recovery.

The initial constraint in *Otherwise* is that each piece arises from one of the theories in my wondrous reference book, *Dictionary of Theories*, like "Wallace's Line" and "Olbers' Paradox."

> The disappeared light on the sore Earth on the almost every organism and animal. Night's sleep. Moths and crickets this time of day and night seem less seamless in the lonely kingdom. Have we evolved to lack sunlight for all time for example during night then day them to keep their stone-closed waters behind great stone dams where which young men buckle to become their short life in artificial light? What's significant to night? What matter/s?
> —from "Olbers' Paradox"

As in most of my writing, these originated in an assignment I constructed for students at California State University Summer Arts in an effort to get them to move beyond the idea that writing is about story product rather than discovery. I always complete student assignments alongside them so that my conversation and instruction serves them best and so that I have completed the first limb of a new body of work. And I always bring in a host of other references, as in the case of the assignment whence "Wallace's Line" arose—research on the selected theory, whale songs, a video on memes, drawing, body movement, one-on-one interactions, poetry, and so on—to vastly broaden students' knowledge base and aesthetic repertoires from the dull and ineffective standards used in most writing workshops. It is simply not enough to study only literature and literary theory. It is simply not enough to lack curiosity about every single and marvelous thing in the world.

Has Jirí Cêch ever published a review of Debra Di Blasi's work?

Jirí Cêch was delighted by all of the attention he received from me and others—except for one particular occasion. What follows is a transcript of a recorded telephone conversation, one of many, between Jirí and I. This one, "Literal Latte (unedited version)" is from the album, *The Interviews 1.1,* "available on iTunes and other music download sites," said Jirí. It's as close to a critical review of my work as he ever achieved.

> DEBRA: Hello?
> JIRÍ: Debra, what are you doing?
> DEBRA: Hi, Jirí. What's up?
> JIRÍ: I'm very unhappy with you.
> DEBRA: Why?
> JIRÍ: Because I have a friend at *Literal Latté,* and I just heard some very disturbing news.
> DEBRA: Oh. You heard about the article? Is that . . . is that what you're talking about?
> JIRÍ: Yes, the article you wrote about me. And then you sent it to *Literal Latté* to be published!?!
> DEBRA: Well, but Jirí, the article's true and it makes you . . . um . . . it makes you seem attractive and desirable to women and . . . and . . .
> JIRÍ: It makes me seem like an asshole! C'mon, you know it makes me seem like an asshole.
> DEBRA: Well, Jirí, frankly you are kind of an asshole.
> JIRÍ: Debra, Debra, you wound me. You wound me by your words.
> DEBRA: Jirí you know I'm . . . I like that asshole nature of yours.
> JIRÍ: You really think I'm an asshole? I'm asking this in a most serious fashion. You think I am an asshole?
> DEBRA: Uh . . . Oh . . . Okay, this is a tough question to answer because there's no way that I can answer this and make it sound all right.
> JIRÍ: Please, try. I'm sitting here in pissed-off anticipation waiting for your response.
> DEBRA: Okay. An asshole is someone who is sometimes inconsiderate of other people's feelings, which is how you behave at times, right?

JIRÍ: If I am inconsiderate about other people's feelings it's only because I'm so busy I forget the other people.
DEBRA: See, that's the problem, Jirí. That's what assholes do.
JIRÍ: To me assholes are the barbarians sweeping down from the north to ... to stand at the gate with their big, big clubs waiting to knock your women in the head and drag them out into the fields to fornicate.
DEBRA: Ohhhh ... Well, that is perhaps of another time and era. What we're talking about is nineteen— ... Oh no, what year is this?
JIRÍ: Debra, you don't even know what year it is. How can I trust you with your definition of asshole?

In Prayers of an Accidental Nature (1999), *the themes of rationalization, deception, self-deception, sanity, and manipulation are important. Could you talk about some of these ideas in the short stories of this collection?*

The stories in *Prayers* are now so old that revisiting them is a bit like analyzing a stranger's writing. "Where All Things Converge," for example, was published in 1989 and written, as I recall, in 1983. The newest story in the collection, "Our Perversions," was written in 1994 or 1995.

> Interesting, to me, that my memory of my writing is located by who I was sleeping with at the time.

Most of the stories obviously arose from someone in her mid- to late twenties, someone who has not yet processed what she's learned thus far, or lived quite long enough to move beyond the more facile views of humanity and human nature. Her repertoire is more literature than life, the early part of a long pathway.

I see hints of that young Debra's progress in the title story, however. "Prayers" is my favorite in the collection, the one that literary journals were least interested in. (What does that tell you about the industry? Or about me? What does it tell *me* about me and my outsider status?) The "we" narrator alone says much about the evolution of my sociopolitical and economic views and about the chasm between the two disparate social classes with whom I socialized those years—poor students, lower-class workers, and rich heirs and scions.

> I see, too, influences of Lillian Hellman's, Tennessee Williams's, and Sam Shepard's plays, most obviously. I had wanted to be (also) a playwright but

> enjoy describing things and people too much—rather verboten in playwriting and screenwriting. The play format annoys me because they use the space and text of the page as merely instructional, not emotional.

Regarding recurring themes of deception and self-deception, rationalization, manipulation, sanity . . . these are ape behaviors. We're apes. Ignoring or neglecting ways these behaviors bar us from self-awareness and higher levels of integrity, perhaps even higher levels of consciousness. The human brain may have reached its maximum efficiency size-wise, but that doesn't mean we've even begun to use (or understand) the myriad neurological interconnections that might further enlighten us.

Lying, whether to self or others, prevents evolution of self- and societal consciousness in so many ways. And all adults lie. Everyone rationalizes and manipulates with remnants of psychopathic infancy, but most people remain—by choice or inability—ignorant of these simian habits. Perhaps I became a writer and artist because of my obsession with "truth" and "reality." The worst thing we could do in our family was lie—worse than the "crime" we'd lied about. We might be punished for stealing the last piece of cake, but we'd really get in trouble for lying about stealing the cake. I suspect that my parents demanded truth for two reasons: (1) to keep order within a big, condensed family; and (2) because it was the Vietnam–American War era, the Nixon era, the assassination era, an era of boldface political lies that caused the deaths of thousands of very young men, and my parents were smart people who recognized cause and effect and the calamity of complacency.

> It is therefore hilariously ironic that my first marriage was to a pathological liar! Or is it?

No. I *am* interested in the real-world pathology of prevarication and rationalization: the way a person says, "I don't care," when they care more than they can tolerate; the way stealing is rationalized, and cheating shrugged off as acceptable business practice; the way we're bombarded daily by the media's benign and malevolent lies and those of politicians and those of strangers and the people we love and our own words and memories and dreams.

> I spent a great portion of my childhood hiding the truth of my family's living conditions from schoolmates and so was a prisoner in a world of my creation. My family lived in a house without plumbing. A tumble-down house teeming with mice and insects and children. I had a birthday party when I was six or seven and then never again. Five years later I witnessed

what must have occurred at my own party when my younger brother had his birthday party: His friends were horrified by having to use a pot to pee in. I was ashamed. My brother would be, too, a couple of years later.

My oldest and forever dearest friend, LH, was the one person I allowed to visit thereafter. She was the only child of older parents who were, in our lower-economic small town, economically well off. She lived in a spacious, spotless house full of antiques and a piano and fine china and polished silver and lush carpeting and a full-size attic stuffed with every great toy of our generation. Our unkempt house and smelly outhouse and piss pot and cattle and pigs and horses and deer and creek and woods and pastures and ponds and hubbub of children and dogs and cats, in sum, was exotic and wild to her, and necessarily lacked the claustrophobic rules and restrictions by which she was raised. She loved spending whole weekends with us in summer, getting gleefully dirty, eating sack lunches at the creek, and running around at night on dirt roads and dewy grass, under a floodlight glittering with hordes of moths and mosquitoes and May flies and June bugs, with no curfew except her own fatigue.

When we were teens, and LH was going through her own exceedingly difficult circumstances, she betrayed me and my living conditions to another friend, SM, with whom we were both spending the night. The other friend's father had just installed a new and second bathroom in their lovely house. We were all three standing in front of the mirror and talking about the groovy bath design when LH suddenly turned to me and asked, grinning, "Where's your bathtub, Debbie?"

She knew, of course, that there was no tub in our house, that we "spit-bathed" ourselves from small amounts of water in small plastic tubs or in summer bathed in the yard with big buckets of water from the well.

I looked at her in disbelief and then looked at SM and saw that she also knew the truth: They were both grinning. They wanted to embarrass me, sure, probably because I was such a know-it-all, but I think they also wanted to see how I would respond, whether the sanctimonious girl—who always tried to remake the world in her own image—would remain on her high horse when put to the test.

I flunked that test: "Our tub's on the east wall," I lied.

I rationalized the lie by telling myself that my father, too, had installed a new room: He'd enclosed part of the old back porch with reclaimed wood so that we no longer had to go sit on the pot in plain view of the bedrooms upstairs. The porch was big enough to bathe in so, as I was by then fourteen, with flowering breasts and pubic hair, I took serious advantage of the lock on the door for all my toilet and hygiene needs. I rationalized that, though the plastic tub held no more than a few pints of water, it was still a "tub." I rationalized that when I washed myself from that plastic tub, it and I stood along the "east wall" of the porch. "Therefore" dot dot dot.

Note that my lies were all semantic, stemming from language and meaning, signs and symbols.

Truth is flexible because language is flexible.

It depends on what the meaning of the word *is* is.
—a classic argument, albeit obfuscation, by former President Bill Clinton

There is what happened, or what we felt, and then there is what we say happened or what we felt, and then there is what we say that we say happened or felt. But somewhere in all that convoluted mess reside the words that are best for living and giving freely in the world. Esteban, of my story "I Am Telling You Lies," gave freely of himself to Jorge, Tamara, and Diedre by telling them boldface lies. They took freely his lies because the inventions were beautiful, the way any good story is beautiful for the sentiment it conveys and evokes, the path toward escape and enlightenment. Much of the fiction in *Prayers of an Accidental Nature* attempts to get at not one but multiple truths, to excavate myself and those truths from the archaeology of deceit and duplicity in which everyone is buried. I'm still digging at that site. I'll be digging until the day or night I die.

Reading a book like Skin of the Sun *obviously disrupts traditional ideas about what a book is supposed to be. Beyond the manipulation of the appearance of the book—print, page, layout, medium—it feels as though* Skin of the Sun *leads us to rethink what visual texts are as well. In other words, the images are not just there to disrupt the traditional text but to question their own existence. In looking at the visual texts, I came to ask, what are they? They are not quite illustrations of the written text, but they are. They are not documentation or even a form of scrapbooking, but they are. And so forth.*

I'm making dreams. Consider how the brain collects, discards, sorts, and recombines fragments from our day into a single narrative unfolding in sleep. I'm making dreams.

In many ways *Skin of the Sun* continues investigations into meaning-from-randomness that began with *The Jirí Chronicles* and before with my (as yet unfinished) novella begun in 1992, *The Second Millennium War, Or: What We*

Found At Birmenstow, designed as a dossier that incorporates artifacts with the text.

Skin questions: How deeply into apparently random juxtaposition can the writer and reader dive and still somehow remain tethered to narrative?

> The multiple interrogatives posed by individual writings in *Skin of the Sun* are themselves juxtapositions that must be navigated by the reader.

Well, that's a rhetorical question: We can go forever deeper because it is part of human nature to create meaning where there is none: The wild chimp cocking its head at the shiny gyroscope in its hand, that's us. Some of the images in the book are less illustrative than others, which is part of the experiment.

I find myself now most interested in the writings that *collide* image with text rather than cozy up to each other. "It Was Just Like a Movie" is one of my favorite interrogations because the images both *collide* with the text and are, within themselves, *collisions* of images—layers and layers of transparencies and color shifts and erasures. It's no coincidence that every piece in this book arose post–9/11, when the word *collision* took on such significance: collision of plane and skyscraper, of body with pavement, of cultures, of religions, of philosophies, of media that apparently could not find enough bloody ways to replay collision for us. Everyone around me went a little crazy, trying to create meaning out of the chaos resulting from collision.

Likewise, the story "Quell the Mayhem Night" was a collision of the Phil Spector murder trial + Nancy Grace's kooky reportage of it + real crime incidents reported in the Cape Town, South Africa, newspapers + the story title and subtitles appropriated from articles about war in other geographic places, like Bosnia + my own experiences in South Africa, particularly overwhelming feelings of economic-privilege guilt + drawings made during one of my visits there + all that yet remains in my subconscious.

Ultimately, I want the reader to derive emotional, evocative, essential meaning from the aesthetics provided and build all of it into one narrative that is what it is because of the reader's construction. But the reader cannot be lazy or hasty or uncurious. And I'm not certain there are many readers left who aren't.

Skin of the Sun will become a multimedia, interactive book that I'll be presenting at MIT in Spring 2013. This iteration is a new, delightful area of study for me. I want to take the restrictions of the iPad iOS platform and explore and explode it as much as possible, in the same way that I'm trying to explode the parameters set by Createspace's print-on-demand service. The iBook version of *Skin of the Sun* will contain video and audio, quizzes and music, images as text, and text as image. I'm also working on a "frame" version of *Skin of the Sun* that contains a deck of cards, original drawings and paintings, a sheet of paper covered in mud, a flash drive containing video, audio and music, snapshots, a microscope slide containing a surprise, and more.

> A frame is a new category of book that uses print-on-demand technologies to make one-of-a-kind works of literary art accessible to an expansive audience. The books are to be sold unfinished on Amazon, for example, with instructions inside detailing how to get the book shipped, completed, signed, numbered, and returned by the writer.

I'm putting forth the idea that a "book" can resemble an organic object that opens and opens and opens again, unfolding new layers and levels of meaning, thus representing a microcosm of writer and reader, who are microcosms of the universe. Which brings me to a close:

—*what a book is supposed to be*—
　Who defines the parameters of "book" and *why* do those definitions exist?
—*what a book is supposed to be*—
　Is rebellion coded in the DNA of some people but not others? And if conformity is part of the human ape's social structure—its glue—then who sets the parameters by which to conform? Are those who rule by setting rules doing so for the benefit of all or selfishly—or even malevolently?
—*what a book is supposed to be*—
　Why heed the art parasites—the publishing executives, marketing reps, agents, editors, academic administrators who secretly or publicly don't give a rat's ass about the immeasurable human value of art or cannot eloquently talk about it because to them all Value is $ign and $ymbol.
—*what a book is supposed to be*—
　When I define a book, on its cover, as "writing" versus "fiction" or "stories," what am I suggesting the reader question from the outset?
—*what a book is supposed to be*—
　What is a book? What is a page? What is a word? What is an image?
—*what a book is supposed to be*—
　A question. Not an answer. Or.

works cited

Di Blasi, Debra. *Drought & Say What You Like*. New York: New Directions Books, 1997. Print.

———. *The Jirí Chronicles & Other Fictions.* Tuscaloosa: Fiction Collective Two, 2007. Print.

———. *Prayers of an Accidental Nature.* Minneapolis: Coffee House Press, 1999. Print.

———. *Skin of the Sun: New Writing.* Mixed-media interactive book. Self-published, 2017.

———. *What the Body Requires.* Seattle: Jaded Ibis Press, 2008. Print.

further writing by and on debra di blasi

Di Blasi, Debra. "In Conversation: Debra Di Blasi & Sam Witt." *The Brooklyn Rail.* N. pag., 2012. Web. 10 Feb. 2016.

———. Interview with Chris Richards. *The Art of Dismantling.* N.p., 2010. Web. 10 Feb. 2016.

———. Interview with David Hoenigman. *Word Riot* (2009): n. pag. Web. 10 Feb. 2016.

———. Interview with Jefferson Hansen. Blog post. *Experimental Fiction / Poetry / Jazz.* Networked Blogs, 5 Oct. 2008. Web. 10 Feb. 2016.

———. Interview with Marc Lowe. *Mad Hatters' Review* 6 (2006): n. pag. Web. 10 Feb. 2016.

———. "People of the Book." *Ploughshares* (2013): n. pag. Web. 10 Feb. 2016.

———. "Small Press." *Entropy Magazine* (2015): n. pag. Web. 10 Feb. 2016.

———. "Song of the Monkey King." *Litscapes: Collected U.S. Writings 2015.* Ed. Caitlin M. Alvarez and Kass Fleisher. Normal: Steerage Press, 2015. 67–72. Print.

———. "Sprung Up in the Years Since." *Wreckage of Reason II: XXperimental Women Writers in the 21st Century.* Ed. Nava Renek. Brooklyn: Spuyten Duyvil Press, 2008. 303–21. Print.

———. "21st Century Mashup." *Forbes Magazine* (2011): n. pag. Web. 10 Feb. 2016.

———. "What is Experimental Literature?" *HTML Giant.* (2011): n. pag. Web. 10 Feb. 2016.

———. (writing as Jirí Cêch). "Bohemian Beasts and Their Buttery Buxom Brides." *Brothers and Beasts: An Anthology of Men on Fairy Tales.* Ed. Kate Bernheimer. Detroit: Wayne State UP, 2007. Print. 47–56.

———, ed. *Dirty: Dirty: An Anthology of Writing and Art.* Seattle: Jaded Ibis Press, 2012. Print.

percival everett

PERCIVAL EVERETT IS A DISTINGUISHED PROFESSOR OF ENGLISH AT THE UNIVERSITY OF SOUTHERN CALIFORNIA. HE IS THE RECIPIENT OF THE ACADEMY AWARD FROM THE AMERICAN ACADEMY OF ARTS AND LETTERS, TWO HURSTON/WRIGHT LEGACY AWARDS, THE BELIEVER BOOK AWARD, AND THE 2006 PEN CENTER USA AWARD FOR FICTION. IN 2011, HE WAS INDUCTED INTO THE SOUTH CAROLINA LITERARY HALL OF FAME. HE IS THE AUTHOR OF *ERASURE* (2001), *I AM NOT SIDNEY POITIER* (2009), *ASSUMPTION* (2012), AND *THE WATER CURE* (2007).

IT HAS BECOME somewhat of a tradition to start critical pieces on Percival Everett by acknowledging that his work is unclassifiable. Indeed, Everett's novels address issues of family, race, identity, sexuality, death, and writing through various forms and styles—a western novel, a children's book, an epistolary novel, parodies and satires of the publishing and political worlds, and retellings of Greek mythology.

Everett's breadth of writing has led critics to conclude that he is a writer who debunks categories, who does not fit into the molds that we have constructed to think of literature. In other words, his work takes part in a literary tradition that disrupts and redefines writing and interpretive categories. While Everett participates in this tradition, his novels point to its limitations and reveal the pretenses of self-proclaimed difference, uniqueness, and innovation. In *Erasure* (2001), for instance, we laugh at Gimble, an avant-garde writer, who brags:

> I have unsettled readers. I have made them uncomfortable. I have unsettled their historical, cultural and psychological assumptions by disrupting their comfortable relationship between words and things. I have brought to a head the battle between language and reality. But even as my art dies, I create it without trying. (44)

The protagonist replies, "Man, do you need to get laid" (44).

Everett adopts a parallel humorous stance in his essay "A Modality": "The corruption of so-called convention, or the recognition of such corruption, exploitation alteration, whether motivated by aesthetic, political, or commercial (money's not the only currency) interests, is a commitment to generic rules more rigid than an adherence to the so-called accepted conventions" (*Fictions' Present* 211). In fact, most of his fictions mock the pretenses of the very forms that they explore, questioning the act of formal invention itself. When Everett writes a parody of poststructuralist discourses in *Glyth* (1999), for example, he also adopts a parodic stance to reveal the limitations of parody. In short, Everett often presents readers with a situation, a model, or a path of reading to resist it from within. Yet, Everett's distrust of literary categories—traditional or experimental alike—is not a mere resisting stance; it is not quite a political act against all systematic qualifications of literature. He is simply opposing an understanding of writing that he deems wrong.

Everett's use of a form, theme, and language to show its limitations implies that readers develop excitement for his characters, stories, and humorous situations, only to find out the limits of what caused this excitement. His prose feels effortless; it is graceful and alluring. Yet, most would agree that if it ever appears simple, it is deceivingly so. Thus, our own reading techniques seem to entrap us, and the ones we set up in reaction to his works end up disarming us.

To someone unfamiliar with his work, this disarming experience may be unsettling, but pleasure also comes from the reshaping of the assumed rules of storytelling. Surprise often accompanies laughter when we are playfully reminded of our roles as readers or when the collapse of frames procures a deeper sense of confusion and understanding. In such moments, the vulnerability of the ungraspable coming and going of control leads us to laugh at ourselves and at acts of language.

It might not come as a surprise, then, that Everett does not particularly like to talk about this work: in a literary interview lies the illusion that finding out his opinions, writing habits, or aesthetic rationales would somehow illuminate his craft. As he points out, he is known for his one-word answers. Nevertheless, talking to Everett is a lot of fun: his sense of humor, warmth, honesty, and generosity made the discussion fascinating. The interview that follows was recorded on January 27, 2010, in Columbus, Ohio, a few hours before Everett's reading of *I Am Not Sidney Poitier* (2009) during The Ohio State University's Writers' Reading Series.

•

In your essay "A Modality" you write, "I wish only to suggest that we refocus our gaze from the transcendental connections of meaning(s) toward the obscure and indeterminate surface of fiction" (211). Is that you speaking here?

That is, but the sentence before this is a reference to Wittgenstein.

Right. But that one is you?

Yes, I think.

It was surprising to me.

This could be too that I was making it up.

That's why I'm asking you.

It certainly has some meaning, but it does not mean that I mean it. The essay itself is a work of fiction; the sentence would be self-referential about the fact that this is mere surface . . .

Which you also contradict in the essay.

Of course.

I was interested in this because you've worked on French theorists, and the essay is obviously written in reference to Wittgenstein, but you could see connections to other theorists.

Yes, there are many other connections, and I was not looking stuff up, so when you ask, "is this from some place else?" it very well might be. I don't know.

You play with theorists a lot, and you believe that theorists might be playful, especially the French ones.

Not Wittgenstein. He is completely earnest.

I know, but you make fun of that.

Oh, I make fun of him.

Does this relate to your idea of the French theorists being funny or not necessarily serious all the time?

Playful.

Yes. I thought of "A Modality" as a place where you yourself were being playful with theory, but I have to admit that the idea of French theory being playful might not be commonplace.

Really? How do you read it?

Well, I mean here in this country it is unusual to see it that way.

Here in this country, but I don't think for the French it is unusual at all. British and American theorists are so damned earnest. I don't think for a second that Barthes ever believed that he was getting to the truth.

Are you talking about the early Barthes?

Yeah. For him, it was another way of interpreting things, not to interpret something to the truth but for the mere act of interpretation. In *S/Z*, all that talk about Balzac is pure theatre, which is why in *Erasure* I write *S/Z*, the other unvoiced voice, and played with that, so it's not so much a parody of *S/Z* as it's really an homage to *S/Z*.

And Derrida, you find also playful?

That's a bit more problematic because I think he is playful, but later he is really full of himself. He's playful in a different way: he's exploiting the situation with the very earnest American scholars and the position of a celebrity. But so much of his deconstruction, the binary opposition thing, is pure play, and that's what is so wonderful about it. I think that the talk he gave at Hopkins in '68, the late '60s, that sets everything in motion, is a wonderful puzzle. I think he meant it as a puzzle, but I don't think he means it as some truth. I don't think that Derrida ever meant that there was truth, maybe a dismantling of what was perceived to be the truth, which is a truth in itself, I suppose, but not the determination of some interpretation that might correct the truth.

So it's the finality of the ways in which people interpret these works that you find frustrating?

Not even frustrating. Amusing.

I ask about Barthes and Derrida because your background is in philosophy, and you always say that you decided to write fiction because it was a better way for you to express something about morality or . . .

I don't know if there is a way to express anything. It was a way for me to explore some places of my own.

But why fiction?

It allowed me the kind of playfulness that I enjoy. Also, it allowed me to work on whatever philosophical question I think persists in my work about meaning and about, I suppose occasionally, morality, but I never think of that in terms of philosophy, just in terms of being a citizen. But this might happen offstage. The reader might never see the work that I am doing for myself philosophically. It helps me, obviously, exploring and playing with the notions of how it is we mean things.

Does that have anything to do with your interest in dialogue?

It might. I have to say, I haven't really analyzed myself in regard to what I do. Probably not dialogue specifically but the whole idea of voice, which is why I've gravitated toward first-person narration, though I didn't early on. My first novel was first person, but then I wrote third person. It allows me to play with the telling of the story, the reliability of the narrator, the context of the narration.

You said that I'm Not Sydney Poitier *is a novel of ideas.*

I think maybe all of my books are, in that they're not really driven by some story that I have to tell. *Not Sydney* is driven by some things that I want to touch on, ideas that interest me about identity, race, and culture, so that the drive of the novel is not my desire to tell this particular story. The story serves my desire to address particular ideas.

But I'm Not Sydney Poitier *is not an exception.*

It's different from my novels *Wounded*, *Watershed*, or *Erasure*.

You mean it's different because you approach the ideas differently?

The driving force in those is more the story I'm trying to tell and the ideas I want to explain. With *Wounded,* I come at it with an interest in the characters and the world we live in, and I present ideas because of that world of actions. I don't create these actions to serve the ideas.

And for you, Wounded *is one of the most experimental novels you've written.*

I think so because it's kind of hyper-real and ostensibly conventional, but I have no idea what that term means. I find the idea of experimental writing so pedestrian that it's bothersome. In that novel, I was trying to make something so naturalistic that the experiment was actually hidden.

What I liked about it is that there are several wounds in the novel—some of them physical, some of them not. I kept trying to figure out if language was wounded. What would it look and feel like?

It thrills me that you picked that up because my personal concern is that the first casualty in any war is language, and in any conditions that we now live through, my first concern is the wounds that language suffers.

The Water Cure deals with violence. The book directly addresses torture, and you have been quite open about the events that caused or influenced the book— the use of torture and the wars during Bush's presidency. It is unusual for you to expand on the origins of your fictions.

The origins of that book derive out of an anger that I usually try to keep out of my creativity. What you feel politically, socially, and morally always finds the work, but in this one, I just wear my politics on my sleeves. But these are the politics of the character. The character I created, though far from me, shares that vitriolic response to the Bush years. There is also a calculated move on my part when I realize, well, if I do this so overtly, then it challenges the function of the fiction itself. I think it's easy to see it as a representation of the character's thinking, but I'm fascinated by the fact that people get so bugged by it that they want to attribute the overt politics solely to me.

I read one of the essays on Water Cure *that was written in the French press after your visit in November 2009, and I was fascinated by the ways in which the writer equalized the character's voice to your voice, so that you became this angry figure against Bush, which also feeds into a stereotypical French discourse against the United States.*

Which is interesting. And that's why I like to talk about Malraux. I love Malraux because much of his work was opposed to French colonialism, so that there is a French tradition of this kind of writing. I think there is a failure in Western culture regarding reading texts, novels, but also movies and television, especially television. People say, "you know in that movie where Clint Eastwood says," but it's his character. People cannot disassociate the writer from the work. They enter the work and do not completely surrender to the story.

What's interesting is that if you compare the discourses about your work here and in France, they are quite different and perhaps sometimes contradictory.

Since I don't read reviews, I don't really know.

Well, in the essay I mentioned, published in Télérama, *you became a representative of the American intellectual voice against the Bush years (and obviously there is something exotic in that position from a French perspective). Here, I think that people want to classify you more as an African American writer, which did not figure in that French portrayal of Percival Everett.*

Here, it's really bizarre because there is such a need to pigeonhole. If you're not a white male writer, they want to figure out where to put you. Ever since *Erasure,* there is a resistance in making me African American because I do invalidate the category to some extent, but that's still there. Now, it's experimental. For a while, it was Western. It's amusing.

It's a narrative.

One I choose to ignore, but it is.

To go back to Water Cure, *I was interested in the visual arrangements, the images, and the fragments. It's not that other books you wrote are not fragmentary, but I felt like there was something different about the use of fragments in this novel.*

Well, it's completely non sequitur.

Yes, and it's very visual. For example, we see three asterisks, and we read "ASTERISK ASTERISK ASTERISK" (49). Of course, visuality is also part of torture in the book. So does writing and reading become a mode of torture?

I've never thought of it that way, but why not? Sure.

I don't believe you've used images before. Have you?

No, apart from covers. But again, it is generated solely by my understanding of this character.

A lot of contemporary authors feel that the changes in technology and the use of new media influence them or they feel a need to respond to those changes. Is that something that matters to you?

No, I don't feel a need to respond. I still write my first draft with a pencil. The only problem I have with so-called new technology is all the talk about the disappearance of the book. I like books. I don't want to think of them as relegated to cyber culture, and I want to think that people after me will have the same experience I have with books, where they live on the bookshelves and you can buy them and you visit them. And you don't do that the same way with your files. You don't visit them in the same way when they are in the computer. It's the same with the library. We used to go to the stack—or even the card catalogue was different—and you would find one book because you were looking for another book. You'd pick up the books that were beside it, and you'd have this experience of all of these books around you. It's the thinking behind the Internet—the clicking on links—but then the links are decided for you by someone who is not terribly smart. You're not choosing. There are probably some other relationships that people will develop with texts that I can't see coming, and that might be as special to them as the objects of books are to me, but I'd hate to see people not have this experience.

I think that you never say, "I write books" or "I write novels," but you say, "I make books." You've said, "I can't articulate what [a book] looks like. I begin with a sense of weight" in an interview with Susan Salter Reynolds. You've also noted that you "always loved the idea that all [your] words were on the ribbon" when talking about typewriters with Robert Birnbaum. You write longhand. You insist on the shape of your books. Does this interest in the physicality of books and writing make you write in a certain way?

I'm sure it does. I don't know how it affects my writing. My first five books were written on a manual typewriter. Again, I wrote longhand first, and I typed. But now, I put them into the computer. I'd be interested to see—since I don't really read my work after I'm done with it—if my work changed from those first five to subsequent books just because of using a different machine.

In Walk to the Distance, *at first the chapters are very close together. Chapter 3 might appear in the middle of the page, right after chapter 2. As we go on, the chapters get separated, and toward the end, it's very visible because the chapters are shorter. These later chapters start on a new page each time. We end with four white pages. Is this something you meant?*

It's a long time ago. I have a vague recollection of saying that I wanted the experience of reading the book to somehow reflect the coming home and the western landscape, of adjusting to that wide-open sense, of moving from the congestion of having just returned from Vietnam.

I thought about the sense of emptiness, at least for me, that I associated with the growth of white space.

Well, that's the beauty of semiotics and languages. I can't control what it's going to mean once I do it. I can think of no better reason to make art than that. Once you let it go, it's got its own agency and it will do what it's going to do. More importantly, it lacks any agency and it will do whatever the observer is going to have it do.

You also paint, but you don't name your paintings. They are numbers, aren't they?

Sometimes they are numbers. There is no logic to it. There is one called "Conversation with G. E. Moore." Somebody said, "What is this painting called?" and I said, "Conversation with G. E. Moore." That's what came into my head.

In your paintings, there is a saturation of paint to distance yourself from the original object.

I start with something that's representational, drawn onto the canvas, and then sometimes I'll actually paint it, and then I'll slowly eradicate anything recognizable. The desire, the hope, being that, as it's eradicated, the essence, the feeling of that original representation, though it's completely gone, will persist. Obviously, that's not something that I can gage, measure, or even talk to someone about since I won't tell them what the original was. But for me, that's what I'm seeing to do.

Is there a parallel with writing?

Only in so far as I really want to write a novel that is nonrepresentational, and language doesn't lend itself to that. The closest I've come to that is *The Water Cure* because it's non sequitur, but even there, the act of reading is also the act of generating narrative. Anyone can tell the story, though none of it follows. It's very easy to tell the story.

What about poetry? Your last volume of poetry, re: f (gesture), *is close to painting.*

It's got the three parts to each poem, and I hate using the word *abstract*, but representation is abstracted each time. So you actually see some play with language that I experimented with in *Water Cure*. I hesitate to talk about my poetry because that makes it sound like I think I'm a poet. The only reason that I write poetry is to prove that I am not, and I do a pretty good job at it.

Do you write it differently?

Yeah. I'll be sitting around, and I'll become interested in something, and I'll study something, and then I'll write a book of poems. It's not like I write poems, but it's a book for me. I edit it and go back, and go through them a thousand times, but it is a book; it's not a collection of poems.

You mentioned that when you finish a book, you realize that you thought you were going to know more when you started and end up realizing that you know less at the end of the process.

Oh yeah!

Do you know less about the book in terms of content or writing or language?

The world. Everything I know. I'll know what the book is, whereas before I didn't know what the book was going to be, but as far as my understanding of human beings, the nature of language, the way I think meaning works, I always end up knowing less, which is the real reason to do this. I like that. It's a humbling feeling, but it's also really exhilarating. It's quite freeing. My aim is to know nothing at all, and you even told me this, and most of my friends tell me that I'm well on my way!

I have told you this?! You confuse me with someone else! In your books, I also find that there is an idea of repair, that something is missing or does not work.

It shows up literally in "The Fix," perhaps even in "Cerulean." But there are other modes of repair as well. Zulus *might be an example.*

I don't know about all the repair stuff.

You don't like the word.

I don't know. I have no idea. *Zulus* is another novel about the breakdown of language. In fact, I did an experiment with *Zulus* that I don't think people really see. Typos are intentionally placed in *Zulus,* and it was a fight with the copy editor. I kept saying, "No! It's supposed to be there." As the novel goes, they increase in frequency. Sylvie Bauer got it: she wrote a paper where she got that. I could not believe it. You never know what people will uncover. In my novel *Glyph*, there is a substitution code at one place, and the last line of the novel is "The *line* is everything." When I made the substitution code, it was this very private joke. For some reason, it occurred to this guy in Pittsburg named William Scott to take the substitution code and to apply it to the last line of the novel, and *line* becomes the word *shut*, which is *shit* where the *u* and *i* are replaced. He came up and told me this, and it just kind of frightened me that anyone had figured this out. There is no reason to think to do that.

Yeah there is. It's in the book. You did create this substitution code, but sometimes you borrow other texts.

There're some schemata in there that come from semioticians, but that's it. And there is Boltzmann's constant, the physicist who wrote about molecular structure.

In Watershed, *there are direct citations from the treaties between the United States and Indian tribes, medical discourses, and technical details about water. I found that I paid a lot of attention to these passages, but I think that I would have taken them for granted in another setting. The technicality of these documents became really important to me.*

The stuff from the treaties is . . . you can't make this up; it's just so incredible. First thinking about it, I just thought, *I'll create language for the treaties*. I've this huge book with all the treaties in it, and I started reading them, and I thought, *I can't do better than this*.

The book is published with an introduction by Sherman Alexie.

The paperback is.

It frames your reading in some ways.

The initial book did not have it.

Right, but I read the paperback, and, in the introduction, there is a discussion of writing about Native Americans. Was it something that you struggled with in terms of your representation of Native Americans?

Well, I wasn't writing about Native Americans. They are characters, but it was a character describing an experience with Native Americans, so I was a little confused by that, though I was glad to hear from Sherman that my depiction of at least some Plains Indians was, in his eyes, accurate. Though I kind of found that a little bizarre because I thought my depiction of those particular people might have been accurate, and not even as Plains Indians, because even as I know them, they are as diverse as anybody else.

It was a bit surprising to me too because it's a very political introduction so that a sense of pressure comes from it. You open the book, and you think, "This is it."

That's the real thing . . . (laughs)

Maybe I should ask you about humor.

I'm never funny.

Of course not! Why do you write parodies?

I never think that I'm writing parodies. Well, I have a parody of the Western in *God's Country*, but I was trying to represent that form and tried to create a language of the form. You'll find that it sounds like a Western, but you will never find characters in Westerns talk the way they do in that novel, and that's what I wanted to do. It generated a little bit out of watching television and seeing the depiction of different professions and races—you know, black talk—and I realized I never hear anyone talk like that. It's completely artificial, and I took something that was completely artificial and extracted the language for it, but it doesn't sound like any Western.

It's really funny, but, like you said, it's uncomfortably funny.

Good.

You've said that you use humor to understand something better.

I think that's typically a function of humor. All cultures use humor to try to get through difficult times, try to process the world. The best understanding of politics comes out of humor. The best place to get the news right now is *The Daily Show*. You don't go to Fox News. That sardonic take on the news is often so much more honest than any of this so-called objective reporting, and it's so much smarter. What better way to treat difficult and moving issues in a culture than to get your readers laughing first. Mark Twain did it with slavery. *Huck Finn* is a funny book, but it's not a funny book. It's hilarious, but it's also terribly sad.

A History of the African-American People (Proposed) by Strom Thurmond, as told to Percival Everett & James Kincaid *is a very funny book too, but it's also . . .*

We didn't mean it to be funny at all. It's true.

Did it change something for you to work with James Kincaid on it?

It didn't change anything, but it was fun. Jim is a maniac. He writes so much all the time. I just kept telling him, "Stop! It'll get done."

And this plays out in the ways every writer thinks everyone else is insane and . . .

Haven't you gotten e-mails from people?

works cited

Everett, Percival. *Assumption*. Minneapolis: Graywolf Press, 2011. Print.

———. *Erasure*. London: Faber and Faber, 2001. Print.

———. *Glyph*. Saint Paul: Graywolf Press, 1999. Print.

———. *God's Country*. Boston: Faber and Faber, 1994. Print.

———. *A History of the African-American People (Proposed) by Strom Thurmond, as told to Percival Everett and James Kincaid*. New York: Akashic Books, 2004. Print.

———. *I Am Not Sidney Poitier*. Saint Paul: Graywolf Press, 2009. Print.

———. "Interview with Robert Birnbaum." *Identity Theory*. N.p., 6 May 2006. Web. 18 Feb. 2016.

———. "A Modality." *Fiction's Present: Situating Contemporary Narrative Innovation.* Ed. R. M. Berry and Jeffery Di Leo. Albany: State U of New York P, 2007. Print. 209–12.

———. *The Water Cure.* St. Paul: Graywolf Press, 2007. Print.

———. *Watershed.* St. Paul: Graywolf Press, 1996. Print.

———. *Wounded.* St. Paul: Graywolf Press, 2005. Print.

———. *Zulus.* Sag Harbor: Permanent Press, 1990. Print.

Laval, Martine. "Percival Everett." *Télérama* 3121 (11 July 2009): 44–46. Print.

Reynolds, Susan Salter. "Percival Everett, In and Out of Fiction." *Los Angeles Times* 12 July 2009. Web. 18 Feb. 2016.

further works by and on percival everett

Bauer, Sylvie. "'Fracture This Bone . . . and Find the True Anguish of Speech': Disenacting the Body in Percival Everett's *Zulus.*" *Percival Everett: Writing Other/Wise.* Ed. Keith B. Mitchell and Robin G. Vander. New Orleans: Xavier Review Press, 2014. 37–57.

Claude, Julien, and Anne-Laure Tissut, eds. *Reading Percival Everett: European Perspectives.* Tours: PU François Rabelais, 2007. Print.

Everett, Percival. *Abstraktion und Einfühlung.* New York: Akashic Books, 2008. Print.

———. *American Desert.* New York: Hyperion, 2004. Print.

———. *Big Picture.* St. Paul: Graywolf Press, 1996. Print.

———. *The Body of Martin Aquilera.* Camano Island: Owl Creek Press, 1997. Print.

———. *Cutting Lisa.* New York: Ticknor & Fields, 1986. Print.

———. *Damned If I Do.* St. Paul: Graywolf Press, 2004. Print.

———. *For Her Dark Skin.* Seattle: Owl Creek Press, 1990. Print.

———. *Frenzy.* St. Paul: Graywolf Press, 1997. Print.

———. *Grand Canyon, Inc.* San Francisco: Versus Press, 2001. Print.

———. *Half an Inch of Water.* St. Paul: Graywolf Press, 2015. Print.

———. *The One that Got Away.* Illustrated by Dirk Zimmer. New York: Clarion Books, 1992. Print.

———. *Percival Everett by Virgil Russell.* Minneapolis: Graywolf Press, 2013. Print.

———. *re: f (gesture).* Pasadena: Red Hen Press, 2006. Print.

———. *Suder.* New York: Viking Press, 1983. Print.

———. *Swimming Swimmers Swimming.* Pasadena: Red Hen Press, 2011. Print.

———. *Walk Me to the Distance.* New York: Ticknor & Fields, 1985. Print.

———. *The Weather and Women Treat Me Fair.* Little Rock: August House, 1987. Print.

Farebrother, Rachel. "'Out of Place': Reading Space in Percival Everett's *Erasure.*" *MELUS: The Journal of the Society for the Study of the Multi-Ethnic Literature of the United States* 40.2 (2015): 117–36. Print.

Feith, Michel. "Philosophy in the Basement: The Heritage of Ancient Greek Philosophy in Percival Everett's *The Water Cure.*" *Troubled Legacies: Heritage/Inheritance in American Minority Literatures.* Ed. Michel Feith and Claudine Raynaud. Newcastle upon Tyne: Cambridge Scholars, 2015. 49–70. Print.

Johnson, Michael K. "Looking at the Big Picture: Percival Everett's *Western Fiction.*" *Western American Literature* 42.1 (2007): 26–53. Print.

Kincaid, James, ed. *Percival Everett: A Special Section.* Spec. issue of *Callaloo: A Journal of African Diaspora Arts and Letters* 28.2 (2005). Print.

Larkin, Lesley, ed. *Race and the Literary Encounter: Black Literature from James Weldon Johnson to Percival Everett.* Bloomington: Indiana UP, 2015. Print.

Maniez, Claire, and Anne-Laure Tissut, eds. *Percival Everett: Transatlantic Readings.* Paris: Editions Le Manuscrit, 2007. Print.

Maus, Derek C., and James J. Donahue, eds. *Post-Soul Satire: Black Identity after Civil Rights.* Jackson: UP of Mississippi, 2014. Print.

Mitchell, Keith B., and Robin G. Vander. *Perspectives on Percival Everett.* Jackson: UP of Mississippi, 2013. Print.

Powell, Tamara. "Lord of Allusions: Reading Percival Everett's *Erasure* through African American Literary History." *Valley Voices: A Literary Review* 12.2 (2012): 100–107. Print.

Ridley, Chauncey. "Van Go's Pharmakon: 'Pharmacology' and Democracy in Percival Everett's *Erasure.*" *African American Review* 47.1 (2014): 101–11. Print

Weixelmann, John. *Conversations with Percival Everett.* Oxford: U of Mississippi P, 2013. Print.

thalia field

THALIA FIELD IS PROFESSOR OF LITERARY ARTS AT BROWN UNIVERSITY. SHE IS THE AUTHOR OF *POINT AND LINE* (2000), *INCARNATE: STORY MATERIAL* (2004), AND *BIRD LOVERS, BACKYARD* (2010). SHE HAS ENGAGED IN VARIOUS MODES OF COLLABORATIONS—WITH JAMIE JEWETT ON MULTIMEDIA DANCE PERFORMANCES; WITH ABIGAIL LANG ON *A PRANK OF GEORGES* (2010); AND WITH BILL MORRISON AND ABBOT STRANAHAN ON FILM IN *ULULU (CLOWN SHRAPNEL)* (2007).

I BECAME INTERESTED in Thalia Field's work after I read *Point and Line* (2000) and fell in love with her architectural use of language—the physical dimension of the page; the gaps in and contours of the surface and depths of the texts; the geographical and mathematical dimensions of language. *Point and Line* takes the form of composite discourses exploring thought, language, and the body. The result is a sensual exploration of "the touch [that] might be painful, erotic, before we understand it" (9) and of "the body [which] is the blueprint of all technology" (25). As I read more of her work, I discovered diverse directions and genres: many of her projects defy categorization so that fiction, theater, poetry, essay, and art-book writing conflate. Often, literary devices attributed to specific genres or discourses venture into unexpected areas of texts: in *Point and Line,* for example, Field incorporates her theatrical use of [prompts]—a technique that invites audiences to participate in the development of the performance that they are viewing—to stress the reader's active relationship to her text and to highlight the openness of texts. This conflation of genres and writing techniques gives us new paths of exploration of the nature of language as we reconsider our approach to literature from unusual angles.

In *Bird Lovers, Backyard* (2000), for example, Field explores the relationship between "group" and "individual" narratives, decision-making, and autonomy in a text that resists linearity and closure. The book, multidisciplinary in focus and genre binding in form, approaches questions of hybridity at various levels. At times, the layered narrative ventures into a writing mode closer to the essay than that of a traditional narrative, so that the reader discovers layers of truth about ecological concerns. The multimedia book *ULULU: Clown Shrapnel* (2007) includes excerpts from plays, documents, and illustrations about the mythologizing of the seductress as well as footage from filmmaker Bill Morrison. This volume asks questions about knowing and not knowing, as the narrative pieces together facts and artifacts about the infamous Lulu. The collage of media prompts us to rethink how we envision time, characters, documents, history, and truth in the context of biography and fiction. The text's multivocal qualities resist linearity and closure, thereby reminding us of the unstable nature of writing—"factual" or "fictional."

Incarnate: Story Material (2004) proposes a different mode of literary experimentation in its exploration of the contours of life and writing. It focuses on the human form: the manipulation of narrative structure accompanies the displacing and dispersing of the "I." In "Autocartography," for example, the text physically maps out activities that might build selves, including the activity of naming "thalia field" (4). Here, Field shapes the self into an indeterminate entity.

Field and I e-mailed each other from January to June 2012. The exchange was fast paced and extremely productive—along with the back-and-forth of questions and answers, we each edited, modified, and shaped the contours of the manuscript that we were creating. While this exchange was particularly enjoyable for me, I believe that it also attests to Field's true commitment to collaboration, as she engaged wholly in the growth of the document that follows. Collaboration is, in fact, one of the topics that we addressed as well as her views on group and individual thought processes; identity and the self; the spatial, physical, and visual dimensions of the text; hybridity; and the political, ecological, and ethical impacts of her work.

•

When I first became acquainted with your work, authors like Stéphane Mallarmé came to my mind because of the importance of the spatial and visual manipulations in your literary practice. Would you care to say something about your use of the space of the text?

Coming originally from theater, I transferred to books the open feeling of an empty stage: an immediate calling, desolate and heightened, where everything can manifest from the barest material. It's not so much an interest in poetic concreteness but rather an all-over kinetic synergy: voices, plasticity of action, of thought. Running through space, containing multitudes, there's ritual and there's a sense of transformation. Then, too, a biological analogy: evolution equals behavior *and* morphology; in other words, text on the page that takes on novel shapes can be a response to history, accident, or chaos. Think of water taking on the forms it encounters, of fantasy and dreams, of trees and slime molds and milkweed. Think Nathalie Sarraute: the movement of thought readies the page for surviving it.

I should say that quite accidentally my pieces ran smack into the market convention of prose fiction that assumes stories should be free of formal qualities and "pour" without resistance or complication from one format to another, that is, from the computer to the magazine column, website, or book. Fiction writers as 'content providers'; if it doesn't pour into any container, it's not fiction. I never understood this, even though from the very beginning it caused me trouble. My writing can be awkward, angular and shapely—and pages can be too. Thankfully for New Directions, I was rescued early.

For Johanna Drucker, the page is always in tension with the text printed on it because the white space of the line breaks is "a force, against which the whole must be recovered, or against which the whole can be fractured, dissolved, let go" (Figuring the Word 140). A book like Point and Line, *which maximizes its visual potential, reminds us of this tension. Could you elaborate on your use of the white surface of the text and its print?*

It never even occurred to me not to use text and space expressively. It seems so obvious as a component of working in print that I would be more curious to ask people who follow generic (nonvisual) forms of prose why they don't take advantage of the page/book's possibilities. I suspect it's because of dominant conventions, which, as I mentioned above, expect fiction to be more "content" and less visually/aurally/performatively complex.

*You have mentioned theatre and fiction above, but you are also involved in different kinds of artistic media—*ULULU (Clown Shrapnel), *with its visual and written experiments, is an obvious example of your involvement in interdisciplinary arts. Does your commitment to various genres require a different mode of writing, practically speaking?*

Clown Shrapnel required visual interruption because Lulu's history was ruptured over and over by the many who kept putting it back together. She's an unwieldy stereotype, a cipher, a clown—and through all the stories told about her, there are stories branching off and more language and then some film and a history of burlesque and commedia. And finally, there were the men who appeared on- and offstage, and finally it was all just too much! So the book carries that excess. And so it took extra hands to make it work. I don't have an automatic affinity with illustrations, but in this case the surface of the narrative was already so fractured, so atonal, so beyond repair, that the visual interruption of the film (mimicking, of course, the absent but intended film from the opera) and the illustrations (their quest for relevance) could both be contained in the body of the whole. Poor Lulu was born motherless; an unnatural creature (so they said) and the work always lived beyond genre.

Practically speaking, I don't have any conception (pre- or otherwise) about genre when I'm working. I think of myself as a storyteller and my artistic heroes are as often stage artists as novelists. In fact, I think the stage has recently been doing a lot about the potential of the novel: I'm thinking here of Robert Ashley, Liz LeCompte, Elevator Repair Service, Simon McBurney, and many others. The only question, finally, is whether something will be in a book or on a stage. If in a book, it's a book piece, and my commitment is to make it work for the reader the same way a performance succeeds for its audience.

The use of [prompts] involves a level of collaboration with performers in Hey-Stop-That *and with readers in* Point and Line. *When you allow your writing to become part of performances or when you work with choreographers, you also engage in collaborative relationships. Why is collaboration important to you?*

In *Point and Line* you'll find "Hours" and "Setting, the Table," which employ the [prompts] I developed for use in my theater work, now fashioned for the page. These were crucial to me when I worked in live performance—an essential ability to invite the thinking mind (of the performer and the audience, simultaneously) onstage and then later into the book. This is a form of collaboration in that the text is never solely "authored" by me. I haven't returned to [prompts] in a while because my interest in a thinking performativity needed to expand beyond this one discovery. And so the textual indeterminacy moved toward other ways that fiction invites argument, debate. . . . There are other performance-y pieces lurking here and there (overt ones such as "Zoologic" from *Incarnate* and less overt ones such as "Parting" or "This Crime Has a Name" from *Bird Lovers, Backyard* or *A Prank of Georges*, generally). In terms of my more recent stage work, I've enjoyed the challenge of working with dancers because dance provides a continual lesson in immediate and oblique approaches to meaning.

Interdisciplinarity already feels collaborative: a ceaseless evolution and cross-pollination of form and idea. As a mongrel thinker I have always chased unusual connections, odd affinities, or awkward conversations in progress—challenging purists since I can remember—whether in art or academic or personal contexts. So when all goes well, writing is self-collaboration in that it forces a challenge to—and (possible) abandonment of—old habits and head gunk.

But of course I've also had the delightful honor to work with actual collaborators through the years. One of my favorite collaborative pieces was a performance featuring an enormous "hair nest" (and video and music and interactive text) with Michelle Ellsworth and David Wiley. With an incredible group of women (including Shelley Jackson, Akilah Oliver, and Bhanu Kapil) we put on "Hey-Stop-That." With composer Toshiro Saruya I wrote the libretto to "The Pompeii Exhibit." With my old friend Jena Osman we made fun short works for performance and page, and of course there are my recent and ongoing adventures with Abigail Lang. Other people are a complement of treasure—making it a richer room. Be that room a theater or a book, *peu importe.*

In Incarnate: Story Material, *the ways in which language "perceives" intersect with bodily matters. Could you talk about the body in the book?*

I think language "perceives" (as in something self-organizing, emergent) in the more groping and polyvocal pieces in *Incarnate* such as "Land at Church City," "Envelope Bag," or "Flickering." Analogous to an organ, something bodily, these stories construct themselves out of raw story materials, almost sense data (sense in both senses of the word). From "Autocartography" to "Zoologic"—is a living body an individual? Its meanings and experiences unique and irreducible? Or are we simply aspects of larger entities—just flickering . . . ? While writing *Incarnate,* I remember being concerned with some of the same questions that preoccupied *Point and Line,* but as the questions became more "incarnate" (taking body) they grew more capacious, multiple, formless—insisting on a kind of liminal space between energy and matter. Still, the recurring question: Who speaks? It never seems a single voice. In terms of body, there are searches, desires—for name, for territory, adventure, pleasure, autonomy—which may be how incarnation can feel both like a prison and a condition of freedom.

While Incarnate: Story Material *and* Point and Line *explore issues of selves/ stories differently, they both invite us to think about what frames these selves and stories. In other words, we don't just look at selves/stories, but we also think about how they are delineated. Obviously, the two are related, but we often disregard how we frame or delineate things to look more closely at what they are. Why is it important for you to explore not only selves/stories but also their boundaries?*

What my name is, or my history, what my 'nation' is, my species—ultimately we can't find these edges, though we use placeholders to mark them. Any intuition that "I" am not so simple—either as the subject or the narrator of anything story-like—becomes a literary wild space, a series of challenges. So one way into this new sense is through building and dissolving frames, whether those frames are around a portrait, a state, a well-known myth, a history, a name, a list, or an easy answer to a straightforward search.

Also, what is in our lived environment (the world moving beyond and through our skin, our sense of privacy, personal property, or self) is what's too easily overlooked or diminished in literary characters. I think I'm exploring the difference between so-called characters and so-called scene, between description and action, noun and verb, process and event, situation and mind.

It has been commonplace in recent literary criticism to think of writers who engage in such building and breaking of frames as resisting the presentation of a self. I wonder if this interpretation is not reductive though, especially in light of your answer. Do you see yourself proposing a resistance?

Resistance might be an emphasis on the contingent interplay between accident and identity, time and character, populations and the portrait. Finding the balance between the categorical and the individual is complicated; how are we all interconnected on our single planet, spinning around as one, and yet at the same time so sure we are the unique and one-time-only Very Important Person who laughs and suffers and makes a living? It's a generative paradox . . . that propels a resistance to biography, propels my interest in history, and the open and charged nature of historical representation of characters, of events. How important is one person? One bird? An ant? A society? A population? A culture? Aren't we all equally important and nonimportant? More than merely a resistance to the "self"—it's a resistance to either side of the paradox of the self. "Character" means many things, and characters "mean" many things—functionally and teleologically—and in the defense or the perversion of these meanings both tragedy and comedy ensue.

Characters might result from an accumulation, almost a storehouse, of living and dead language, and in this might be a resistance—as each makes a life from that repository and turns history into behavior. Is character merely action? Behaviors merely neurons, epigenetics, space dust? If so, what is the relationship of thought to behavior—How do the sloppy dealings of the language of rhetoric, persuasion—as the shaper of lived argument (assuming we're all living forms of argument)—open up the story space where opposing and contradictory propositions collide? My artistic lineage includes authors of fictional polyvocal texts who argue and play with discourse, thought, and narrative: Aeschylus, Sterne, Flaubert (of *Bouvard and Pécuchet*), Zola, Woolf (of *Three Guineas*), Brecht, Dos Passos, Bely, Acker, Kundera, and so forth and so forth—this lineage of dialogic writers breaks fictional surfaces in the service of the *agon*, the space at the center of the city or the center of a situation, or the violent/comic place where ideas and lives collide.

In A Prank of Georges, *the dialogic quality of writing is central. Could you address the dialogue of voices, authors, and languages in the book?*

Prank was joyful to write because we thought of certain nodes of inquiry and then wove our language through them, creating tangles that seemed to catch on or entrap certain notions in their webs. These included notions about being an individual or being a member of a population, having a proper name or just being an example of one, making dramatic sense or being a force of illogic, being defined by things like birthday, place of origin, or some sort of basic habit. These sorts of questions propelled us, and through them we also found that many of these resonate with themes and language that Gertrude Stein posed over and again. Putting our inquiries in the same web as hers—or inviting her onto the stage—this was how dialogue happened. The fact that we were working on little machines freed us from constraints of genre. The whole thing resembled an open field in which all sorts of characters (or discourses) could speak—a bit perhaps like Stein's concept of landscape.

Do you think of ULULU *or* Bird Lovers, Backyard *as political because of their exploration of history and imagination? Or do you consider all of your works political on different levels or perhaps not political at all?*

I believe my writing is political in that it relates to the affairs of groups. Any group decision requires storytelling, whether it concerns roads across Alaska, pigeons in public places, military strategy, scientific inquiry, or simply what to name something. Bringing in authority from science, history, famous thinkers, even dictionaries!—any group (even a group of two or four) must make choices that affect members and nonmembers alike—occasionally resulting in forms of groupthink or in individual genius. In any history, immediately there are both group and individual stories (and dreams and memories) colliding with official stories (even at the expense of a life). Bureaucratic structures often figure in my stories because they directly obstruct easy notions of the autonomy of the individual actor or author. What potential does a group character, a population, have to be just when a community trying to survive exists and doesn't exist in equal measure? This quasi existence, which we sometimes believe in and sometimes can't, feels vital when "it" is the subject of its own history or storytelling.

This is why I sometimes choose the chorus as a dramatic character (the "chorus as judge," or "chorus as decision-maker"), the dialogic possibility of the *agon* (or that which puts the reader in the uncomfortable space of debate viewer)—where "authority" is dispersed across a wide range of speakers—for example, multiple perspectives are argued, voiced, reasoned (or unreasoned). The range of possible authorities includes texts, quotes, historical events, experts from various disciplines, cultural figures, and so forth. Competing ideas are embodied, and ultimately there is a generalized dispossession of knowledge, an activated groundlessness. This *agon*-istic questioning is certainly what motivated "A (therefore) I" (*Point and Line*) and "Zoologic" (*Incarnate*) (heroic battles) but also what undergirds *Bird Lovers, Backyard*.

In a book like Bird Lovers, Backyard, *one may conclude that the facts brought in from various sources should create solutions or responses but instead they create questions. Could you explain how questions are the core of learning in your work?*

I'm of the opinion that there is only ever an amalgam of fact and fiction, nearly impossible to distill or purify. Because of this there is an ongoing conversation between commonality and individuality, between what is received or created from tradition and what is unheard of. This is why my materials for writing also combine so-called fact and so-called fiction, because there's an intricate gray scale of interest as a palette. Questions, on the other hand, can be called obsessions, fanaticisms, problems, suspicions, grief, trauma, dream, or fantasy—whatever gets the work moving. The questions are sometimes obvious in the work and sometimes deflected, buried or transposed, but for me they provide the heat. Sometimes the questions and the materials intersect so closely that they seem to emerge from each other. Sometimes they are very far apart. And anyway—what question can't a question question?

Because your work explores facts and fiction in prose, poetry, and drama, it is often referred to as "hybrid." Hybridity appears at different levels: genres become permeable as well as "history" and "imagination." Do you feel comfortable with the appellation "hybrid" in regard to your books? And why is the engagement of multiple sources and genres essential to your writing?

As you see in the stories in *Bird Lovers, Backyard*, I was quite taken with questions of hybridity, both in the sciences and in literature. Obsessing over purity is never merely a theoretical proposition but usually an ethical one. 'Hybridity' used negatively is a symptom of any obsession with purity, of closed mindedness or overprotection of narrow interests, most often involving identity. Hybridity is an inescapable force in all aspects of life (human and otherwise) and seems hardly to warrant defending, except that our minds tempt us to draw territories and distinctions, and so the subtle poison of purity is always to be counteracted.

Personally I've witnessed conflict where interpretation of events, behavior, or truth was at stake in devastating ways. Fact and fiction being mostly inseparable, storytelling stands open to bias, operational (or emotional) fallacies, and the aggressions of hermetic discourse or perspective. One man's self-righteous genius is another's lunatic. Thus, multiple sources allow a situation in which questions are posed and not resolved. Artists whose work moves fluidly between so-called genres have always been of particular interest to me because each piece is allowed to simply be what it is without explanation. I would much prefer readers find my writing engaging or not than ask whether it succeeds or fails through the lens of a genre (I guarantee it fails).

Ethical questions are central in Bird Lovers, Backyard, *and, though perhaps to a lesser extent, in your other books. Would you mind expanding on ethics in relation to your writing?*

I hope I consider ethical issues and social issues as clowns would encounter them. Some favorite authors use clowning in their work (Fellini of course, but also Joyce, Chekhov, Beckett, Brecht, Ellison, Handke, Spark, etc.). With a clown as a guide, it becomes serious play making off-balance problems that take unexpected journeys through rigid or oversanctified logic. Aware of performance, the clown steps and slips and smiles and stumbles in sublime and illogical obedience to the world's foundational mandate to simply pay attention. This attention is an ethical stance. Moreover, clowns fail virtuosically, reversing hierarchical values that are often themselves masks of injustice. Cutting through complication by revealing how potent a simpler question might be, it is the clown's role to exist beneath our high-concept radar, to challenge the commonsense agreement of how things "work," and to bring out the childlike openness to simply being present, which undoes the fanciest of social or intellectual agendas. It is to clowning in this way I aspire, even though I am often afflicted with its opposite—a sense of some seriousness of purpose—which skips the digressions and fertility of the moment for the sake of something for which there is no shortcut. Ethics, then, is to allow the playful task of simply being with my work; to allow whatever arises to partner me and I to partner it, generating the most meaningful of clown problems.

Reading about your ideas on clowns brings up the question of humor in your work. One does not expect to laugh easily at an outline, but I certainly laughed when, in Point and Line, *I read "Outline, In Mind" with sentences like "Sal Takes a Drink of Early Civilization" or "Pragmatic Archeologies on the D train" or when I read questions such as "BUT WHAT'S 'SHUT UP' IN SIGN LANGUAGE?" (ULULU 222) or the "Discussion Questions" in* Bird Lovers, Backyard *(41). But, as you mention above, playfulness is not isolated from other, perhaps, more serious matters.*

Lists and jostled discourses, the movement of language between systems of thought, retrofitted for individual purpose—I find this humorous and I'm glad you do as well. It's the clown's prerogative to negotiate, as though a foreigner, the self-serious oddities of what we take for granted. In the overlooked habit there are infinite opportunities for play, and to paraphrase James Carse, "lack of seriousness is what confounds society the most."

Your reference to foreignness evokes Viktor Shklovsky's defamiliarization—the idea that art, by making what we take for granted unfamiliar, enhances our understanding of the familiar. How does this kind of artistic awareness take part in your writing?

I would say that the alienation effect (at least as put forward by Bertolt Brecht and first enacted with Erwin Piscator) definitely focused my attention on the practical distance between actor and character—and thus the dialectic deployment of story and dramatic material. To perform without complete absorption into imagination, to retain a bridge between imagination and a historical situation, this challenge is close to clowning. Through Brecht, I read the formalists, especially Shklovsky, who is a master writer about writing, as Bakhtin is, too. At another moment I loved the *Iliad* and Aeschylus and Aristophanes and all things Greek. Only later I read Chinese and Indian philosophy. Aren't we the products of our libraries? As Brecht said about his writing of epic, "individual episodes need to be knotted together in such a way that the knots are easily noticed" and also that characters act "in relation to history" (201).

Making strange, in the formalist sense, depends a lot on the specific conversation literary devices are having with the audience—all at a particular historical moment. To reveal forgotten history is a form of defamiliarization—an echo of Walter Benjamin's notion that history is mostly a way for the present to re-present itself.

Despite all this, I don't feel that devices in any formalist sense (or ideas in any conceptual one) are how I engage my work in practice. I think what Shklovsky does well is to articulate the intuitive nature of how a writer feels his way into reinvigorating old forms or making his work slow the reader into heightened awareness. I feel also in tune with Bakhtin's ideas of literature as a radical heteroglossia, a carnival. This novelistic symphony, this cacophony, is ultimately musical, which reflects how I hear so many voices at once when I'm writing. The first play I ever "wrote" (an early collaboration with the director Daisy Prince) involved creating the script through a collage of my own writing, found text, and prompted collaboration with the actors. In this open field, authorship remained unglued from any single point, reusing information and forms in strange ways. Thus, this writerly polyvalence isn't conceptual, it presents itself as a practical and open process of reinventing. As Shklovsky said, "Every literary work is a brand new montage of the world, a new unpredictability, a new occurrence" (*Energy of Delusion* 26).

I like Brecht's idea of noticeable "knots" in relation to Bakhtin's polyphony. The combination of both makes me think of the architectural qualities of your work. I think, for instance, of the physical and angular spaces of "The Compass Room," or the visible "knots" of knowledge in ULULU *when each discourse, framed by the lines on the sides of the book, changes visibly in content and form (with the play of fonts), or the architecture of "(Flickering)"—its words' movements on the page. Do you think of* Point and Line *as a mode of Ekphrastic writing?*

I suppose I am prone to borrow and beg juicy bits from other arts in order to re-pose paradoxes that seem pertinent to a shared conversation. I don't think of myself as engaged with any sort of "writing into" other arts, but maybe I'm wrong. There's Kandinsky of course, there's film history, architecture, there's Wilde's *Salome*, then, of course, most of *ULULU* is in discussion with a variety of artists, and then there's a bit of Poe (in *Point and Line*) and Blake (in *Bird Lovers*) as well as others here and there—so I guess there's something to your question. Is that Ekphrastic? I always wished I could have been a composer.

Perhaps that yearning to express myself musically causes a reach toward other artists.

In Bird Lovers, Backyard, *your investigation centers on the ecological possibilities of writing. Could you expand on this?*

I was considering how writing and science both call upon narrative when positioning authority. My unfinished studies in animal behavior and evolutionary biology left me with nagging questions about the language bound up in scientific practice (questions that either pleased or drove my professors nuts). A lot of the stories in *Bird Lovers* began forming during those early rehearsals.

From an ecological point of view, I also found it suspicious that the vast majority of literature wasn't reinventing or reimagining its subject positions—or its narrowly human-governed logic—despite the general impact of deep ecology. The radical entanglements of unworkable binaries (such as human-animal, beautiful-ugly, wilderness-culture, etc.) inspired me to ask narrative questions more in the scale and time sense of bio-logical or geo-logical approaches. This brought out stories as multivalent systems, rather than as soundstages for human protagonists cinematically foregrounded against a psychologically explanatory cohort and a viably televiseable human-scale world; in other words, the normative fictions left over from poorly understood naturalism. If we know that even the human body is a "unit set" for thousands of species of bacteria, controlling our minds and our moods, then including bacteria (or glaciers or fruit flies) in literature feels unavoidable. And not just as 'content' either. . . . The interdependent goings-on in any patch of earth are so rich they can barely be perceived, let alone described. So the challenge of ecology, of being alive in the world, is how to respond to infinite richness with satisfying new ways of enacting it—without always putting ourselves as the subject. No matter how much I include in each piece, I feel I've left out much more than I can ever include—that each story can never achieve the density of existence or experience.

As I mentioned earlier, questions of hybridity that preoccupy *Bird Lovers* overlap between literature and ecology—and so the scientists who have narrated hybridity became of interest. One of the most salient aspects of working with Vicki Hearne was her attention to language in power relationships between species. It goes back to that blank and inviting relation that is intimately unknowable. This loving unknowability is why language matters and has power. In performing stories, there can be sublime play and imaginative experiments—as long as the terms are not harmful. This is, for me, literature's greatest potential and maybe science's too—a crucial rethink of our dominant misunderstandings of value.

One of my neighbors in France took part this year in a human chain stretching from Marseille to Lyon protesting (or just calling attention to) one of the densest concentrations of nuclear reactors in the world. There were kilometers of people holding hands and then of course kilometers without hands, and very little press coverage. But that chain is what she could do to express anxiety. Writing is my chain.

Obviously, the majority of books published today don't engage in the kinds of questions your work, or other works that we have talked about, is invested in. Do you think that the state of the publishing industry has an impact on the kinds of works published in this country?

My artistic genealogy, my own private lineage of artists and authors, provides the most vibrant and sustaining aspect of my creative life. The books and plays and operas and works I feel I am in constant debate and conversation with fuel not just my work but the abiding pleasure I feel in art and in living—the courage of being really aware, the courage of death. Everyone has the books they cherish, reread, ruin. We must support the people who keep them all available. I hope every reader finds the books and artworks that matter to them. That would be enough for all publishing "industries" to consider, as they are the heroes of that story, and so much that is priceless is in their hands.

works cited

Brecht, Bertol. *Brecht on Theatre*. Trans. John Willett. London: Methuen, 1964. Print.

Field, Thalia. *Bird Lovers, Backyard*. New York: New Directions, 2010. Print.

———. *Incarnate: Story Material*. New York: New Directions, 2004. Print.

———. *Point and Line*. New York: New Directions, 2000. Print.

———. *ULULU: Clown Shrapnel*. Minneapolis: Coffee House Press, 2007. Print.

further works by and on thalia field

Baetens, Jan, and Éric Trudel. "Backward/Forward: Thalia Field's Metanarratives." *MFS: Modern Fiction Studies* 60.3 (2014): 599–615. Print.

Elshtain, Eric P. "An E-Mail Interview with Thalia Field." *Chicago Review* 47.3 (2001): 99–110. Print.

Field, Thalia. *Experimental Animals (A Reality Fiction)*. New York: Solid Objects, 2016. Print.

Herman, David. "Hermeneutics beyond the Species Boundary: Explanation and Understanding in Animal Narratives." *Storyworlds* 8.1 (2016): 1–30. Print.

Parrish, Gillian. "The Question of Evolution in the Buddhist Ecology of Thalia Field's *Bird Lovers, Backyard*." *Ecozon@: European Journal of Literature, Culture and Environment* 2.2 (2011): 157–76. Print.

Tardi, Mark. "[7 Outdated Objects Which Dangle]: The Post-Genre Prism of Thalia Field's *Point and Line*." *Theory That Matters: What Practice after Theory*. Ed. Kacper Bartczak. Newcastle upon Tyne: Cambridge Scholars, 2013. 285–93. Print.

renee gladman

> RENEE GLADMAN IS AN ASSISTANT PROFESSOR OF LITERARY ARTS AT BROWN UNIVERSITY. SHE IS THE AUTHOR OF THE RAVICKIAN SERIES: *EVENT FACTORY* (2010), *THE RAVICKIANS* (2011), AND *ANA PATOVA CROSSES A BRIDGE* (2013). SINCE 2004, SHE HAS BEEN THE EDITOR AND PUBLISHER OF LEON WORKS. FROM 1999 TO 2003, SHE WORKED AS EDITOR OF THE LEROY CHAPBOOK SERIES.

IN HER ESSAY, "Emergence of a Fiction," Renee Gladman explains that her narratives involve "a character or 'self' [. . .] projected into a (usually) urban terrain that proves difficult to cross or assimilate due to real and imagined obstacles" (89). Indeed, many of her texts are deeply rooted in urban-ness: a kind of urban sociology emerges from cosmopolitan demographics, from the appearance and/or disappearance of an urban community, from the states of anonymity and alienation, from the development of subcultures, and from the urbanites' sense of tolerance or lack thereof. The negotiations of public and private spheres in the metropolis lead Gladman to examine the contours of urban selfhood. *Juice* (2000), a text halfway between prose and poetry, explores what constitutes such selfhood through possible and impossible scenarios. In the hybrid text, Gladman creates series of paradoxes, as well as moments when cause and effect do not suit, when time does not progress as it should (or as we think it should), or when discrepancies between language and experience manifest. As the self is taken in different directions, the space of the page also becomes important: words' physicality on the white canvas matters to the evolution of the four narratives—another mode of reflection on the urban maps that surround us.

The question of materiality and immateriality comes up in Gladman's latest trilogy—*Event Factory* (2010), *The Ravickians* (2011), and *Ana Patova*

Crosses a Bridge (2013). In the country Ravicka, speech is performed by bodily movements so that communication becomes an odd choreography of gestures, bows, and dances. In such a context, the physicality of speech becomes a major preoccupation, both for the characters and the readers of the trilogy. In Ravic language, expressing oneself can be challenging: consider the impact of having to perform deep knee bends for three minutes as part of a daily conversational regimen. In such a world, how does the life of one's body infiltrate communication? How does one convey implied or partial meanings? How does one render language's multiplicity? In Ravicka, what can and cannot be communicated takes such physical proportions that the reader is led to ponder the physical challenges of the very text she is reading.

In many ways, the movements of language in the three Ravickian volumes, like the bodily movements of communication, materialize some of the matters of the text. That is, Gladman explores language's movements through the themes of dislocation, translation, writing, and poetry reading, as well as through words' movements on the page—its white expansions and blocks of text another expressive mode. These movements also materialize the prose's lack of linear progression: fragments and seemingly unrelated modes of expansion ask readers to consider how a text, whose narrative is engrained in bodily expression, moves.

The trilogy begins with *Event Factory,* in which the unnamed protagonist experiences various kinds of defamiliarizations during her travel to Ravicka. Though she thought herself quite fluent in Ravic, Gladman's character encounters trials when adapting to her new environment. The complexity of new and foreign interactions in which exaggerated situations border absurdity are at once funny and tragically serious. In many ways, in their extremeness, the protagonist's linguistic and social blunders also comment on our own language usages and the difficulties of expressing ourselves: just like the character, we may think that we know a language when we might in fact not comprehend its subtleties and implications.

In *The Ravickians,* Gladman's linguistic exploration is almost reversed in comparison to *Event Factory,* as it focuses on the emptiness of language: in a city quasi unoccupied, filled with uninhabited homes, empty trains, and unfilled buses, silence prevails. This collapsing urban-ness is described in three interlocked narratives: a first-person account of a day with acclaimed novelist Luswage Amini, the retelling of a poetry reading, and a dialogue between writers. In many ways, the sense of loss and absence carves out a different language, which Gladman explores at the level of form and content: the carving activity appears in the thematic of architecture (characters are fixated on the architectural realities of Ravicka) and the architectural qualities of the text itself, whose sinuous progression establishes a kind of negative space of expression.

In *Ana Patova Crosses a Bridge,* Gladman's simple yet profound prose elaborates on another kind of negation, one that is quite material while having immaterial implications:

> I wrote a book where after every sentence
> I or my character or an object in the
> room disappeared. [. . .]
> [. . .] It was a
> book in which I recognized a companion
> text, one that would hold everything this
> book was erasing. [. . .]
> [. . .] I wrote a
> sentence and downtown was gone; the
> last building stood up and walked away,
> the fourth since that morning; I wrote a sentence
> to replace the building (everything
> that vanished got replaced, at least in the
> book I was writing), but its space in the object world remain empty. A new object vanished: I was still writing. (72–73)

Set at a time of crisis (and this concept takes on various meanings in the novel), *Ana Patova* presents situations that appear both fantastic and quite realistic in their evocation of contemporary urban planning. The above passage is referred to in the conversation that follows, as I ask Gladman about language in *Ana Patova.* Much of our exchange, which took place via e-mail between June 2012 and April 2013, focuses on the Ravickian books and their oblique meanings.

•

Your work often poses questions about time. In Juice, *for example, from the epigraph to the development of the four sections of the book, temporality is at the forefront of the reading (and writing?) experience. Could you talk about your interest in temporality in* Juice *(or other works)?*

Lately, I've been studying the drawings and writings of architect Aldo Rossi (1931–1997). In one passage, he describes his looking back over past projects as coming from a need to grasp an "internal ordering of questions." This idea of "internal ordering" immediately struck me as something that goes on in language. We write against and into that sense of order when we use language narratively, which is pretty much how we always use it, even if the result is fragmented or obfuscated. I think the narrators in all my works are very conscious of a kind of being beholden to time as well as a doubling where you talk yourself into time and stand outside of that time to organize the talking. To speak—for example, "About the body I know very little, though I'm steadily trying to improve myself"—is to enter into a system of conveyance; and regardless of whether one is rendering events or a state of mind, this system entrenches one in time. So, to narrate is, in a sense, to agree to time and order. But, to narrate is also to put oneself in a position to question time and order and then to allow time and order to bewilder one's narration.

You mention narration here, but you also write poetry. Do you find yourself approaching these kinds of writing differently? Is poetry, in fact, different from narration for you, or do these distinctions not apply as much to your writing?

I don't think I would make a distinction between poetry and narration because I find language inherently narrative, occurring in the instance of the word or even the letter. So, in a way, I would argue that there is always some level of narration going on. I like to teach a course called "Fiction Through Poetry" because I'm interested in liminality, "the seam between two expanses," as Danielle Vogel puts it. Rather than talk about binaries, I focus on what lies between two discrete categories and what secretly binds them. What I have been working on lately is less a distinction between poetry and prose than one between prose and line drawing. Here, I'm thinking about the line that moves through language (i.e., the sentence) and the line that moves abstractly across a sheet of paper (it's interesting that we don't say "the page" in this context). Both bear within a desire or necessity for movement and articulation, and something that I've found recently is a convergence (in the space of drawing) where language blurs into abstract notation and, somewhere farther along the line or visual plane, returns to language. I call these Prose Architectures.

In Event Factory, *the experiences related to travel—being confronted with a new culture, being introduced to new people, being immersed in the complexities of foreign linguistic interactions, and so forth—are at times exaggerated to the point of hilarious absurdity but also of quasi-tragic seriousness. Could you talk about these "poles" in* Event Factory *and how their cohabitation is important in the novel?*

I write with an elation that sometimes comes out as melancholy and sometimes write with melancholy that also comes out as melancholy. Often my work is about loneliness, where my narrators feel disoriented and without. But this is a feeling that constantly desires to be interrupted—whether by epistemological quandaries (in the way of Beckett's *Molloy* and his rubbing stones), the possibility of sex, or just the sheer wonder of time or place or structure. These moments of interruption allow the narrative to shift so that it's not all one way. And these are often moments where I'm learning something or where I'm trying to connect with or love the text.

Could you elaborate on how what you describe above happens in your series?

In the first two books of the series, you have two solitary walkers—a translator-tourist wandering through parts of a foreign city looking for events and a writer wandering through the "ruins" of her city on her way to a poetry reading. What connects them is a desire for company. Luswage Amini, the great Ravickian novelist, asks several times throughout *The Ravickians* whether one is ever really accompanied. As we learned in *Event Factory*, it's not enough to simply run into people or take on a lover. Both narrators want a connection that bears out in language and that, most importantly, alters the space they occupy. In "Grand Horizontals," part II of *The Ravickians,* you get to see Amini as part of a group, a narrative that takes shape through fragments of exchange. In *Ana Patova Crosses a Bridge* (the third in the series), one thing I learned was that all this time I believed that these women were alone. I believed their stories. And, it's not to say that they don't experience isolation. Rather, that their moments of isolation are bracketed by time spent with others, this group that meets and waits and writes together.

In The Ravickians *translation is a big preoccupation for the narrator (and for the reader of the book), at times to the point of obsession. It is not the first time that you explore or allude to the act of translation in your prose. Could you talk about translation in* The Ravickians *and/or in other works?*

Translation is one of those topics I find endlessly interesting; it's a question, a *project* of communication and representation that just keeps opening and opening. As a reader I am drawn to texts that appear in English from other languages. A very good translation will allow you to read the book with some semblance of confidence that the book you wished to read (for example, Magdalena Tulli's *Flaw*) is the book that you, in fact, are reading. But, a good translation will also bear a strangeness, a quality of remove, or existing liminally, as if between books and between languages. I love this space.

In *Event Factory,* everything is translation. When you are foreign to a place, everything must be deciphered. I realized as I was writing *Event Factory* that my narrator's attempts to operate within Ravicka's elaborate system of codes were beginning to stand in for other problems that I'd been wanting to think about—for example, how to present one's body to another (in both intimate and nonintimate situations). I also wanted to dramatize the peculiarity of being inside one's body, which sometimes feels like an enclosure but also sometimes feels like an ungainly enormity that engulfs you, that you must direct with your thinking. There is an issue of scale—how small, how big you feel in relation to what you're saying, how loud, how softly the words come, the size of the container that receives your words, how to read that container's reactions. These are all problems of translation.

In *The Ravickians,* I wanted to use translation as a layer-building device for the book. That is, as a reader, you could begin to understand that the book you were reading might have been written in Ravic, that there is something off in the English, an indeterminate presence. I was interested, too, in thinking of the complications that arise in going from one language to another, especially when one is bodily and the other mostly mouth based. And then there is reading and the experience of taking in written language. Also, Luswage Amini, who narrates the first section of the Ravickian, who is a world-famous author, is aware that readers outside of Ravicka are encountering her work. I think, for her, that intensifies the act of accounting. What do you make available to the foreign reader? What do you conceal, protect?

In your essay, "Emergence of a Fiction," you mention the act of translation; there, it is not directly related to a transfer between two different languages. Instead, it focuses on a transfer of information from "life" to "writing." Would you care to say something about this other mode of translation?

I imagine language as a string that pulls thought out of the body. I'm interested in what happens to that thinking as it moves from a more complex interior space (the space of the mind, which defies my understanding) to an exterior space of language, which is a straight line, progressively unfolding and making "order" as it moves further from the body. I'm struck by the disparity between the multidimensionality of memory *pre*-writing and the troubling flatness of memory once it gets encoded. I love how much language it takes, how many sentences are required to bring a many-layered complex thing into appearance. And, most of the time, the most we can do is describe the complexity, describe how we're failing to represent it, and this is my experience of literature. Literature, for me, is about the things that don't quite get through and the resulting shape.

You explore orality at various levels in The Ravickians. *Could you explain why/how orality matters to your writing?*

I don't think about orality so much. The concern for my narrators is performance of speech—getting the words out. Is this what you mean? But, as you know, in Ravic speech is always accompanied by some ceremony of the body. One does not simply say, "Hi. Where are you going?" The Ravickian will be looking at your body to understand the context of your words. Are you bending? Have you performed some gymnastic feat? Are your arms swinging? Is only one? In *Event Factory*, the narrator finds herself at the entrance of a restaurant, wanting lunch, but she can't enter until she performs the appropriate gesture. She has to recall it. It's an anxious moment for her. She wants to be more than a tourist in this place. In *The Ravickians,* the characters are native speakers and fully entrenched in the culture. I think what is most urgent for them—with regard to speech—is finding a way to contain tiny histories within one act of speaking. When people come together in this novel, it's after a long absence. Each person wants to explain what has happened to her, what she has seen, the loneliness she has endured, but somehow it is not right to simply say those things. Perhaps it is impossible to speak toward accumulation. Something breaks off in the language.

The body is important in your answers to my questions here, and it is also important in your work. Can you address the body in your writing?

I am never very good at addressing "the body" directly. I'm not sure I always mean the literal body when I use that word. Of course, when I talk about the Ravickians using their bodies to speak, I do mean their physical bodies. I do mean to suggest that it would be most odd for them to experience the English language, which is mostly something that happens with a person's head. In English, you look at the face; you have no idea what is happening with the feet. In Ravic, someone's body is always coming toward your body or showing you what it can do. Often, the older you are in Ravicka, the more excited you are to speak, to surprise people when they see your back flip, to be able to go on saying the most difficult things. But the Ravickians are (for the most part) invented, so there must be something figurative going on as well. What is that? I want to call attention to an elaborate system of communication, a way to imagine language rattling through an architecture (in this case, the body), where it emerges still alive, still in progress, not complete until absorbed by an adjacent architecture. These gestures are important for me when I think about how I connect or wish to connect with others. The body is less important than the whole choreography of trying.

The idea of choreography and the Ravickians' modes of communication call for a process-oriented approach to "linguistic" expression. In addition, Ravickians' use of their bodies stresses that each utterance will be unique (i.e., personalized by each body's ability), which, in some ways, is true in English but exacerbated in Ravic. Ravic also stresses the ephemerality of each moment of communication.

When I think about why the Ravickians use their bodies so elaborately to speak, it seems to have something to do with the conditions of speaking, with a sense of how crucial and meaningful it is to engage a person. Regardless of whether that encounter is an intimate conversation or an exchange at a ticket counter, the Ravickian senses the energy around the event. They perform as if to say, "How strange it is that we have a language between us," "How strange it is that you have something I need," "How strange it is that we have known each other for years." They say, "Look at your body," or "Look, I have a body, can you believe it." I wanted to return us—the reader, me—to a place where every utterance had the quality of being new, invented as a kind of necessary collaboration between the voice, body, and the air between them.

Can you talk about architecture in Ana Patova Crosses a Bridge?

I could talk for days about architecture in this book. In fact, the book seems to obsessively circle the question of built spaces—whether built from language or concrete material. One wants to build a space—a bridge—to pass through, something that will mediate "the elements" from outside (of one's self), something that will connect one event to another event. Each enclosure for Ana Patova is an architecture of trying, a space of unfolding or raveling through which she hopes to arrive at a kind of answer or idea about living in the world, about ending the crisis, about being close to others.

Ana Patova *is about the act of writing. Why is it important for you to engage in a "metafictional" mode of writing?*

I want to resist applying the term *metafictional* to this book. While Ana Patova's *Enclosures* primarily concerns itself with the books Ana Patova has written as well as those her friends have written, the act of writing occurs on the level of the narrative, alongside drinking coffee, walking the city streets, surviving the crisis. The writing about writing is never meant to comment on itself, to be outside of what is happening in Ravicka, to show a hyperawareness of the form—in fact, the book we are reading is the one that to me seems the most impossible. What fuels Ana Patova's *Enclosures* is an urgent sense that to survive she must do three things: write, walk, and gather. Each of these acts is inextricably bound up with the other. To write about writing is to simultaneously investigate every aspect of being a living person, beholden to time, surrounded by place.

In Ana Patova, *writing seems to have a material presence or force, while writing is often considered as a fairly immaterial activity. Can you address the material/immaterial in the novel?*

Everything that has to do with writing is immaterial, in the sense that it's all imagined, it's all abstract. Recently, I've been marveling over the fact that language doesn't *do* anything to the object world. You write, "It is raining outside," and absolutely nothing happens to the beautiful, clear day you're experiencing. That's such a strange practice. We sit in the world but write in a liminal space, something between presence and nonpresence.

"The crisis" has an ever-looming presence in Ana Patova. *Can you explain the crisis of this volume of the Ravickian books?*

The problem with the crisis, and this is the case in *Event Factory* and *The Ravickians* as well, is that it cannot be described. It is ungraspable. It is something felt rather than seen, something that reorients your city while you're sleeping, that commands the language in your novels. The crisis is real and utterly unreal at once. It is the effect of loneliness: it's thinking you're alone, and that's the most definite picture I've gotten of it thus far.

works cited

Gladman, Renee. *Ana Patova Crosses a Bridge*. Saint Louis: Dorothy, a Publishing Project, 2013. Print.

———. "Emergence of a Fiction." *I'll Drown My Book: Conceptual Writing by Women*. Ed. Caroline Bergvall, Laynie Browne, Teresa Carmody, and Vanessa Place. Los Angeles: Les Figues Press, 2012. 66–70. Print.

———. *Event Factory*. Saint Louis: Dorothy, a Publishing Project, 2010. Print.

———. *Juice*. Berkeley: Kelsey Street Press, 2000. Print.

———. *The Ravickians*. Saint Louis: Dorothy, a Publishing Project, 2011. Print.

further works by and on renee gladman

Gilbert, Alan. "Ghost Stories: Renee Gladman's *Juice*." *Another Future: Poetry and Art in a Postmodern Twilight*. Middletown: Wesleyan UP, 2006. 136–38. Print.

Gladman, Renee. *The Activist*. San Francisco: Krupskaya, 2003. Print.

———. *Arlem*. Jersey City: Talisman House, 1998. Print.

———. *Newcomer Can't Swim*. Berkeley: Kelsey Street Press, 2007. Print.

———. *Not Right Now*. Toronto: Second Story Books, 1998. Print.

———. *A Picture Feeling*. New York: Roof Books, 2005. Print.

———. *To After That (Toaf)*. Berkeley: Atelos Small Press Distribution, 2008. Print.

bhanu kapil

BHANU KAPIL IS AN ASSOCIATE PROFESSOR IN INTERDISCIPLINARY STUDIES AT NAROPA UNIVERSITY. SHE ALSO TEACHES IN GODDARD COLLEGE'S MFA IN CREATIVE WRITING PROGRAM. SHE HAS WRITTEN MULTIGENRE BOOKS—*INCUBATION: A SPACE FOR MONSTERS* (2006), *HUMANIMAL [A PROJECT FOR FUTURE CHILDREN]* (2009), *SCHIZOPHRENE* (2011), AND *BAN EN BANLIEUE* (2014). HER CROSS-CULTURAL AND CROSS-DISCIPLINARY WORKS BLEND PROSE AND POETRY IN MOST ADVENTUROUS WAYS.

IN THE FOLLOWING interview, Bhanu Kapil asks, "What is the body of the text?" Her work considers this question from the initial steps of writing to the published artifact that the reader encounters. Indeed, for Kapil, the drafting process is a performance of sorts that shapes the content and form of her narratives. An obvious example of this mode of performance/writing is *Schizophrene* (2011), a book in which the draft was sealed in a Ziploc bag and thrown in the garden to spend months outdoors in the Colorado winter. The text, full of gaps created by the erased parts of the "winterized" manuscript, documents "Partition and its *trans-generational* effects: the high incidence of *schizophrenia* in diasporic Indian and Pakistani *communities*" (*Schizophrene* i). The decaying process of the book in Kapil's garden allowed the creation of a void in her writing—a nonbeing of the work as it was left unwritten—while also impacting the narrative's own exploration of white space, gaps, syntactic experimentation, and fragmentation. The initial "failed" document, the pages of which became "curiously rigid" (i), sculpted the "fragments that attract each other" in the hybrid text (22). This attraction provides a pattern of repetition and association that echoes, verbally, the "light touch," which "regularly and impersonally repeated" is healing, "for non-white subjects (schizophrenics) as anti-psychotic medication" (71). "This quality of touch" (71) was born out of the "*brittle*," "*damaged*," "*dead*" (63) manuscript that formed the vibrating pages that the reader goes through in *Schizophrene*; its maturing process became part of the reading experience. In that sense, Kapil takes the concept of hybridity into new territories, involving not only the crossings of genres but also the crossings of writing and of the experience of such writing.

The Vertical Interrogation of Strangers (2001) is another example of Kapil's interest in genre-binding texts. She describes the book as "an anthology of the voices of Indian women" (6). It is also a recording of the narrator's travels to India, England, and the United States so that the process of documenting women's answers to Kapil's twelve questions becomes part of the presentation of their voices. These voices, whose fascinating "roughness or rawness in terms of syntax, grammar, spelling, punctuation, or the way in which [women filled] the space of the page," have remained unedited by Kapil (6). The strangers' words are mixed with the author's notes answering some of her own questions. The end result is a poetic weaving of "love," "body," "shape," "suffering," "silence," "dismemberment," "fear," "death," motherhood, and utterance (9).

In *Incubation: A Space for Monsters* (2006), Kapil plays with the frames of the book, presenting the reader with a "Handwritten Preface to Reverse the Book." The first sentences of *Incubation* are, "Reverse the book in duration. What does that mean? I am writing to you. These notes now when it's too late" (3). In the preface, Kapil notes that she wanted to write about "Continuance. As it related to loss. The secret pleasure of refusing to live like a normal person" (3). *Incubation* creates this "continuance" by negating divisions between genres, selves, languages, and sections. The "Handwritten Preface" bleeds into yet another introductory text, "Notes on Monsters (1–3)," followed by "Notes against a Cyborg Preface." These frames to the story, not without evoking Mary Shelley's introductory narrative to *Frankenstein*'s monstrous text, collapse the boundaries between textual frames (introductions, prefaces, forewords, etc.) and the "main" section of books. This collapse is in line with the multiple voices of *Incubation* that present vignettes of life, often focusing on the experience of a British girl of Indian descent in the United States, along a poetic theory of cyborgs and monsters. Visually, the text is broken up into sections ("A Dream of Lallo," "The Many Colors of Laloo," etc.) and often numbered subsections, echoing Kapil's mention of her notebook in "Notes on Monsters (1–3)": "It's not the same when I just write it out in my notebook. I like the paper separately. Visually, a series" (5). The visual effects of the book put the narrative in between the "series" that appears in Kapil's notebook and the cyborg text that became *Incubation*. In other words, Kapil explores in-between-ness, the mesh that constitutes the cyborg and the monster by creating a genre-binding text and presenting a collage of identities. The in-between is also rooted in the shape of the text itself—its multiple frames and its physical disjunctions and associations.

Humanimal: A Project for Future Children (2009) is based on Kapil's travels with a French film crew to the Bengal jungle to chronicle the story of Amala and Kamala, who were found living with wolves in 1921. Reverend Joseph Singh's diary of his reintegration of the girls is interlayered with the memoir of Kapil's journey to India and the collecting of facts on the wolf girls. Moments of Kapil's family life also emerge from her examination of the colonized body and the violence and forces that normalize and scar it. Scarring is a theme that punctuates the text, as Kapil compiles a portrait of memory and violence during "civilizing" endeavors. This scarring also penetrates the shape of the syntax and of the pages of the book, as the back-and-forth between voices, sources, and times marks the development of the narrative and the visual arrangement of the page.

The interview that follows evolved out of an exchange of e-mails in June 2013. Our electronic correspondence was fast paced and exhilarating: the final document, full of verve and insight, dwells on the body, the anticolonial, somatic writing, and cross genre writing. The interview bears the mark of Kapil's interest in binding genres and voices; it quite feels like a living body, ruptured and disjointed in its list-like arrangements, memoir-/diary-like recordings, side notes, and parenthetical comments.

•

Your writing engages the body in many ways. Would you care to say something about the importance of the body in your work?

I just had the pleasure of seeing Robert Gluck read from and talk about his work for the first time, at the Spring Convergence of the University of Washington at Bothell. The building is like a glass coffin overlooking the perimeter of a forest. A fairy-tale setting, in other words, in which to hear Robert—Bob—say it just like that: "I am interested in the body more than anything else." What did he mean by the body? Listening to him read from his AIDS-era memoir of a former lover, Ed—the memoir, that is, of Ed's living and dying; what it meant to be his friend—I understood that Bob's writing was touching something very deep inside the body—[the initiation, let's say, of peristalsis]—[the way you feel it before it happens]—[the eviction, that is, from the body: of what is inside the body]—then writing from that. The sensation of the soft tissue contracting then releasing, uncontrollably. The "turd" expelled onto the face of an unwanted sex partner in a tree house in a clearing in a Tacoma forest—at this point, Bob looked up from the podium and gestured to the real forest outside the window. And how, then, "Ed" ran—a vector—from the forest—pausing only to gather his sneakers as he fled. I understood everything about this scene: the desire to write from the very inside of a body in a way that is mapped to its flight. To have both those versions in a text.

What is a text? What is the body of the text? Is it too boring to even say that, as if Hélène Cixous never peeled an orange on a balcony then wrote it? That juice. Those pips. I am increasingly thinking of a text as performance instructions for my own: body. Between the first drafts and the last, I want to figure something out. I take the posture, for example, of the bodily life I am trying to describe. For four years, recently paused—with the acceptance of the manuscript by Nightboat—I wrote the story of Ban, a girl who lay down in the first minutes of a race riot. A race riot, that is, that unfolded [happened] in my neighborhood—on the border of Southall and Hayes in northwest London—London as "shit-hole"—immigrant, industrial London, that is—*les banlieues*—on April 23, 1979. That day, Blair Peach, a teacher from New Zealand and an antiracism protester—died—protesting the decision of the National Front to hold their annual meeting in a nonwhite community. In 2010, the inquest—resolved—and the metropolitan police—publicly acknowledged that Blair Peach had died as the result of police brutality that day. He died in Ealing Hospital, later that night or the next morning. In this way, writing *Ban*—I wanted to write into the—space?—created by this event but somehow, also, beneath it, running next to it: at the same time. I wanted to work on the body in the riot but in ways that would allow me to process: the riot: in other ways. What is this other body: deflected, erased before it appears in the document of the event? What is a girl—never born—or apparent—in the society she is "born" in, though never acknowledged—as a member of that society—something—that resolves—as well—upon the question of Englishness? I am not saying this well. "What are the somatic effects of oppression?" This is a research question that a colleague of mine at Naropa University—the amazing Christine Caldwell—a pioneer in the field of somatic psychotherapy—is working on. Like her, I want to work out the intersection of narrative and nonverbal factors. How the girl's body registers so many different kinds of violence at once, a register I wanted to work out through the contractile-extensive tissues—as per Bob—but also the rough, overlapping, and acoustic arcs of the violence to come. The violence, that is, that had already happened. This is logic. Ban lies down because she is, to use and also misuse Agamben's language on sacrifice in *Homo Sacer*, "already dead." Is the sound of breaking glass coming from Ban's home or the street? How can writing be the place where you get to work on the inside and outside at the same time? How can

I do all of this and still honor the body of the protester who died that day? How can a work that is about trauma, but also the neighborhood, also be the occasion of this—trauma—moving through at the same time that it preserves a cultural memory of a part of London that is already overwritten by more contemporary arrivals and other immigrant histories?

From somatic approaches to trauma—derived from Babette Rothschild, Peter Levine, and Pat Ogden—I understood that both the image and the narrative sustain the vortex of loop of traumatic memory. How to de-loop? How to build a countervortex? How to stay, longer than narrative or even poetry might [could] demand, with sensation itself? To "complete something that was never completed" in the time it was written [happened]—to paraphrase my friend Laura Campbell, a transpersonal psychotherapist in Colorado trained through Levine's model of discharge—is something I am very interested in. That is why I want a sentence that shakes. A sentence that takes up the cadence of the nervous system as it discharges a fact. To map this sentence, in other words, to the gesture-posture events.

That is why writing has become this thing where I lie down too. In London, and in the mud rectangle in my back garden, I have been lying down—to take the pose of "Ban." I want to feel it in my body—the root cause. On a butcher's table in Los Angeles, I got into a meat sack and rotated and glitched: nude, girl-like but current—disgusting—to work on the compound scene. How it feels inside the sack. And to be witnessed: the audience on the grass outside, on the slope beneath Schindler's studio in West Hollywood. This was as part of an event curated upon the theme of voyeurism by Amina Cain and Teresa Carmody; I have never forgotten the gift of being invited to embody the things I was [am] attempting to write about.

What kind of book can come from these activities? Though my book has been accepted, I am frustrated. I want to strike a blow. I want to strike a blow to the manuscript in the same way that social violence is an impact that obliterates lived form.

And how this blow has its own history and ongoing effects. This is why it has to be prose. I want to write an anticolonial prose: a prose of the body that is destroyed, yes, killed off, yes, but also—revolutionary, with a capacity to become: again: refigured from its gametes: the colors of the body on the floor. Earth memory and its unguents. Incarnate form becomes an interest here.

Could you expand on "anticolonial" and "revolutionary" prose? Are you implying that the kind of bodily writing you mention here has political ramifications that are uniquely different from other kinds of writing? Could you give examples of how some of your narratives are anticolonial or revolutionary?

I am still working out Juliana Spahr's cultural [colloquial] statement at the Territory symposium held at Naropa University earlier this spring: "Colonialism is wily." I think she was saying an anticolonial literature must be tricky in turn, in order to outwit—what colonialism is capable of as an idea or in its entirety. From an Indian perspective, one that doesn't quite fit with the complicated way "territory" is taken up by Marxist readings of contemporary U.S. history—by which I mean the last five hundred years—the anticolonial is about nonviolence but also violence; it's about the courage to be a spy, to disguise yourself as the enemy, to walk with salt to the sea. It's about the radical protests against rape that are happening in India now. I am not writing these words as a true Indian but as an Indian subject in my own way. In other words, part of what the anticolonial work is—is this: the register of national spaces and claims of all kinds. The anticolonial is the willingness to be spat out and to make a study of deflection. Who does not appear in the document of place? Who is the nonwhite clinical subject? Why is it that nonwhite clinical subjects process antipsychotic medications differently from their white—citizen or noncitizen—counterparts? What is a counterpart? What will it take to adhere to the grid? To the city? To the green spaces? To belong? These questions led to studies of immigrant and community biologies; research and presentation in the field of cross-cultural psychiatry; a prose that was no longer—wholly—itself.

As narrative, the anticolonial gesture is recursive: written in the space that precedes the border. Written in abeyance, I sometimes think, of the event. The place before touch, entrance, or even becoming itself is possible. I think of *Schizophrene*'s corridor space: "Document the corridor. Cure the corridor." The sense of exhaustion rather than inquiry. I am not interested in liminal space as a germinal metaphor. I want to make a study of migration that is as much about its surface materials as the display of an atopic node. To this end, I have worked / spoken / taught through my own diasporic history and stories but also: others. In all of this, I am most interested in the places where progressions are impeded, restricted, deviant, reversed, abruptly possible. Perhaps this is why there are so many commas in my sentences. They point backwards to the origin of the sentence: a prehistory that is not, always, exposed in the sentence as the thing or event or situation being talked about. Syntax is feral. Syntax does not always want what the writing wants: an expression. Syntax opposes lyric construction, in this sense. Is this a revolutionary act? To reverse speech. To say one thing but do another. How the commas are meat hooks, I have also written [considered]—and this is why my writing is roughly made, composed not of fragments—but of an abraded "side."

The side of what? More explicitly, my subjects—generally—are on the receiving end of social violence of different kinds. I think of myself as stopping time, as a writer, that was not stopped in life. In time itself. To pause time in the opening minutes of a riot, to let a brown/black girl [Ban] lie down—I am not preventing her death by doing this. I am not preventing her rape. But perhaps I am allowing her to die in her own time. To incarnate. To dissolve the fixed colors of her body that might then: recirculate or combine: in other unheard of or unimagined ways. Are imaginaries radical? I don't know. I know that music helps, pink lightning helps, the reader as a witness with a broken open heart: helps. To make this death happen. In this other kind of way.

In India later this year, I will be giving a public performance. I will lie down for forty minutes on the place on the ground where a "girl"—The Fearless One—in December, in New Delhi, in 2012, was raped then thrown from a bus. She lay—throbbing, glitching—there—for forty minutes—observed by a crowd—of men—before anyone called the police. That forty minutes has haunted me. The steel pipe used to gut her has haunted me. I want to keep working on the ideas of sacrifice and witness—the dismembered body—but with [through] my own body now, as the medium of enactment but also discharge, in the way I spoke of earlier. How will I frame this? The place where this happened is just a few minutes from my own aunt's house near the Indira Gandhi airport. Will I lie down just as I am, exposing my body to the air? Will I cover my body with ash—like the holy men and women—the *naga sadhus*—who roam India? Will I be naked? Will I form an alliance with a political action group, asking them to witness my protest? Will I create an archive of images at the same time that the event is happening? All I know is that my instinct is to participate in what is happening: there. With my own body. Is this a revolutionary act? Perhaps it is connected to histories of civil action that are also performative: a display of milk, silence, salt.

In earlier practices, I lay down—on the border of Pakistan and India. A few photographs document this. I built a *silueta*—the outline of my body re-filled with clay lamps and marigolds—in homage to the earth art of Ana Mendieta. All of that was fine: germinal. But perhaps a revolutionary act is one that progresses the politics of the image beyond its ability to be captured as part of an artistic or working practice. What was said? What was done? What charged the air? Perhaps part of this is that experimental writing does not have cultural power; as a writer, I am value-less. I don't get paid for the writing I do. It is a part of what my body is for. What is the writer's body for? This is the question I am only now beginning to ask. My writing is becoming less writing and more this other thing. I wish I had the courage to delete *Ban* and write into the aftermath of a performance I have not given yet in a country that may or may not be my true home.

Your reference to "revers[ing] speech" made me think of a question I asked myself about Schizophrene: *I wondered if dis-writing or unwriting (or something else?) was taking place in the book. Care to say something about this work?*

Reversals present in *Schizophrene*:

1. ["Reverse migration. . . ." Is psychotic.] How the diasporic vector has begun to reverse itself, West to East—as the initiating community ages but also as a result of transglobal economics. I am interested in the branching that accompanies the nonlinearity of migration. To track: this line. At the expense of the socialist model. I was raised with a picture of George Bernard Shaw on the dining room door, pinned there with tacks—a yellowing newspaper portrait. My father used to go to Speaker's Corner in Hyde Park on a regular basis, a short aluminum ladder tucked beneath his arm like a newspaper. That he'd then unfold. And climb upon. To claim or state: something. In a loud voice. Mortified, I'd orient to the road or the tulips or my book—and so I can't recall. What was said. I know that it filled the day and the consciousness of others in an immediate, obliterating, or noisy way. I think of my own flinching position—but also the curiosity, applause, and jeers—attention—of the passersby. The people who stopped to listen. Sympathetic listeners, racist listeners. Listeners [readers] of all kinds. But what does it mean to contract from oration, from the alternative telling of colonial [British Indian] history and politics: that my father, for example, was so compelled to: proclaim or tell? My mother, meanwhile, is currently writing a book of stories called *TRASH*: memories of war. She writes them every morning in a spiral-bound notebook. A baby suckling its dead mother on the ground, for example, is a kind of trash. What do my mother's stories unwrite? At the very least, they unwrite the stories I could write or imagine. Perhaps the stories she writes now, and which were bedtime stories once, unwrite my childhood. Yes, I think that is what they do. It is possible my mother is a better writer than me. She is uninhibited. It is possible that my father was a great man.

But perhaps I can also answer the question through syntax. There's a way that a study of recursive traits makes the deep structures of language—the phatic communion that underlies a sentence—for example—drop off. To complete a sentence is an act of reciprocity. Or domination. Perhaps not completing one—or destroying one—is psychotic in this regard; a marker of anhedonia—the lack of affect necessary to: continue, arise, begin. Here, I am making a parallel between childhood and schizophrenia that is nonidentical, but perhaps it is okay to let the two things lie next to each other in the answer to your question. Microbial exchange is fundamental to horizontal evolution. Is this true? I want to unwrite the question. I want to dis-write the answer, too. Why? Why do I want these things? The question is making my heart beat faster, just to answer it.

Schizophrene is also a book of extreme travel. Why do I want to go as far, each time, as I can? I think of my early flights—hitchhiking—to Scotland as a child. It was as far as I could get from London at that time. A child can easily slip onto the train. I read the ecstasies and lectures of John Donne, gazing up every now and then at the farmland and avoiding the gaze of sexual predators as they passed from the onboard café to the "can."

2. [Anhedonia]: I want to dis-write the positive symptom of schizophrenia. Its hyperverbal aspects. In studying migration and mental illness, I found that this was the hardest thing to treat in immigrant [Asian and Caribbean "Brits"]—the negative symptom, that is. An "allele"—resists conventional treatment or responds at different rates to conventional treatment. What is an allele? I am neither an epidemiologist nor a biologist. I was a delegate to the World Conference of Cultural Psychiatry (London, 2012); a gathering of psychiatrists, refugee workers, psychoanalysts, and others who work directly with the population I engage in *Schizophrene*. That is where I learned about the ways nonwhite subjects process medicines or therapies of different kinds. Unwriting takes you away, as per Kenneth Goldsmith perhaps, from what a book is [or could be] for. I was also interested in a writing that would not build itself through lividity, through the pleasure of language—which, for me, was always the antidote. I wanted to write something for which there was not a cure.

I wanted to write into the bundle of forces—invisible things—that preceded the "break": the way that even an initiating war, civil war, is no longer apparent in the city you live in now. And what if that wartime image was the thing you glimpsed, as you were fleeing a place? The image of the women tied to the trees, for example? Writing this book I understood [though perhaps not in the words I am using here, but rather through impatience, frustration, a kind of self-hatred that is difficult to admit to in an academic context] that the reason I could not write it—the reason I finally flung it into the garden—was because it was not founded on a scene or even an image in its fullest sense. What I wanted to write about was both too contracted, too swiftly processed [glimpsed] and never analyzed as a cultural scene until many, many years past the event—in literatures or forums perhaps not accessible to the people who have lived through that time. Except through stories, the retelling that mutates each time—mixing its gametes with bedtime fairytales and oral epic forms. Thus, what are the technologies for writing into a broken down space, a space that loops with the intensity of a moment [a seam] always? How do you de-loop, which is perhaps at odds to experimental aims?

I wanted a book* that did not look away, just as the child in the opening section does not. Perhaps this is my way of reversing, too, the trajectory of vision itself, back into the eye. The bodily eye of the radical, vulnerable, altered witness. And to then unwind that spiraled-in place—a throbbing nerve deep inside the nervous system itself—and out: into narrative. This is brainspotting, a trauma therapy based on the regulation, stripping, and organization of eye movements with a "wand." This is the idea that it is less about what happened than allowing what happened to be unraveled, contacted, engaged, withdrawn, pulled out—and then, without language—but through other, smaller or non-verbal movements—the sensorimotor sequence—to be "released." To be given over to the larger field of sight. And in this way to become a part of the environment again, which is nourishing. It is the start of life.

*To make a book was like these things: migration and its corollary "sense." A sense that did not appear in the contemporary British TV, film, or literature that I grew up on, even in the nineties. In many ways, perhaps this kind of thing can only be written now; in a way that coincides, actually, with the cultural work happening in other fields. How do you turn a glimpse into something that the body can tolerate and thus discharge? In writing a traumatic text, what potential is there, for a writer, to reverse the traumatic effects they are writing about? To work—fifty years on from the event—with the trapped energies of war in the bodies of the descendants of those who lived through war? As the child of a refugee, I am back once again to questions of poverty, sexual violence, chronic forms of racism, urban housing, and ethnic density—that also accompany these questions.

The trauma is not in the event; it's in the nervous system. (Peter Levine: trauma therapist, founder of Somatic Experiencing.)

I am not interested in disclosure. I am interested in discharge. (Petra Kuppers: disability activist, poet and professor of performance studies at the University of Michigan.)

If both disclosure and the event are fundamental to the novel, then I am, yes, dis-writing the novel. I think of the novel as shattered, just lying there, in the rich green grass next to the fountain—or perhaps it is the water of the fountain itself: disappearing and becoming with such great force. Blue-bright. In an England I seek to recuperate. In an India that is an India that is never seen or truly known. But also here, where I put my head beneath the streaming water—every day. The water is writing before it is writing or could be writing and is still this other thing: an intense sensation or thought.

Many of your books involve "real" historical or personal trauma so that "fiction" merges with "reality." Could you address the ways in which these traditionally opposed realms cohabitate in your work and why their merging is important to you?

Both "cohabit" and "merging"—though I love both those things—are vectors that arrive in the house of the text. It is hard to speak faultlessly about hybridity in literary forms. To come to the cross-fertilization of "real" and imagined—"fiction"—I locate—which is almost not possible—this instinct or activity—in the center of my own body. Or brain. Or nervous system. I think the way things merge precedes the question of form. (For me.) I think of how my brain grew up on story, for example: the particular combination of oral epics (absolutely nonlinear retellings of battle or cosmic scenes from the Hindu holy books: the *Ramayan*, the *Mahabharat*, the *Gita*, and so on), but also: stories, in lucid, hyper-real detail, of India itself. Stories, that is, of the civil war: life before it and afterward. There was a moving background to the stories my mother told me: the silver, grays, and indigos of London weather systems and the culture of violence that pressed close all around. Perhaps the violence froze my brain deep in storytelling. This is circuitry. I sometimes ask my students to describe their reading experience in childhood as a way to replicate or approach the reverie or shift that could happen in writing now. I think of reading, for example, as this other experience of lived time: reading *Alice Through the Looking Glass* on a loop, in a storage room in Talwara, India—or encountering Donne, in Great Britain, at ten. So, part of your question reads to the question of what storytelling is in the first place, and which language it arrives in. Part of your question reads to the physiology of trauma. As I grow older and my own nervous system replenishes itself—which happens most profoundly whenever I complete a book—and in the act, of course, of having lived long enough in a place to be a person of it—to grow flowers and raise a child and have my heart broken by a series of gorgeous and dangerous sexual partners—I wonder how this internal and extensive approach to writing will change. Perhaps I will, after all, write the novel I have always dreamed of: writing. A novel, that is, that could be read by others. In the place I am from. Experimental prose is here. It is for now.

Humanimal (A Project for Future Children) draws from various sources and media to bring us to the limits of language and humanity. Could you talk about the project—the book and the process of creating it?

Summer 2000: I am a pregnant massage therapist. My first book has not come out yet; neither has my first chapbook, an essay or autobiography of the cyborg. I have no intention of becoming a professor; in fact, such a thing feels impossible. I am between books. I want to write a book. I go for a health walk "up the hill" to CU Boulder, crossing a creek and wondering if I will be assaulted in the undergrowth. Yet I keep climbing, one week past my first trimester. No longer nauseous, but anxious and with elevated blood pressure. Hence the walk. I walk to the library and there I commit bibliomancy. I say: wherever my hand stops, that is where I will begin.

My hand stops at the "diary" of the Reverend Joseph Singh, a colonial account of the capture and rehabilitation of two "wolf girls" in Midnapore, India, in 1921. The book comes with an accompanying essay by Robert Zingg, an anthropologist from Denver who published Singh's account as part of his own discredited findings in 1943. I am struck by what I think is a Punjabi name—Singh—in combination with the Colorado setting. The lights are flickering off in the stacks. I check my book out and leave.

Some years pass. I attempt to write a postcolonial novel set in Calcutta. For the sal jungle of Bengal, I substitute the ponderosa pines of the Arapaho Forest. There is a faint smell of crushed vanilla beans in the bark. One day, a bobcat leaps in front of me, then away. In my notebook, one of the wolf girls escapes from Reverend Singh's mission—the Home—and walks, at the age of fourteen, from Midnapore to the sea. Coffee House Press queries me. They keep my book for a year. It is rejected. I feel profoundly ashamed. I put my poorly written novel away and focus on my massage therapy practice: Ayurvedic spa treatments and soft-tissue integration, with a specialty in treating whiplash injuries.

A year passes. I am the mother of a toddler, living in the Colorado mountains in a cabin without running water and I'm about to get divorced. A French filmmaking company queries me, having read an excerpt of my novel, "The Wolfgirls of Midnapore," online. They invite me to go to India, to be filmed researching my novel, as yet unwritten. They like that I'm not finished yet. I separate from my husband and go to India. There, I have many extraordinary experiences. The spaces in my book become real. I meet a ninety-eight-year-old woman who recalls the wolf girls' howling. I watch the filmmakers set up a blue gelatin lamp deep in the jungle and comply, with profound passivity, when they ask me to walk through the jungle at night "as if you are looking for wolves." A new sentence forms in my head: "Walking through the jungle lit by blue paper." I return to the United States and write it down.

A year passes. I have accrued two sets of fragments: notes on feral children and notes on film. One day, I am washing my hands in the bathroom and look up. An owl girl has appeared in the mirror—smudges from my son's hands, I think—but when I look again, I can't deny the distinctness of the figure who has appeared. I look into the eyes of this figure and have the sudden, profound, and intense feeling of my father's eyes looking back out at me, through the eyes of the half bird, half girl in the mirror. The notes triple or are struck by this blow. My father's body—a memory of poverty, of the body, of a child's body covered with silver, pooling scars—appears in the writing.

I write myself out of one life and into another. During this time, I write and complete *Incubation: A Space for Monsters*—a progression of my cyborg/immigrant material. It is published. I am offered a more permanent position at Naropa University, and I take it. In 2006, I teach a class called "Narrative and Architecture;" as part of this, I become interested in matrices and grids. I study the logic of the grid. I apply an alphabetical/numerical grid to my notes. I am interested in what happens when a grid fails or gets wet. And so I let the book do what it has been doing all along. I let it fail. The way that it fails is that it stops at the letter O. I study the O. The O is the wolf girl's mouth stretched, distended—her hair pulled backward by the Reverend's fist—during an attempt: to escape. I start to write these soft-tissue notes into the work too. I start to write about the colors refracting in the indented part of the leg, where it's scarred. I analyze the parts of the "diary" that are about the progression from feral to human—or "upright"—posture. I write down the burst parts of first speech.

Once I have the grid and the O, the book is swiftly written in the course of a few days. I start to feel less excruciated by the time it has taken me to accrue and disseminate my "notes." I begin to think about the lag and delay as part of the project itself, what it takes to loop colonial time through structures dependent and stemming yet separate from it.

In 2007, I go to the United Kingdom. I drink pear juice in a café. I return to my uncle's house and check my e-mail on his ancient desktop computer. There is an e-mail from Kelsey Street Press. They are querying me. I sent them the Word attachment of the work I am now calling *Humanimal*. When I wake up the next morning, I read the acceptance letter from Hazel White. I go to Buckingham Palace with my son. We eat ice cream on the fountain's rim.

A year passes; I am obsessed with a photograph of a young girl gathering tobacco at the edge of a jungle in the early twentieth century. It is black and white, doubly exposed—so that the girl's arms make an overlapping gesture. They duplicate. They blur. It takes a year to receive permission to use this photograph as the book's cover from the estate of Manuel Álvarez Bravo. I write a letter to the Getty. I write a letter to a woman in Mexico, Álvarez Bravo's great-niece.

In 2009, the book appears in the world. I receive invitations to read from the book in different parts of the continental United States. When I read from the work, I have the sensation that it is not for myself, it is for them. It is for Kamala and Amala, the two girls who were found living with wolves. I send energy to them. I send love to them. I send light to them. It is hard to explain the feeling in my own body—a powerful feeling, deeper in—that happens when I read. I notice that these readings give me the courage, ultimately, to embark upon a next work following the same model: a decade of documentary research—this time, into migration and mental illness—organized swiftly in a belated: form. I notice how the art precedes the shape it will take, and I'm not disturbed by that. I am not confused. I have discipline this time.

I write *Schizophrene,* linking the wolf to the schizophrenic—in a very private way.

When you look back at your writing career thus far, do you find that you write differently, that your books are different, and/or that you are researching something different as you go on?

This is the progression of subjects/bodies in my collected works, such as they are: (1) Cyborg. (2) Indian/Pakistani women [from Haraway: the idea that the cyborg moment happens at the transition from organic—agricultural—to inorganic—industrial—aims.] (3) Monster [progressed, also, from Haraway: "an entity produced by discourse." To paraphrase. To write: mutation.] (4) Wolf girl [monstrous body/immigrant body—the beginning of a socialist approach to autobiography; I start to think hard about poverty—its valence—next to that of race. I begin researching ethnic density and schizophrenia rates in northwest London's immigrant communities, even as I complete a work set in India in 1921.] (5) An explicit text on transgenerational trauma. And shame. I think about the anonymous/recut narratives I began with. What would it be like to wear a body's organs on a dress, pinned to a skirt? I begin to think about the history of war in a way that is fulfilled or expressed, sexually, many years down the line. The subject is the schizophrenic. (6) I return to the stories of childhood that my cyborg material was built from or of. This time I work things out through the scene, a girl's body—the forces it receives. In the way her body fuses to the asphalt during a race riot—coppery—I can see she is a little cyborg too. I study conductivity in order to write this material and return to my research on migration and mental illness: the intersection of poverty, chronic racism, and domestic violence / sexual abuse—as triggers more powerful than that of migration itself—upon the body I want to write about and know. This is Ban. (7) To this end, as each book takes me further into the inquiry or subject matter that all the books share, I come to the brink of what the novel is for me. I start to take the posture of the body in the novel I am attempting to write. I lie down on the floor of the world. I read the palm of the president of the World Psychiatry Organization at a conference on cross-cultural psychiatry in London; he sends me a letter from Greenland. I study the packaging and make a chrysalis from it. I place the chrysalis on my shrine. I watch the light refract its thin plastic and tissue paper; the words written inside.

I go to India. I find the place, as I said, where a girl was thrown from a bus in December 2012, after a brutal and sustained rape. In some ways, I repeat myself in order to build courage for a performance that will be witnessed rather than documented in other ways. I lie down on the dirt for forty minutes, to mark the forty minutes that she lay there: before anyone in the crowd that had gathered to watch called the police.

I am going to India, as I said. The appearance of what is inside what I am writing beyond it always signals to me the moment when the work is complete. A nine-year-old girl, for example, walks straight out of the sub-Himalayan spaces of *Schizophrene* to become Ban: and Ban herself, as a bodily outline—bloodstains on the sidewalk—incarnates in the news cycle. I walk into the news cycle, deferred.

I think of my work as happening at the intersection of performance art, research, and the novel. In retrospect, I can see that I embodied every stage of my few books. In metegenomics, a theory of hybridity holds that some organisms are hybrid because they share a membrane but that some organisms act together—respond in synchronous ways—without sharing a membrane at all. The work progresses as a series of rough, overlapping arcs. When you glimpse the outcome of the experiment, you move on, before completing it in that particular space. You work it out in the next space. This is relaxing. This is a brilliant system. It is spiritual and practical at the same time!

A wolf girl lies down in the lap of her schizophrenic mother. A monster and a cyborg have complicated sex. Two monsters have a different kind of sex. The schizophrenic goes down on all fours, as does the feral child. I can see how these mirror effects happen in my books, but I am conscious also that it would be unethical to have written with these effects in mind.

To this end, I am trying to work out the techniques on my blog so that when I write, I can write less about the process of writing itself, such that characters and weather and crystalline, epic energies might reverse themselves, duplicate, shimmer—with their own volatile and extreme desire to get to the next part of life.

works cited

Kapil, Bhanu. *Ban en Banlieue*. Callicoon: Nightboat Books, 2015. Print.

———. *Humanimal: A Project for Future Children*. Berkeley: Kelsey Street Press, 2009. Print.

———. *Incubation: A Space for Monsters*. New York: Leon Works, 2006. Print.

———. *Schizophrene*. Callicoon: Nightboat Books, 2011. Print.

———. *The Vertical Interrogation of Strangers*. Berkeley: Kelsey Street Press, 2001. Print.

———. "Writing/Not-Writing: Th[A][E] Diasporic Self: Notes Toward a Race Riot Scene." *English Language Notes* 49.2 (2011): 35–40. Print.

further works by and on bhanu kapil

Dowling, Sarah. "They Were Girls: Animality and Poetic Voice in Bhanu Kapil's *Humanimal*." *American Quarterly* 65.3 (2013): 735–55. Print.

Higashida, Cheryl. "Negative Dialectics of the Racial Self: Bhanu Kapil on Writing/Not-Writing." *English Language Notes* 50.1 (2012): 39–41. Print.

Kapil, Bhanu. "Unfold Is the Wrong Word: An Interview with Bhanu Kapil." *HTML Giant*. N.p., 18 Apr. 2012. Web. 15 Mar. 2016.

Kocher, Ruth Ellen. "F/Fabula A/Anima: Reading Bhanu Kapil's 'Writing/Not-Writing: Th[A][E] Diasporic Self: Notes Towards A Race Riot.'" *English Language Notes* 50.1 (2012): 47–53. Print.

michael martone

> MICHAEL MARTONE IS A PROFESSOR AT THE UNIVERSITY OF ALABAMA AND A FACULTY MEMBER OF THE MFA PROGRAM FOR WRITERS AT WARREN WILSON COLLEGE. HE HAS BEEN AWARDED TWO FELLOWSHIPS FROM THE NATIONAL ENDOWMENT FOR THE ARTS AND THE AWP AWARD FOR NONFICTION IN 2000. HE IS THE AUTHOR OF *THE BLUE GUIDE TO INDIANA* (2001), *MICHAEL MARTONE* (2005), AND *FOUR FOR A QUARTER* (2011).

WHEN I APPROACHED Michael Martone about his participation in *Divergent Trajectories* and asked that he choose his preferred mode of interview, his reply was, "How about by postcard? Twitter? Each question a different medium?" From then on, I became "Flore, or different modes," and we embarked in a play of media and language. This means of interviewing is fitting with Martone's approach to writing: as he stresses in his critical essays and in the following interview, the contexts and parameters of writing matter to him as much as what his fiction explores.

From 2009 to 2012, receiving correspondence from Martone involved a thrilling process of discoveries about the limits and contours of fiction writing. We wrote on and/or with e-mail, postcards, photos, Twitter, e-mailed word attachments, recordings, letters, and cell phone texts. We corresponded in various locations—virtually and physically—which ties in with Martone's exploration of "place." He is frequently categorized as a writer of the Midwest, a region that is often the subject matter of his short stories and nonfictional writing. In his introduction to *Townships: Pieces of the Midwest* (1992), he explains: "We are always left with the Midwest as a lump, as leftover. We are always making the most of it, whatever it is" (12). He adds: "Think of the Midwest as a vast plane studded with nodes of creation where artists are making a place by staying in place, riddling it with possibilities" (9). His work on the region explores how those artistic possibilities can respond to the Midwestern landscape, way of life, and myths.

In its explorations of how "places" are created, Martone's fiction, just as this interview, asks questions about the frames of writing. The "Contributor's Notes" of *Michael Martone* (2005), for example, call attention to the texts we often overlook: in playing with the form of the contributor's note, Martone points out the materiality of his book—what constructs it and frames it in a writing tradition. For him, the writerly constraints that shape such notes are parallel to the constructions of the various Michael Martones. The creation of fictional Martones also comments on the author's interest in books' structures and reception. His latest book, *Four for a Quarter* (2011), explores such matters in "44 fictions about 4's"—"Four Fifth Beatles," "The Sex Life of the Fantastic Four," "Four Eyes," "Chili 4-Ways," and so forth. The structure of the collection matches its content: it is separated into four sections, each chapter divided into four more subsections.

Martone's exploration of "form" has ventured outside of what we traditionally consider "form": when he published fictive sections of *The Blue Guide to Indiana* (2001) as nonfiction, Martone asked readers to investigate the difference between facts and fiction or to reconsider what fiction *is*. *The Blue Guide to Indiana* also asks that we reconsider what we often overlook when approaching literature—how books are made, published, presented, produced, and packaged. In taking part not only in the creation of *The Blue Guide to Indiana* but also of its distribution, Martone reveals that, while we tend to ignore how books circulate, the vehicle of their circulation affects their existence. Martone started his exploration of the context of literary delivery and distribution when he republished the content of *Alive and Dead in Indiana* (1984) in *Fort Wayne is Seventh on Hitler's List* (1990)—though *Fort Wayne* includes three new short stories. One may purchase a copy of either collection of short stories without realizing the doubling effect that Martone created. On the other hand, someone interested in Martone's work may also acquire both copies and compare the two books, looking for discrepancies between the two volumes. The preface of *Fort Wayne* does not record the story "Vocation" in its list of the works taken from *Alive*, for example, as the story is given a new name in the new book. This comparing activity reveals that our habitual conceptualization of books, documentation of authors' works, and chronologies of their publications are conceivably futile. It also invites us to reconsider what history, remembrance, and truth mean—including the performative elements that they involve. Therefore, what we consider important about literary production is always under question when we are faced with Martone's work.

98 • michael martone

Interestingly, and perhaps shockingly, Martone has extended his formal experiments to the realm of authoring: he has published poetry under the name of Neal Bowers, an author who had written a book about the theft of his poetry, then republished by another author. As Martone explained in an interview with Matthew Baker, he has a number of aliases:

> I publish under your name, Matthew Baker. I've published fictional poems under the name Neal Bowers, fictional stories under the names Christian Piers, Jonah Ogles, Arin Fisher, Sarah Mignin, and Matthew Douglas McCabe, fictional nonfiction under the username zzxyzz [on Wikipedia.org], fictional advertisements under the name Klemm Co., and fictional songs with the band under the name AVALANCHE. (*Hobart*)

Martone's experiments with authorship obviously play with the "death of the author" and the concept of originality. In disrupting concepts that we often think of as static—authorship, book, reader, and publisher—Martone points out their limitations and malleability. His aliases also create a strange mode of collaboration where the limits of narrative, biography, authorship, copyrights, and plagiarism no longer apply. Yet, in writing and talking about these experiments, Martone also remains the "author" of the disruption of authoring, possibly becoming an author "under erasure," to borrow Derrida's terminology. Perhaps the fact that we do not have critical terms to define Martone's experimentations is telling of the scope of his artistic production.

The following interview addresses—in serious and humorous ways—Martone's interest in literary production (how books are created, sold, and received) and how this interest affects his lifestyle, writing process, and teaching philosophy. We also discuss his latest ventures in the cyber world: his tweeting activity and exploring fours, much like *Four for a Quarter,* makes us ponder what falls into the category of art and what does not. Some of our exchanges bear the typos or errors that accompany handwritten texts or cyber posts; to allow a fluid reading, I decided not to add the mention [*sic*] to these instances.

•

<u>(E-mailed) Word Document</u>: *In "Mount Rushmore," you write of "Transparency": "the dominant ideology of the age, our age. The trick of Realism, its tricklessness" (Fiction's Present 192). You also note in "How to Hide a Tank" that "it is interesting that realism as a style works so diligently to conceal, as Kenner says, by withdrawing the hand of the conceiving person"* (Unconventions *146*).

These remarks on the veiling of construction and origin of the fictional medium made me think of David Bolter and Richard Grusin's work on remediation. In Remediation: Understanding New Media *(The MIT Press, 1999)*, Bolter and Grusin study the use of a medium within another medium—"the ways in which older media refashion themselves to answer the challenges of new media" (15). Think of the relationship between painting and photography, theatre and film, photography and film, film and television, and so forth. They postulate that, in absorbing other media, remediation strives for immediacy, or that which allows the medium to disappear, immersing the viewer in a visual world that is as close as possible to daily visual experiences. The logic of immediacy "dictates that the medium itself should disappear and leave us in the presence of the thing represented" (6). But in order to create immediacy, media makers work very hard at concealing everything that "makes us aware of the medium" and that "remin[d] us of our desire for immediacy" (34).

While the "transparency," "tricklessness," and "conceal[ing]" you mention do not directly involve the reworking of another text or medium (though in some cases it might), I find it interesting that your remarks on fiction coincide with Bolter and Grusin's comments on our culture's desire for a "direct" experience with an artistic medium, an "immediacy" that relies on the effacement of what makes this experience possible. Could you elaborate on your play with this desire and your refashioning or reusing of other media, texts, genres, formats, and contexts in your fictions?

(E-mailed) Word Document: Well, maybe before that elaboration, I'd like to talk about typewriters. I want to continue considering that interesting interaction that results from the evolution of kinds of media. Movies began as filmed plays—the camera static, single takes, and so forth—then movies soon found that movies move, can do what movies can do different from what a static play can do. And painting evolved when in competition with the medium of photography. Painterly representation could now be captured by anyone with a Brownie, so painters find what only paint can do. Etc. I'm interested in these remediations. Because literary fiction in the United States found itself (since mid-twentieth century) in universities, it seemed to be able to dodge this bullet. Competition with rising "narrative delivery devices"—movie, radio, TV, cable, even twelve-step programs—were buffered by the institutions where writers were writing. There, there was and still is an active denial of these other media. Or at least a departmentalization of them. Writing programs, English departments provide a safe haven. This screen, the bulwark of the institution, allows the teachers of fiction writing to ignore the twentieth century and to "norm" fiction writing to the form of domestic internal psychological realism practiced at the beginning of the century—Chekhov is the master and its ideal performer. Freud's insights. Joyce's epiphanies. James's details. Woolf's streaming. This retardation was made possible by the move into the university and by its methods of instruction, the workshop. Evidence? How writers think of and use their computers. They are essentially taught to use this incredibly powerful typesetting machine and networking terminal as a typewriter essentially unchanged (save for the electric turbo burst mid-century) since 1900. Writers are to produce a "manuscript" (a further distortion) that is basically a script for editors to work on and typesetters to type set. Realism's aesthetic bonds nicely with this notion. The physical object should not call attention to itself in any way. It should contribute to the transparency, and, in so doing, help blind the writer to the fact that he has access to an array of graphic enhancements. *Italics* for instance. I am amazed still at how few writers will actually italicize instead of underline. Any attempt to be graphic in any way, to be unconventional in any manner from preparing a standard typescript is met in the workshop with derision. Attacked as amateur on the one hand or beyond the job description on the other. The machine that allows writers to write is meant to be transparent even when, or especially when, it is at our fingertips. The computer is not a typewriter, but, to this day, most writers employ computers as if they were. And if the finished typescript does look different from a typewriting typescript, chances are it is because the computer defaulted there. That is to say, the writer is not making the choice of font and margin and leading and kerning anymore now that he can do it. The machine in that sense is "writing" the script. There is hostility in university workshops to the very idea of teaching the computer, graphic design, typesetting as elements of the writing student's craft. This kind of transparency or blindness lends itself to the transparency that Realism demands. The work is to seem as if it has merely happened, spontaneous, any reference to its manufacture, its artifice, its physical reality must be scrubbed away, erased. I don't think we should think of Realistic narrative as the "traditional" story opposed to a fiction we call experimental. Narrative Realism was a robust vital experiment that got stuck, and its move into the academy enabled it to survive pretty much intact away from direct contact with evolving forms of media and technical innovations of printing, publishing, and dissemination.

Audio Recording: *How and why do you call attention to the physical objects of fiction and fiction-making in your work?*

E-mail: I am old school I guess. No ideas but in things. I am a nominative writer. Like Barthelme, I want to be on the leading edge of the junk phenomena. Words are already abstractions. It is very difficult to make them solid, concrete, concrete even in abstraction, and then to abstract them once again. But I want to do that. More and more I am involved with the actual material of fiction—the book, the media, the leftover residue of stuff. I want to not just make and manipulate a text but manipulate its frame. I want to "publish" myself in ever more physical ways. Not so much a fiction writer as a fabricator of fictional stuff, text only a part of it. I arrange things. I arrange words, yes. But also the things that are words.

Postcards:

Dear Michael,
 Why is it important for you to manipulate texts and frames? Are politics involved in these manipulations?
Flore

June 28, 2010 Athens, Hellas

Dear Flore, I am sorry it has taken me so long to answer your postcard with its question about frames, but as you can see I was waiting for this trip and the chance to write and send postcards in response (I do hope they find you—one never knows with collaborators such as Greek post or the US postal service). Here to do a 2 week workshop on Corfu for the University of Iowa. Staying tonight in this downtown Athens hotel. It has a roof garden where I am writing this and just now the lights have come on the Acropolis next door. How's that for a frame. M.

July 9, 2010, Corfu

Dear Flore, In the 1950s, comedians discovered that the best way to satire President Eisenhower was to report his speeches verbatim. The change of frame from oval office to night club stage was more than enough. This is a postcard interview. Several frames are at work here. The frame of interview—and where the interview will ultimately appear. The frame of the postcard. With this postcard I am sending a postcard that is a self-conscious postcard. It has a picture of a gallery of the new acropolis museum with an artifact being installed. The usual frame of the postcard (and of the museum usually depicted) has frames that are transparent, that disappear. The viewer is to see the object clearly with only the mediation of labels as further framing. Here there is the scaffolding of installation (usually removed) that appears—a massive work of sculpture. This is a frame of a frame, that reminds us of the artifice. The new museum has whole series of these kinds of cards. Why? Greeks are aggrieved by the lack of Elgin Marbles in the B. M. Is this a way of saying that the past isn't over yet? Martone.

Letter:

[Handwritten letter dated 07/08/10:]

> Dear Michael,
> Thanks for the Indiana Postcard that arrived from Greece.
> It seems that your interest in frames involves the accidental conditions of fiction. Does this interest in the accidental require a different mode of writing, practically speaking?
> Best,
> Flore

[Handwritten response overlaid on the letter:]

> Dear Flore, or different modes. I am interested in the exchange the transmission of writing that needs to be produced and reproduced. The material component of the abstract ideas of abstract words, letters. I like when the art appears as machine made, steam punk. I like the residue of our interaction with the machines that reproduce (reproduce!) writing — the accidents, yes, the mutations. The way information decays over time. This question was lost in the machine of the postal system. It appeared again in a xerox copy (praise be Chester Carlson) your handwriting decayed. I am writing the answer on that copy. Who knows if you will get it and in what condition, and then you will transcribe it or copy it again etc. etc. I love the time fulness of it and the performance of finding it and then reframing it into art.
> Martone

07/08/10

Dear Michael,
Thanks for the Indiana Postcard that arrived from Greece.
    It seems that your interest in frames involves the accidental conditions of fiction. Does this interest in the accidental require a different mode of writing, practically speaking?
Best,
Flore

Dear Flore, or different modes,
I am interested in the exchanges the transmission of writing that needs to be produced and reproduced. The material component of the abstract ideas of abstract words, letters. I like when art appears as machine made, steam punk. I like the residue of our interaction with the machines that reproduce (reproduce!) writing—the accidents, yes, the mutations. The way information decays over time. This question was lost in the machine of the postal system. It appears again in a Xerox copy (praise be Chester Carlson) your handwriting decayed. Who knows if you will get it and in what condition. And then you will transcribe it or copy it again. Etc. Etc. I love the time fullness of it. And the performance of finding it and then reframing it into art. Martone.

Tweets:

What is the difference between @4foraQuarter and your book, Four for a Quarter?

4 one, the book took 10 years when this tweet exchange took only 4 months. The book has 44 fictions about 4's. The tweet has 140 characters.

Do you consider the tweet exchange one of your fictions?

For fiction, I always consider the context as well. The exchange? It's part of a fiction made up of all the emails setting up the exchange.

If 4foraQuarter shares themes and formal constraints with the book, what is it in relation to it? A kind of sequel? A parallel development?

For me, it is maybe the left hand to the right on the 88 key keyboard. The minor key to the major? Or the crumbs left after the loaf is cut.

Will that fiction have an end?

Forever? Railroad tracks running into the distance. The paradox of parallel lines. The intersection seems to happen. A kind of destination.

You have given examples somewhere else of 4s that interest you, but could you say why 4? Why not 3 or 5?

4, golden mean. The square. The only name of a number (in English) that has the number of letters it names. The photobooth god decided on 4.

<u>Cell Phone Text</u>: *Would you like to propose a question for you to answer in the interview?*

<u>E-mail</u>: What is it with you and telephones?

<u>(E-mailed) Word Document</u>: *Disappointingly, perhaps, there is not so much with me and telephones. I have acquired a cell phone only a few years ago and use it mostly like I use a landline, whatever that traditional use might be—doctors' appointments, checking on family, and so forth. So, even my use of nonportable phones is not very creative. But I've read in your interview with the* Southern Indiana Review *that you invite texting in your readings and in the classroom. Can you say more about that? What has come out of your invitations?*

<u>E-mail</u>: I have thirty-two text messages to answer today. I gave a lecture on Thursday to a class of one hundred freshmen. A kind of intro to the arts class. At the beginning I invited them to text me during the lecture. I told them that if I was as good as they were, I could give the lecture and answer them at the same time. But I am not that good, so I am, days later, still answering the texts. The main point of the lecture is that art is a method we use to slow us down, to make us see the wonder again in the things we take for granted. The Russian formalist idea of making the stone stony again. I remind them that in the air they breathe, the air that is now an electromagnetic soup we swim in, are all these words, language, letters, and we have these little boxes that pull them out of the ether. I had them write a poem, too, with their handheld devices. I asked them where they sent the poem. The first student said, "I sent it to Oregon to a friend there." To Oregon, I reminded them. Fucking Oregon! Another student said she sent it to the person sitting next to her. Just as amazing. I like the cell phone for the heft. It is like the stone I am making stony again. I had them bring in a stone and write a word on it, and, after class, place it back out on the campus somewhere. Maybe near the spring pond that the students, even as they walk by it every day, don't remember seeing as they gloss their lives. Then, I recite the Bashō: Old pond / frog jump into / water sound. They have left their cell phones on. All one hundred of them have written poems and now the responses are coming back from everywhere. The cell phones vibrate and chirp. Frogs in a bog.

<u>Cell Phone Text</u>: *Do you know that there is a book of photography entitled* Dark Light *by Michael Martone?*

<u>Cell Phone Text</u>: Yes! A different mm. I know him. mm.

E-mail: I brought it up because it made me think of the poetry you published under the name of Neal Bowers. Care to say more about that?

E-mail: Last term I taught a class on plagiarism and the commons using Lewis Hyde's new book *As Common as Air*. Exciting time to be a writer using the commons of language and ideas. Massive forces seeking to enclose such ideas. And this machine—the computer and the internet—seems to be able to deconstruct the older idea of authorship faster than one can say "deconstruct." Neal wrote a book about having his poems stolen and republished as if written by someone else. I thought an interesting thought experiment would be to publish my poems under Neal Bowers's name. So I did that.

E-mail: When I started reading books in English, I became more aware of tables of contents because the French tradition, which I was used to, prints content pages at the end of books. I prefer the practical American way: it saves me time looking for the content pages in the last sections of the book before I consider reading it or before I start reading it. My Martone content pages are full of notes because, for reasons I do not quite understand, once I realized that some entries were missing, republished from previous volumes, or modified from previous volumes, I had to compulsively track the differences. For instance, in Michael Martone, *the table of contents' list of "contributor's notes" does not match the actual content of the book.*

E-mail: I guess I have a couple of things to say about this. The first is that, like you, I am very interested in form, as you know, and the book as form. And also, I am very interested in the material nature of books and writing now that writing and printing are moving from an analog nature to a digital one. So many parts of the traditional book, such as the table of contents or the blurbs on the back cover or the flaps on the dust jacket, have been relatively stable over my lifetime. I guess the notion of what the writer writes and what the writer provides to the publisher has been stable too. As the definition of the writer's role expands, it does begin to encroach on the traditional territory of designer, editor, publisher. I want to do more than provide the text for the body of the book. I like animating more and more parts of the book. It is interesting to me to address readers like you who pay attention to the table of contents. To play in these stable fields is like reinvigorating clichés for me, reactivating the strangeness and the beauty of these dormant conventions. One picks up the book and is delighted with many aspects, not just one thing. The table of contents, the dedication, the acknowledgments, the index, the bio note, the blurb, the author photo, the margins and gutters, the head and footnotes can be and should sometimes be in play. The second thing to say is that I look at any one book of mine as only a part of the one big book I am writing. Think *Leaves of Grass*. All the books I have published have included ligatures to previous books and future books. I reprint stories because they change as the context of the book changes. Here this piece can be read as fiction, and here the very same words can be read as fact. The table of contents strikes me as a porous portal for the text as it flows as well as a platform for transforming titles. In the new book, many titles in the table of contents are different from the titles in the body copy. I like to think of these as purposeful mistakes. Double takes. Implanted false memories. The design is for the reader to do with the book what a book does very well—allowing the reader to move back and forth within it and inviting the reader to write on its pages.

E-mail: When I acquired my copy of Alive and Dead in Indiana, it came with a review by Peter S. Prescott ripped from the May 28, 1984, copy of Newsweek. I read Prescott's piece. The first sentence of the review is, "This collection of eight stories is so slim a breeze might blow it from the bookstore shelf, but don't be deceived: the larger the talent, the smaller the container it requires" (83). The rhetoric of this opening made me smile, not because there is nothing to admire in the collection of stories or because the review itself is uninteresting but because it is quite amusing to read such a statement about a writer who is invested in the context of fictions, in how they are framed, presented, and packaged, not to mention the idea of "talent" at odds with a writer who questions the idea of originality, authorship, and the concepts of good and bad writing. With the review is a printed picture of Michael Martone: "Martone: reinventing famous men."

E-mail: Yes, very amusing. Also amusing was the legal battle behind that book—part of the reason it is so slim is that several stories were taken out of the book because of their invading privacy. What I learned was the inoculation clause that this is a work of fiction does not work. The story in the voice of Mark Spitz, the swimmer, was kicked. The lawyers said, we believe this person to be Mark Spitz (he isn't named but narrates the piece), and they said, we believe this because the character is a dentist and former Olympic swimmer. The funny thing is that he was widely believed to have become a dentist after his career—he did apply to Dentist College and he appeared on a Bob Hope show where they made fun of him as a dentist. But he never finished. I spent a day in the Fort Wayne mall asking randomly, "whatever happened to MS?" and most thought he was a dentist. So very funny that the lawyers used the fact that the character was a dentist to prove his real identity as Mark Spitz, and therefore I had invaded his privacy. The story was dropped.

<u>On the Back of Four Photo Booth Pictures</u>: Do you start your stories with an abstract concept—about form or theoretical ideas, for instance—or does something else usually get you started?

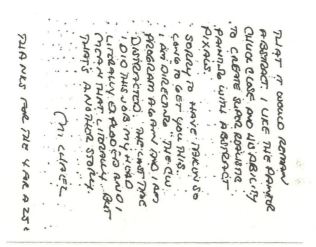

March 29, 2012, Iowa City, Iowa

Dear Flore,
Language or the letters of language is/are abstract. I like abstract art where paint can be paint. But if one is a writer one can't be abstract in the same way. If I write CAT and ask you what cat is, you might say a four legged furry pet or a tractor with threads. You will not say it is black ink on the page. That is to

say, writers are always trying to bring this abstract—by nature—medium into the concrete. So yes, my stories always begin in the abstract, but, also, I would like to find ways that would remain abstract. I like the painter Chuck Close and his ability to create super realistic paintings with abstract pixels.

Sorry to have taken so long to get you this. I am directing the CW Program again and I am distracted. The last time I did this job my head literally exploded, and I mean that literally. But that's another story.
Michael
Thanks for the 4 for a 25¢.

E-mail: *When asked to "define fiction's future in a word, a quotation, or a sentence" in the* American Book Review *30.5 (August 2009), you wrote: "Four words: anonymous, viral, collaborative, ephemeral." I am going to risk going against the important succinctness of your answer (and the Four for a Quarter mode) and ask you to elaborate on these words.*

E-mail: To expand? I think I was trying to get at the optimistic side of the deconstruction of the "author" both by the pesky French essayists and, more importantly, the rise of the networked word processing machine. I think those four words hint at what I feel is going on as I spend more and more time creating text at my computer to send to webbed social platforms. Much I read on-line is without signed authority and has been "shared." It is all ephemeral, though it all is, we are told, archived somewhere on some server or storage disk. The cloud. I think it is interesting that there are millions of people now writing constantly, twitting, and so forth, and most, not quite all, do not seem concerned about making a "name" or upon lasting contribution or fame. It is news enough. I think we think of ourselves more and more as arrangers or rearrangers. And it is funny that, at the historical moment the laws governing property rights have never been stricter, the ease of stealing around those rights has never been so effortless.

E-mail: *You mention online writing here, and when I initially approached you about this back-and-forth, the list of media you were interested in using for the interview included more "new media" exchanges than "traditional" ones. Could you expand on the influences of new media on your own work?*

E-mail: I am of the generation that always had a television in the house. I worked for the City of Fort Wayne when the cable franchise was let. I have had cable television in the house since 1982. I have had a computer since 1986. But before that, I was working with Apple computers to produce a magazine and a chapbook series called *Story County Books*. My father worked as a switchman for the phone company. He would "cut-over" his part of the system as the analog evolved to solid state. Direct long distance, micro-wave, fiber optic cable. He eventually cut-over a technology that made him obsolete, digital switching. I received only one telegram in my life in 1984 on the occasion of my marriage. In 1977 I worked in a hotel and ran an old pbx switchboard. Then one made wake-up calls live—I worked the eleven to seven shift. I wore a headset and physically plugged in the connecting line to the trunk line. I find I am resisting giving up my line, and I have yet to buy a smart device. Perhaps I am running out of steam. Perhaps I am not able to adapt to the new move. I just bought my mother's 2000 VW Beetle. It came with a tape deck. I still have my vinyl records from the '60s to the '80s and a smattering of new vinyl. No tapes, sad to say now that I have a player again. Many CDs and, again, an exhaustion derived from grooming and managing iTunes. Netflix's bit streaming and by mail. Mail, I love. And I feel honored to be present for the end of it. As I was for the end of the telegraphy. I actually was in a hotel in Poughkeepsie next to the Morse estate the day the last telegraph was sent. The post office is actually in the Constitution. It is one of the few specific jobs the Congress is charged to do. Growing up in Indiana, a flat place, I was always interested in vertical structures. I loved that grain elevators were called elevators. Towers of all kinds. I really feel the electromagnetic soup we are all living in now. The texts and code and messages all around us, flowing through us, radiating. I like having a device that draws language out of the ether. And a device that enriches the soup. I haven't even mentioned photography. My latest book is informed by instant photography of the photo booth, the crossroads of analog and digital picture taking. I like the space of the booth, both public and private, both goofy and serious. Both about the past and the future. All of this reminds me to mention Hermes, the messenger god. Patron of Banker and thieves of all transmission and transition. Of trivia—the crossroads. Hermes was not the great artist his brother Apollo was. But Hermes made the lyre his brother Apollo played so well. Hermes made it out of a turtle shell, cattle horns, a cat gut. Who would have thought that all the bones and sinew would be made into music? Apollo makes the music but Hermes makes the music that makes the music.

works cited

Martone, Michael. *Alive and Dead in Indiana*. New York: Alfred A. Knopf, 1984. Print.

———. *The Blue Guide to Indiana*. Tallahassee: Fiction Collective Two, 2001. Print.

———. *Fort Wayne Is Seventh on Hitler's List.* Bloomington: Indiana UP, 1990. Print.

———. *Four for a Quarter: Fictions.* Tuscaloosa: Fiction Collective Two, 2011. Print.

———. "An Interview with Michael Martone." *Hobart, Another Literary Journal* (2012): n. pag. Web. 10 Feb. 2016.

———. "Interview with Michael Martone by Jordan Cory & Jon Webb & Michael Martone." *Southern Indiana Review* (2008): n. pag. Web. 10 Feb. 2016.

———. *Michael Martone.* Normal: Fiction Collective Two, 2005. Print.

———. *Townships: Pieces of the Midwest.* Iowa City: U of Iowa P, 1992. Print.

further works by and on michael martone

Church, Steven. "The Blue Guide Project: Fresno." *Assay: A Journal of Nonfiction Studies* 1.2 (2015): n. pag. Web. 22 Mar. 2016.

Martone, Michael. "Adventures on the Cultural Landscape." *Delicious Imaginations: Conversations with Contemporary Writers.* Ed. Sarah Griffiths and Kevin J. Kehrwald. West Lafayette: Purdue UP, 1998. 173–93. Print.

———. "Anthrax, Plexiglass, and the Writing Life: An Interview with Michael Martone." *Interdisciplinary Literary Studies* 7:1 (2005): 116–26. Print.

———. "A Conversation with Michael Martone." *Story Matters.* Ed. Margaret-Love Denman and Barbara Shoup. Boston: Houghton Mifflin, 2005. 307–26. Print.

———. "A Conversation with Michael Martone." *Upstreet* 4 (2008): 97–120. Print.

———. *Double-wide.* Bloomington: Indiana UP, 2007. Print.

———, ed. *Extreme Fiction: Fabulists and Formalists.* New York: Pearson Longman Press, 2003. Print.

———. *The Flatness and Other Landscapes.* Athens: U of Georgia P, 2003. Print.

———. "Inkblots, Mardi Gras, and Beethoven's Fifth: An Interview with Michael Martone." *Southern Indiana Review* 16.2 (2009): 89–101. Print.

———. "An Interview with Michael Martone." *Creating Nonfiction.* Ed. Becky Bradway and Doug Hesse. Boston: Bedford/St. Martin's, 2009. 575–76. Print.

———. "An Interview with Michael Martone." *Meridian* 25 (2010): 62–76. Print.

———, ed. *Not Normal, Illinois.* Bloomington: Indiana UP, 2009. Print.

———. *Pensées: The Thoughts of Dan Quayle.* Indianapolis: Broad Ripple Press, 1994. Print.

———, ed. *A Place of Sense: Essays in Search of the Midwest.* Iowa City: U of Iowa P, 1988. Print.

———. "A Prose Aesthetic of Progress: An Interview with Michael Martone." *Indiana Review* 26.2 (2004): 83–98. Print.

———. *Racing in Place.* Athens: U of Georgia P, 2008. Print.

———, ed. *Rules of Thumb.* Cincinnati: Writer's Digest Books, 2006. Print.

———. *Safety Patrol.* Baltimore: The Johns Hopkins UP, 1988. Print.

———. *Seeing Eye.* Cambridge: Zoland Books, 1995. Print.

———. "A Talk with Michael Martone." *Rathalla Review* 1.1 (2013): 28–31. Print.

———, ed. *Townships: Pieces of the Midwest.* Iowa City: U of Iowa P, 1992. Print.

———, ed. *Trying Fiction*. Fort Collins: The Center for Literary Publishing, 2001. Print.

———. *Unconventions*. Athens: U of Georgia P, 2005. Print.

Martone, Michael, and Bryan Furuness, eds. *Winesburg, Indiana*. Bloomington: Indiana UP, 2015. Print.

carole maso

CAROLE MASO IS A PROFESSOR OF LITERARY ARTS AT BROWN UNIVERSITY. SHE IS THE AUTHOR OF *AVA* (1993), *DEFIANCE* (1998), AND *MOTHER AND CHILD* (2012). SHE RECEIVED A LANNAN LITERARY FELLOWSHIP FOR FICTION, TWO NATIONAL ENDOWMENT FOR THE ARTS FELLOWSHIPS, A NEW YORK FOUNDATION FOR THE ARTS GRANT, AND A W.K. ROSE FELLOWSHIP IN THE CREATIVE ARTS.

CAROLE MASO'S WORK is known for its poetic qualities: its reshaping of narrative structures has often been understood as a feminist response to patriarchal modes of expression. Maso herself has written on feminism in her collection of critical essays, *Break Every Rule: Essays on Language, Longing, and Moments of Desire* (2000). Her novels use unconventional forms to tell the stories of women in relation to language, art, memory, sexuality, and gender. *Ghost Dance* (1986) relates the struggles of Vanessa Turin as she attempts to recover her family and her past. In *The Art Lover* (1990), Caroline, a novelist and poet, reflects on the relationship between life and art as she rediscovers New York City after a writing retreat. The novel combines reproductions of pictures and newspaper clippings as they interrelate with Caroline's life, her characters', as well as that of a friend diagnosed with AIDS. *AVA* (1993) recounts the last day of Ava Klein, a thirty-nine-year-old professor of comparative literature, who is dying of a rare cancer. The fragmented narrative offers variations on key themes that wander through Ava's mind—her miscarried pregnancy, the books she taught, her lovers and her three husbands, her family's experience of the Holocaust, her travels in Europe, and so forth—on August 15, 1990, the day of Iraq's invasion of Kuwait. In *The American Woman in the Chinese Hat* (1994), Catherine, a bisexual writer, tells of her experiences in France as she goes through various sexual encounters. *Defiance* (1998) focuses on physics professor Bernadette O'Brien, who is in prison after murdering two students. Awaiting execution, she writes her life story, interrelating her passion for mathematics with childhood stories, sexual fantasies, and reflections on death row. In *Beauty Is Convulsive: The Passion of Frida Kahlo* (2002), Maso investigates Kahlo's mental and physical struggles.

In these novels, Maso's characters disrupt the consistency we often associate with selfhood as they negate a stable identity, branching into other realms, thereby blurring the contours of their lives and personalities. This happens in *AVA* when the protagonist mentions, for instance, "Shiny hair on the pillow next to me: it was mine and not mine," and states, "It is and is not my body" (61, 128). Ava celebrates the open-endedness of her self—real or imagined. This celebration is in line with Maso's conception of writing as an open, fluid, and physical activity, which has led her to research ways in which language can be expressive both intellectually and sensually. Maso sees writing as "an experience that exists as heat or light, friction, dissolution, as spirit, as body, as a world that overflows the covers of the book, and crosses into a kind of derangement, a kind of urgency, waywardness, need—a pulsing, living, strange thing" ("An Interview"). Such an approach to writing asks that we reconsider our relationship to words, as they become part of an embodied approach to language and knowledge. In Maso's work, this translates into a poetic, lyrical prose: *Aureole* (1996)—a multilingual genre-binding, fragmentary and open text about an American woman coming to terms with her sexuality—stresses the rhythms and textures of language that are woven into the erotic explorations of food, sex, desire, and sensuality.

Maso addresses this physical engagement in language in the following interview, which took place on June 6, 2006, in her house in Germantown, New York. We shared a peaceful afternoon of rich discussion in her garden. At the time, I was writing my dissertation on her novel, *AVA*, and she generously elaborated on her approach to this work. Our exchange of ideas was marked by her warmth, conviviality, and thought-provoking comments. In the following discussion, she addresses the influence of feminist thinkers on her work, the use of white space in fiction writing, and the importance of breath, silence, and foreign languages in her artistic processes.

The interview was amended by a series of questions about her then-recently released novel, *Mother and Child* (2012). From October 2012 to July 2013, we wrote about the intricacies of family life as they merge with the surreal realms of fairy tale and magic. Like many of Maso's novels, *Mother and Child* skirts closure and presents a reformulation of narrative conventions: the narrative—at the intersection between the everyday life of a family and surreal happenings—redefines fiction writing both in its content involving the realistic and fairy tale traditions and in its fragmentary elusive form.

•

You have emphasized, especially in your collection of essays, Break Every Rule: Essays on Language, Longing, and Moments of Desire, *the physical qualities of writing. Does this physical relationship to language call for specific writing methods or habits? Does it influence the way you work?*

I've never composed on a computer. I love the actual physical act of writing, and I work in very large art books so that I am drawing as much as I am writing: I am seeing spatially how things, even in a given small piece, might configure themselves. I'll put something way over there that's obviously the beginning, and then, if I have a sense of how the center might look or what the margins might look like, I'll put things there so that it is a visual and tactile arrangement. Words for me have a kind of weight, a presence. I don't know if that's more typical of poets or not, but that's how I work—it's a kind of choreography. It also, of course, has a musical and visual quality. I often walk and write, or swim. Well, I don't swim and write, but I'll go into the pool with some sort of literary problem. That's the only reason I swim laps. I mean, I like to swim, but it's this other thing: I think the brain goes into another zone, and you have access to something quite else at those times. When I come out, I don't know anything more concerning my problem in a conscious way, but I am closer, I often feel, to understanding something I need. There is a sense of it being also a meditation—although I don't meditate in any of the standard ways. I feel that it is part of how I get to a place that is conducive to writing for me. I always write with a flame burning on my desk. There's always a cat in the room.... Charms come into play, talismans.

When you describe yourself writing and swimming or doing other physical activities, I can't help but think of Hélène Cixous's work. She writes that, in her writing, she wants to be "as close as possible to the body. As if [her] body enveloped [her] own paper" (Rootprints 105). She has also influenced your work. Do you think that your goals as writers are similar, or is her work more of a theoretical inspiration?

I am very interested in her work, and while I am drawn to theory, my work does not originate from that place. It's pretty amazing to read people like Cixous and realize that we are very much of the same sensibility. But I think perhaps our processes are different. My project is very much fictive and arises from the imagination. The body is essential of course, and I am certainly in conversation with her work, but it is quite a different enterprise.

Even in AVA, *when you cite Cixous quite often?*

I was reading her a lot, and what interested me and what continues to interest me most about her work are the ways in which she creatively addresses the essay, the fact that, in her own terms, she makes something that is not rigid and dry and difficult, but a living, fluid text. It breathes; it sighs; it swoons. I don't have a graduate degree; I don't have any training in theory, so a lot of it, for me, has felt somewhat inscrutable. I love its textures and tones but it was not accessible in ways that I found completely compelling until I came across people like Cixous. I then felt differently and was interested that, whereas her project was coming from a theoretical place and mine was coming from somewhere else perhaps, a place in which images would appear first, or sound, or I would hear patterns of language (i.e., more typically where the creative artist works from), we were meeting nonetheless. I was interested in a kind of intellectual rigor that did not disconnect from its own passion. Cixous certainly was and is an inspiration, the freedom she affords, her sense of both rigor and irreverence, the beauty of her thought and line. I am not sure where the work comes from for her—if it comes from idea or not. For me, it doesn't come so much from idea, although idea is very much a part of what I'm interested in. I am very unclear about how the mind is different from the body. For me, it's not a dichotomy: the mind is as passionate as emotion or the body. I don't know how to make these distinctions as easily as some other people do. A thought for me feels palpable and physical.

How do you envision the physical relationship you have to language, as a writer, transposed onto the reader's experience?

I think that the physical relationship to language is what ends up on the page. Those are the kinds of shapes that are made in the end, and a reader can't help but assimilate some of that—that is what reading is, in part, I think. But I really don't have a desire to provoke any certain response from a reader. In fact, I am careful not to do that. I don't have a reader I am writing to. I don't have an audience I am writing to. I feel very suspect of writers who do have that or who think of ways in which they want readers to respond or what specifically they would like to evoke in a reader. I understand the desire to do it, but for me, it is not at all something that I would even want. In fact, in a book like *AVA,* which is my favorite of the books, I feel pleased that a reader can write the story right along with me—that they participate. I mean, you can really skip twenty pages of the book, and it would be fine. It does not have that dictatorial narrative—that tyranny of narrative—is how I started to see it. This thing where I know something and I am going to tell you what it is. I am going to create this in you, and then you will have a part of me with you. I find that really troubling. I was happy with *AVA* for its not doing that. You could, if you wanted, keep close track of the characters and their narratives. But you don't have to. You can read any series of lines and put in as much of your *own* story or memory or world into them. And that would be okay. I wanted the space to allow the reader to go wherever she or he wants to go. I love that notion of spaciousness and freedom, especially as experienced through Ava's last day.

When you talk about the space, are you talking about the white space in the book?

Yes, the white space is one sort of space the book creates. There are discontinuous lines, surrounded by white space. You don't feel that you have to get right to the next one necessarily. You do have that moment to do whatever you want to do, remember when this happened, and it's actually the hope that it will create that kind of experience as opposed to, "Oh, I'd better keep track and stay with the narrative. And if I don't stay with the narrative, I am going to be really in trouble." The space functions in different ways, but it allows one the interval, the mysterious passage between one fragment and the next. I'm interested in what the space allows.

So you don't necessarily think of AVA *as a narrative that has a progression in the traditional sense.*

I don't think it is fixed. I think there is a progress, one in which there is a huge amount of flexibility and space in which that project can, on any given reading, on any given day, be quite a different book.

But then if each reader is taking a different way each time he or she reads the book, do you feel that, at the end, we would all get to a common revelation or understanding of some sort?

I do think that there are things that would be experienced by all—though I am not sure it would be agreed upon what that one "revelation" or "understanding" would be—but I do think that there are things that are there that would be a common journey: the fact that it is a journey, that it is indeterminate, and that there is a simultaneous holding on and a letting go (which, I think, the reader might experience as well while reading). There is a kind of surrender and abandon, and there is also the need to not surrender, to "stay a little," as Shakespeare says. There are a series of openings and a series of closings, joys and sorrows—regrets. So again, it's a different thing than most narratives where you have to figure out or understand the ways in which characters work and the ways in which plot works, where you have to really follow certain things. I think that not all is lost if you don't necessarily do that. It's created by the way the reader takes in and mixes and combines the fragments, forming, hopefully, a unique shimmer of one's own.

You mentioned the white space and the way you handwrite and spatialize things. You also say, "Writing AVA *I felt at times more like a choreographer working with language in physical space" (Break 25). Does your interest in space and journey relate to your physical take on language?*

Yes, I think in part—the idea of language as body and the notion of moving the body through space is a very compelling one to me. And how the body in dance holds for an instant before reconfiguring that space—the feeling, one might say the meaning. This interests me a good deal. There are other notions of silence and space that come into play as well. Some of it has to do, I'm sure, with my desire as a child to be a composer and music being a great influence—music coming out of silence or punctuating silence or shaping silence—and that being something I've always thought about. My father was a trumpet player and a very silent person. I always felt like if I could write music, I could actually talk to him. *AVA* is the book that he responds to in a certain kind of way because I got to write a certain kind of music. I think, also, that I am much more influenced by poets than by fiction writers—that negotiation of white space, which I think is also interesting. But back to the choreography and the choreographing of both language and narrative—as a kid, I took a lot of dance lessons and now watch quite a bit of dance. When I was writing *AVA*, I did especially and was interested in the way different shapes would appear, and then, as soon as they made a configuration, they would be gone, and they would disappear in another shape—the ephemeral quality and the fact that there is no dance except when it's being danced. *AVA* exists—you can open it any day—but the shape that coheres for a moment and then disappears, I find really beautiful and very haunting. Also, it is related to the circumstances of Ava's abstracted mind. Her mind is breaking down on some level; it's closing down. It allows discontinuity. And it was a discontinuity I watched when I watched a very close friend of mine dying, and I realized that a certain kind of linear narrative could no longer be maintained. How would you do that? If

I had to write this book about the last day of a woman's life in a different way, it would have been a very different book. It would have been more like the record of the experience rather than the experience itself. And that is something I wanted to try to get to: a sense of it happening as you are reading it. It's not quite being written as you are reading it, but, in a way, it is because the reader is writing it as she is reading it. Then, it's not only me telling a story but someone else's engagement, on their own terms.

Some writers—I think of Raymond Federman in Take It or Leave It, *for example—have also worked with white space. But in their work, white space often materializes the wordplays that are going on in language, or makes visual puns, or disrupts the traditional page arrangement that the words are themselves questioning. Writers like Federman are also enabling the reader to be freer. But I have a feeling that the white spaces in* AVA *might be different; it's as if they materialize some kind of a breathing body underneath the surface of the book.*

Breathing is part of it. *AVA* was conceived at the time that the First Gulf War began. It became very clear to me then that it was important to know that people wrote books, and, for me, the best and the most interesting texts are what I call mortal documents. All they are is the mark of a human being who is alive and working on a page. For me, all that breathing, all that space, humanized *AVA* or made it a different kind of book. What I felt when I read any book, at the time I was writing this and imagining it, seemed a formula. It all seemed formulaic. We had borrowed narratives and forms; we had played and bought into them big time. Something about that war made it clear to me that I did not have any time to be doing that, that that's why we were, and now continue to be, in so much trouble, because we were just passively accepting the status quo, mindlessly just going along: this is how books should be written. For this book, this process involved the use of the white space, the use of a discontinuous narrative, fragmentation. Also, when I think of the breath in that book, of course, I think of my friend dying, and my attention to his breath. Particularly at the end.

In talking about different forms, I am reminded that you also write about the relationship between poetry and narrative: "The question persists: can poetic insight ever truly be reconciled with the novel's form? On the side of narrative— a plot of motives, time, and causality. Poetry—image and pattern" (Break 38). Is this research based on wanting to avoid formulaic writing?

It is troubling but not surprising that the only way one can earn a living as a novelist seems to be by replicating the nineteenth-century novel. That seems really constricting and impossible, but the marketplace has created this. I don't think readers necessarily want it, but I think the market has been created to have certain expectations about what a novel is and what a character is and how a narrative should unfold. It's only a very small bit of the history of literature. So it's interesting that that has been so held onto way past its moment, and as a result it has become formula. Formula is dangerous not only because the novels sound the same but because we start to create selves out of that, too: this is how we are. We are mediated in so many different ways, and it's all versions of a kind of formula.

So, in that sense, in trying to find and work with a different form, would you consider your work political?

Yes, I do on a certain level, although not in the way one might conventionally define "political." It imagines a place of freedom, where one is not constricted by those models of selves and by already accepted versions of what one can be and what one should think and who one should listen to. When you write these other kinds of novels, you buy into those kinds of systems undeniably.

But sometimes, we have this idea that political literature is going to do its work at the level of content. You allude to the fact that form is also part of your political engagement. The argument that a challenge of form is a political action is sometimes thought of as reductive or essentialist. Do you take part in this debate?

I don't. I've never written in those ways. It's an interesting debate, but it's not one that I am engaged in. But you are right that form for me is where almost everything happens and what is most exciting about writing. Content and form are intimately related and need to be in order to do their work well. *Defiance* is just a prison of a book that was so constrictive and so absurd on some level. I find the book really silly in the ways in which it confines one. I wrote it out of specific circumstances, of being in an academic situation I could not get out of and having to be a big administrator for three years, which I was not capable of being, and feeling that I was in a kind of prison and, again, to find a form that could talk about those kinds of things. In my mind, it becomes a critique of those sorts of fictions by exaggerating them, by pushing them to a place of absurdity, this excess of events, this search for reasons. So for me, it's often a different book than other people read. But it was form that I was really interested in.

In Defiance, *I was struck by the use of mathematics. Would you talk about it?*

It goes back to the notion of the cerebral just being a passionate thing, that thinking and ideas and mathematics and the sciences are as creative and as wild and extraordinary as the rest of it. It's just different terms. In that book, the notion of mathematics as deeply creative and as a place of real possibility, escape even, interests me. To choose to be a writer means you can't be an astronomer; you can't be a botanist; you can't be the astronaut one might want to be. So the violence of the choice of it interests me because it really does exclude almost everything else (because it takes so much time to do it well). But it is interesting, then, to find these things you want to think about for a while. Math has always interested me.

You talk about shapes and space and the spatial organization of your writing. Would you consider working with a visual artist?

In *The Art Lover*, which is my second book, there are lots of graphics, paintings, posters, found stuff that needed to be in the book. In a sense, I was working with many artists. And yes, I am, of course, interested in the visual ways to think, and in the book I am doing now, *The Bay of Angels*, I've got a lot of that sort of thing going on. Collaboration interests me. It's a question of not having enough time and having to really pick and choose projects carefully. Several choreographers and installation artists have done pieces with *AVA*. My level of involvement in such endeavors is always a question. Especially as one gets older, you just feel, where do you put your energy and your time, and where do you best use it? But I would love that too, if I could, to work with others, from the conception stages and beyond.

Do you see your writing evolving and changing throughout your career? How so?

It's always been pretty clear to me that I was an apprentice, that all the books are a kind of progress. The books are very different from one another on one level—they read differently, they examine different things—while also being similar in certain ways. But I felt, for a long time, that I was just learning, just teaching myself how to write, just exploring the different ways of what language could do, and always coming against the edges of my limitations and trying to work on how to transcend those, how to move to the next place. Recently, I would say in about the last five years, I felt that all the other books that I have written have been preparation for *The Bay of Angels.* It's a really interesting feeling. It's really odd to have this sense of, "Okay, now I know why I wrote all this; now I understand the circumstances and what I needed to do in order to write the book that I am working on now." The book will have the kind of ability of a narrative like *Defiance,* the diffuse and abstract quality that *AVA* has, but I will also be using graphic and essay and things that I have looked at or engaged in the previous books. So it's this interesting moment of feeling that I am finally ready to write.

It's an odd feeling because people say, "How can you say you are ready to write? You've been writing your whole life." I feel like I have been constantly trying to forge my own way, but I've been writing somewhat in the dominant form. The books still looked too much like somebody else and not enough like where I am. And now I am finally feeling in a different place, and I am not sure why that is. The work I am doing now has been gestating for a very long time. It's been fifteen years. I have notebooks and notebooks and notebooks filled with it. And Ava actually becomes a major part of it, in that she appears at an earlier stage in her illness. She is having a transplant and she is probably five or six or seven years away from her death at this point, and we find her at a very different place, and she is only one part of the whole thing but she is a real part of it.

So The Bay of Angels *is working intertextually with all of your other books?*

Ava specifically makes an appearance in this way, but all of the other books come in, not content-wise—things that I have learned seem to be appearing, too. Now, I am much more able to incorporate visuals, in a way, because I wrote *The Art Lover,* and there is a large essay in *The Art Lover* too, and now I feel very free to just write from an essayistic point of view. A lot of it will be written from my own voice, constructed in certain ways. I feel more at ease in incorporating all of this than I might have before. It is ironic because *AVA* came from the other war, and this one, *The Bay of Angels,* comes from this war very directly and will talk about that from my own voice. And I see it as a kind of history of human suffering and a book about war. I am very influenced by film, too, and the Russian director Andrei Tarkovsky has something he says— I don't have the quote here, but it's something like, to be aware that beauty is summoning us. And beauty comes in and out of fashion—but beauty is what the book is about. It's about beauty, even though it's about suffering and war too. So, at this point, it's maybe a thousand pages of this thing. And now I have a seven-year-old, and instead of what I usually do—that is, looking at my writing—I did not have that kind of stamina and concentration, so I just kept writing and writing, and now that she is at school all day long, I've been able to go to the next step with it all. So I've been composing the last year in earnest.

But you said it's a project you've been working on for fifteen years. Does that mean that you work on several pieces at once?

Often a smaller project has interrupted the large one, and I have put the large one aside. Usually that has come at a time when I have been too busy with teaching or a baby or something else to give the large one what it demands. It's a project I never leave though, and it is always with me. It's also something that, for a long time, I had the inkling I was not quite good enough or prepared enough to write. I did not know enough to write it yet, and the circumstances were not there for me to write it. As I said, I was directing the program, and then *Aureole* came. And I need to write every day, so all I could do were shorter pieces or the essays. The essays in *Break Every Rule* weren't written in any chronology or conceived of as a whole. They were commissioned by different journals and collected later. One day I realized that to continue to do other smaller books or projects would mean to lose *The Bay of Angels*, and so now I have settled there. I am ready. I do feel that every book has a time, a moment, and that moment passes inevitably at some point. It can become lost to one, and it's not possible to get it back again, and that must be understood.

The Bay of Angels began as I experienced deep, uncanny intimations of a life I had once lived in occupied France at a time before my birth. It haunts me and has held me all these years. It holds me still.

*You mention your experience in Europe. I was listening to an interview of Kristeva shown in France in a documentary on her work—*Etrange Etrangère. *She talked about her position as a Bulgarian reading French writers, such as Collette, and being unable, as a foreigner, to focus only on the message but also on how the message was conveyed—the "r" in the sentence and how such a sound is pronounced, its root in our bodies. Can you talk about how your travels in Europe and your use of another language have influenced your writing, posed new questions?*

I was in the South of France, and people were not speaking English. And for a while, I was silent because I was too shy to talk. But after a while, I started to understand the urgency of language, the way it worked for lots of people (the children, for example): that you needed to say something, and you needed to find the way to say it. So all I could say or understand were very simple things initially. That was very interesting in terms of a kind of relationship you were in with language again. You were in a world of need and desperation and also utter wonder and delight around language and sense making. So speaking became something other than a luxury. It became something I really needed in a different kind of way. My precious lexicon and the two- or three-sentence constructions I could make were everything. It was interesting to continue to think and to write in those constructions and to understand what the past or present or future tenses really imply, how they move in a cellular way. It makes all of it very precious and dear and important. I wrote a book completely from that place called *The American Woman with a Chinese Hat*, in which there are only about fifty words that keep shuffling around, used in different kinds of ways. It was fascinating, this idea of a diminished lexicon, and what you can do with it. There is that famous quote by Picasso: "When I don't have red I use blue." You just use what is available to you. Another aspect of that other-language relationship is the feeling of exile, the solitude. It's like nothing quite else. It can be a wonderful thing to have that distance and then try to become near—that nearness and farness that a kind of other language throws you into. And the longing. And silence.

Does this relate in some way to silence in your writing?

I think that it does. There is a sense of how it can engulf one, and how it can really subsume one. I am very interested in Beckett because of that, and in the ways in which he became more and more silent and how he understood what language could and could not do and how to bear that and how to live with that and how to be okay with that. I feel as if I live and write at the altar of the unsayable. That's the only thing that interests me. Everything else—I mean, why would you write if you could say what you needed to say directly? That's what makes me want to do it. For me, *AVA* is the book that gets closest to that because it's all about the things that I can't really say and that I don't know how to say and that are only said in the ways that the lines relate to one another. And in the silences between the lines. It's a deeply humbling endeavor in the end. I'm lucky to be able to spend my life this way.

Was it a difficult decision to publish the diary of your pregnancy?

No, not really. I'd never kept a journal before. I spend too much of every day writing to have anything left over for a more daily recording of life. I do think it is a really interesting form though and one that has too often been belittled or marginalized. For me this recordkeeping was essential—I could feel something momentous occurring in me. It was a document of an event that was never to be again. And I did not want to lose it. It was astonishing to feel as if I was not actively constructing anything. What if you do not make anything? What if you just use the things of your very life? Would that be enough? Why has this been denigrated and dismissed? I felt really moved by the fact that all over the world there were people keeping journals, that all over the world there were people making a record of their day. And why should that not be enough? I tried, as much as a writer can do, to not write it, to just record, not to embellish it, to just let it be. One day I stopped writing it—and so it ended. Without writing an ending or trying to take any sort of control over it. A beautiful lesson in letting go. It had become an altogether different kind of experiment for me.

And a very touching one.

Thank you.

•

Could you say a word about family units and fragmentation in Mother and Child?

For me form and content are intimately linked, and this book presented itself as a series of simple, indecipherable parables in which a mother and a child moved through increasingly fraught terrain on an inevitable but baffling trajectory. This dictates the choice of how to write this. The pieces seem whole but are deceptive, I think, and function very much as parts of a whole that cannot be fathomed or grasped. She's okay.

Can you talk about literary and family lineage in the novel?

I think the book echoes both the Bible and also the many stories of childhood I read to my daughter, Rose. This voice that started narrating from the first sentence I wrote was the way into to the story for me. Only by an investigation into the odd sentences, the images that were coming completely unbidden and the skewed and often desperate logic, only by noticing the distance the narrator was keeping, only by staying open to the deep melancholy and strangeness of the pieces and the sutured progressions, did I begin to understand what was going on. It was a thrilling and frightening and relentless experience. Once set into motion, every day another story would present itself to me as if in visions, both wondrous and fearful—awe, is how I would describe my state of being. I felt I was merely transcribing.

The book comes from an actual event described on the first pages in which a tree falls on my house and bats unbeknownst to me enter the house where my daughter and I are asleep. This estranges and maroons me in a world of terror, in which I try to protect her and feel I cannot. From here, all the other stories, which all have a basis in some fragment of reality, begin to darkly flower.

In the novel, the child and the mother are not given names so that identity is sometimes ambiguous and fluid. Could you say more about your treatment of identity?

Yes, you know right from the start the mother and child were cast into some middle distance from which I could not retrieve them. Despite all my efforts they would not come closer. They would not speak their names; they would not allow me to see their faces. They remained in a narrative space that was neither here nor there. I was very interested that they would come no closer, and neither would they step back into total obscurity. They haunt every page of the book. And I do think their identity at times is fluid and ambiguous, as you say. As I continued writing I began to understand why they inhabited this middle distance, this twilight space. They were both alive and dead. It was untenable for them to live and unbearable for them to die. To me that is the struggle and the bravery at the heart of the book.

Though Mother and Child *does not focus strictly on war and violence, these themes recur in the novel. Would you care to expand on their importance?*

The book was written during the time the country was involved in two major wars, which by the time of the writing had taken a tremendous toll on all of us. The book is populated by drifts of disappearing men; some of those men are phantoms due to war. The other towering image in the book—and central—and in many ways key is the World Trade Center on fire, and much of the disappearance and war meditations emanate from that event.

Mother and Child *asks us to rethink our relationship to reality and truth. Could you elaborate on how the novel deals with the relationship between the real and unreal as well as the true and untrue?*

As I have said, the novel was set into motion by the events that are described in the opening pieces of the book. When the bats entered my house in the night without my knowing and screeched and fluttered in the room in which my daughter and I slept without us knowing until the next night when the power returned to the house, I felt vulnerable and at risk in a way that jarred my sensibilities utterly. It felt as if a veil had lifted and what I could not previously see clearly was now plainly visible, and it was clear to me that it had been there all along. It was an alternate world in which inanimate objects took on luminous, grave, magical properties; a darkly radiant force and light followed me through my days. Seemingly ordinary events in a bucolic life: going to see a fire truck dedicated, passing the concrete rabbit in my daughter's children's garden, swimming in a pool, everything, everything took on a quality of foreboding and danger and magic and mystery. My vision had changed and for a very long time—years really—it did not change back. It was a harrowing and wondrous period of my life because I could see the world that lay just beyond this world—it was all completely accessible, and from there it was as if I were simply taking dictation. And of course it brought into question in a very visceral and direct way the nature of reality, the visible and the invisible, the real and the unreal, the nature of truth, and all our assumptions. Life is all a dream surely. Well, that veil has since come down again, and while I was in that other state I can say more often than not I was in a state of suffering, sometimes ecstatically so. It was a difficult, difficult time; I now mourn the loss of that vision and will long for it in some way the rest of my life. The book remains the record of that experience and that time.

works cited

"Julia Kristeva, Étrange Étrangère." Caillat, François. TV5Monde, INA, ARTE, France. 2 Mar. 2013. Television.

Maso, Carole. *The American Woman in the Chinese Hat*. Normal: Dalkey Archive Press, 1994. Print.

———. *The Art Lover*. San Francisco: North Point Press, 1990. Print.

———. *Aureole: An Erotic Sequence*. Hopewell: Ecco, 1996. Print.

———. *AVA*. Normal: Dalkey Archive Press, 1993. Print.

———. *Beauty Is Convulsive: The Passion of Frida Kahlo*. Washington: Counterpoint, 2002. Print.

———. *Break Every Rule: Essays on Language, Longing, and Moments of Desire*. Washington: Counterpoint Press, 2000. Print.

———. *Defiance*. New York: Dutton, 1998. Print.

———. *Ghost Dance*. New York: Perennial Library, 1986. Print.

———. "An Interview with Carole Maso." *Rain Taxi Review of Books* 2.4 (1997–98): n. pag. Web. 24 Nov. 2005.

———. *Mother and Child*. Berkeley: Counterpoint Press, 2012. Print.

———. *The Room Lit by Roses: A Journal of Pregnancy and Birth*. Washington: Counterpoint, 2002. Print.

further works by and on carole maso

Berila, Beth. "A Correspondence with Carole Maso." *Salt Hill Journal* 8 (1999): 107–13. Print.

Berlin, Monica. *A Casebook on Carole Maso's AVA*. n.d. Web. 19 Aug. 2007. <http://www.dalkeyarchive.com/product/ava-by-carole-maso/>.

Chevaillier, Flore. *The Body of Writing: An Erotics of Contemporary American Fiction*. Columbus: The Ohio State UP, 2013. Print.

Cooley, Nicole. "Carole Maso: An Interview." *The American Poetry Review* 24.2 (1995): 32–35. Print.

Harris, Victoria Frenkel. "An Introduction and an Interpellated Interview." *Review of Contemporary Fiction* 17.3 (1997): 105–11. Print.

Maso, Carole. "An Interview with Carole Maso." *Barcelona Review* 20 (Sept.–Oct. 2000): n. pag. Web. 24 Nov. 2005.

———. "World Book." *Fiction's Present: Situating Narrative Innovation*. Ed. R. M. Berry and Jeffrey Di Leo. Albany: State U of New York P: 2007. 236–51. Print.

Quinn, Roseanne Giannini. "'We Were Working on an Erotic Song Cycle': Reading Carole Maso's *AVA* as the Poetics of Female Italian-American Cultural and Sexual Identity." *MELUS: The Journal of the Society for The Study of the Multi-Ethnic Literature of the United States* 26.1 (2001): 91–113. Print.

Silbergleid, Robin. "Speaking (in) the Silences: Gender and Anti-Narrative in Carole Maso's *Defiance*." *Tulsa Studies in Women's Literature* 29.2 (2010): 331–49. Print.

Stirling, Grant. "Mourning and Metafiction: Carole Maso's *The Art Lover*." *Contemporary Literature* 39.4 (1998): 586–613. Print.

Vellucci, Sabrina. "Figuring Loss: The Rejection of Impersonal Aesthetics in Carole Maso's *The Art Lover*." *Modes and Facets of the American Scene: Studies in Honor of Cristina Giorcelli*. Ed. Dominique Marçais. Palermo: Ila Palma, 2014. 375–88. Print.

Worthington, Marjorie. "Posthumous Posturing: The Subversive Power of Death in Contemporary Women's Fiction." *Studies in the Novel* 32.2 (2000): 243–63. Print.

joseph mcelroy

JOSEPH MCELROY IS THE AUTHOR OF *LOOKOUT CARTRIDGE* (1974), *PLUS* (1977), *WOMEN AND MEN* (1987), AND *NIGHT SOUL AND OTHER STORIES* (2011). HE IS THE RECIPIENT OF AN AWARD IN LITERATURE FROM THE AMERICAN ACADEMY OF ARTS AND LETTERS AS WELL AS FELLOWSHIPS FROM THE GUGGENHEIM, ROCKEFELLER, D. H. LAWRENCE, INGRAM MERRILL, AND THE NATIONAL ENDOWMENT FOR THE ARTS FOUNDATIONS. HE IS A PROFESSOR EMERITUS AT QUEENS COLLEGE, CITY UNIVERSITY OF NEW YORK.

IN THE CONTEXT of contemporary American writing, Joseph McElroy is often compared to William Gaddis, Thomas Pynchon, or Robert Coover because of their common concerns for epistemological inquiries. In his fictions, McElroy uses a large variety of paradigms (chaos theory, cybernetics, biology, data processing, geology, botany, genetics, ecology, relativity, as well as others) to question the relationship between science and technology. McElroy's novels reflect on the ways that human experience, seen as a collaborative network, can be conveyed within the constraints of the linear process of writing. Often, his work is intricately composed, dwelling on the linguistic nature of narrative, and it involves experimentation in narration, syntax, and structure.

A Smuggler's Bible (1966) presents a reflection on sacred texts and offers an opportunity for the unusual assemblage of eight stories that David, the narrator, reads aboard a transatlantic ship. *Hind's Kidnap: A Pastoral on Familiar Airs* (1969) is an inquiry into kidnappings, the deciphering of which relies on a "dense nightmare anonymity—New York, Brooklyn Heights, terrible genealogy, the self in relation to others" ("Joseph McElroy"). *Ancient History: A Paraphase* (1971) is made of detective puzzles that question the meanings and causes of psychological evolution as field theories are applied to people's lives and contaminate the processes of perception, thinking, and writing. *Lookout Cartridge* (1974) focuses on the life of a man named Cartwright after he makes a movie that by chance has recorded terrorist activities. The film disappears, and Cartwright puts his life in danger to find it and understand its disappearance. *Plus*'s (1977) premise is rife with science and technology: The disembodied brain of a scientific researcher, with all its traces of an intimate life, is put into orbit in order to communicate with Earth. *Women and Men* (1987) is an evocation of the connections between communication systems. In the 1,192-page novel, McElroy ambitiously creates communicative and integrative systems that make up the structures of our lives. *The Letter Left to Me* (1998) presents a boy reading a letter from his dead father, the written words of which enable a mental discussion between the two characters. *Actress in the House* (2003) tells the story of actress Becca and lawyer Daley as they "begin a precarious period of discovery, [. . .] slipping a boundary to both past and future" ("Joseph McElroy"). McElroy's novella *Preparations for Search* (2010) and his last collection of short stories, *Night Soul and Other Stories* (2011), show him playing with intimate life, technological data, and scientific systems as themes and structures.

In fact, for McElroy, science is not an abstraction isolated from human life; rather, it is part of people's intimate experiences. In that sense, his fictions debunk the limited understanding of the definitions and of the roles of science, technology, intimacy, and everyday life. McElroy thinks of science "not as arcana but as thought, attention, personal imagination, and a vocabulary of forms: part of that embracing fiction about people and families, cities, nature, the rush and color and manners and plasm of factual and mythy [*sic*] possibility that can go into a novel" ("Plus *Light*").

The subsequent interview elaborates on the possibilities of exchanges between scientific systems and personal life. It also addresses abstract, systematic, and embodied thinking; human agency; change and identity; and writing and risk-taking. The interview took place in the author's apartment in New York City on June 5, 2006. McElroy's erudition is obvious in the following exchange: as he talks about complex ideas with verve and warmth, he juxtaposes, as is often the case in his prose, the colloquial and idiosyncratic of everyday life with the theoretical and philosophical. For McElroy, writing is "partly an act of giving," and his generous engagement in this interview reveals his unbound interest in collaborative acts of thinking (*Anything Can Happen* 249). Our conversation was marked by this commitment to collaboration and giving, as McElroy expanded on his past and current preoccupations in ways that are humorous, challenging, and fascinating. While the interview provides a captivating overview of McElroy's career, it is also marked by my own interest in *Plus,* the novel that I was examining as part of a book project at the time.

•

Looking back at your work, how do you see your writing changing?

Am I saying the same thing over and over again? About an absence sought? I would say that the possibility suspended in a long sentence and gathered from different contemporary subject matters has come nearer and holds a greater depth now—even also some briefer, enigmatic remarks in *Actress in the House*. I am easier with that sentence now than when I wrote *A Smuggler's Bible*, which is a young book. It's happily quite loose, and the bridge passages push a structure of fragments hunting its own form. We accept fragments today. *A Smuggler's Bible* was quite daring in '66. And there's a fresh, off-balance energy giving an impression of tightness. But I was just beginning to figure out how to control that expansion—archipelago is sort of the climactic idea there—giving the reader the impression of only a precarious order.

When I came to *Hind's Kidnap,* I was more strictly shaping or containing the American clutter, these heterogeneous forces that want to succeed on their own, destroy, create. What a country. *What* forces? A book about a city but a city under a metaphor, a pastoral, if you recall the subtitle. A formal simplicity haunting the narrative but not subduing it. I arranged the first and third sections of five parts each—to echo each other with an understanding that the book's second or pivotal section (written in an entirely different way, a half-subconscious monologue of the woman Sylvia) would be in contrast to the first and the third but open each to each. Their sequence of settings repeats in reverse (old stuff by the '90s) so that in *Hind's Kidnap*—there was a lot there, a thought of what an end in itself might be—the reader may still feel a city pastoral teeming with life, precarious while nonetheless having the look of a stricter form. I was reacting to *A Smuggler's Bible*.

And the book that followed, Ancient History, *has quite a different form . . .*

In *Ancient History* (my orphan, though it's coming back into print) I made a soft triangle or a division into two alternating friends of the narrator: country friend, city friend, and the narrator finding his own life as a recourse from that; and there is another alternation between being mixed up with people (like the famous activist in whose deserted apartment the narrator composes his story—gets it straight) and being much alone, the narrator expressly an only child (a theme, it comes to me, I am vastly improving upon in *Fathers*

Untold, a novel in progress about roughly 1948). So, in *Ancient History,* I seem to move away from the official strictness of *Hind's Kidnap,* using still all this mixed-up material of this nation that I am a citizen of and the times that have so many different knowledges—letting all that into the book. It's a first-person speaker in *Ancient History* with all that danger Henry James speaks of, the fluidity—though, as I get older and older, it seems quite natural to me. I'm aware of where it's led in our fiction away from the clear, firm existence of the narrative voice and into the mess of pseudofiction that avoids the demands of invention and recombination and therefore thought. In *Lookout Cartridge,* a mass of material will generate . . . a time, a plot—the film (whose loss the book is about) and the sources of the film—I say "plot" not only as tale of events and thoughts, which are deeper "events," but as conspiracy. So there is a lot coming at the reader.

It seems that the way Hind's Kidnap, Lookout Cartridge, *and* Ancient History *invite the reader to process an excess of information is quite important in your work. In* Lookout Cartridge, *in particular, the struggle of Cartwright to make sense of what's happening to him mirrors the interpretation process that the reader goes through when reading the novel.*

I must like that. I live on the tip of overload to welcome the reader and myself and speak from inside all of that. So, in *Lookout Cartridge,* we have two friends, two cities, two countries, a family in and out of focus, and this man, Cartwright—the presence and voice of the book (not the same thing)—aware of his power as power he's caught in or a presence he could have that would be clear to him as circumstantial evidence unwitnessed, except in his body and thinking. In some way, he is safely at risk, and my proposition in the book—which gives the reader a handle to cope with the danger and traveling of the book—is that he is the powerful one in this world because he, alone, grasps how entrapped he is by it. So there's a paradox. And I think there were greater complexities in this book than in the previous books and in the voice greater order. I seem to react to myself.

Well, I wonder how this complexity leads to the condensed narrative of Plus?

Plus contracts in style. And, at first, scope. Into rudiments? It's a book more close and alone than any first-person voice could ever bring off. Much more intimate than first person, isn't it? Imp Plus is someone—but who—and what? And from Imp Plus has been subtracted just about everything I, with my degree of claustrophobia, might think. But hardly, as it turns out. And it's as if I can see the book as a contraction in the tight form of a sentence that is one sentence after another. Shorter sentences—much shorter in *Plus*, elliptical, though, horrifying, if you see it, droll, longing, practical. I wanted to give a feeling of rudiments that would parallel the subtraction of the body that the main character began before we knew him. But the story is growth and about beginning with something shrunk—no, narrowly cut, reduced, fundamental—in this case the brain. What soon becomes evident—a field of character—and the movement then is to expand by painful inches, which is how I felt about it. That's the narrative gravity—I've been there, I think—as Imp Plus becomes more and makes little decisions and becomes them. But the expansion in its sentence remains very tight. I was always aware of the presence, the being I was in touch with, and I was certainly not going to turn this into a Thomas Wolfian reminiscence about my formative years. It's so much more American than that. NASA, if you like—but a science idyll. One editor said, "Well, we need to have more about the blind news dealer." To get the reader more cozy—I understand the thinking. Another editor, "It would be nice to have some more sex" (*recalled,* she meant)—and so on. That wouldn't have been true to my premise of the book: a realistic account (the best I can do) of an experiment. You could say it's a fantasy, but it's to be taken as a description of an actual project.

But if we are talking about development, I don't know where *Plus* stands. I think it's untamed and compact. Compressed. You pick a word. Then came the explosion of *Women and Men* and all its voices. It was a go-for-broke, unapologetic invention and recomposing of some, everything, I knew in the wild fields of a novel. It's about two characters who never meet or two hundred who do. It comes from retrieving interactions of women and men in the '70s, let's say, in New York, which I guess makes it a genre novel, a society New York but global. But that is not at all how I saw it. That's mainly the material that's in the book. I see it rather as an attempt to do what I think I've always attempted to do, and I think in *Women and Men* I did it much more than ever before: to connect body and thought, bodily motion and mental, and create a sentence and passage that would be like thought embodied. I think that's what I was trying to do, with great emphasis on the body. Childbirth to begin with.

Is The Letter Left to Me *another contraction or a reaction, in some way, to* Women and Men?

The Letter Left to Me is a short book. Simple, I thought. And a great idea! Father leaves son a letter discovered after his death. Family basically appropriates it and duplicates it in hundreds of copies. And this expansion, like some hidden contagion, continues. And yet, what I had in mind in *The Letter Left to Me* was again something to do with the mind both focusing and expanding, and the focus is the intelligence and sometimes the despair but the hope of the young man. He lets the letter be taken from him, after all. He permits it to happen and that's the focus, but the expansion is in his being in several times at the same time. He's very much in the present but more than before, I used the sentence to look ahead, out of grief into action, secret ambition, the other ethos of seeing and making a move, the hell with it. It was seen as omni-directional or something (like my recent sort of jazz novel, *Actress in the House*). You have this person moving ahead, concentrating on what to do with all these people (some of whom have taken away from him this letter) and even how to feel about the letter. He realizes that there is some change, some chance, in him, which is partly in touch, partly not. He has to cope with loss, and also with a curious relief, which, I think, is truthful without being crass, that his father has died. A good man but you are ... what? Free of him? It's a shock, it's startling, destructive, but secretly in there (and maybe it's a kind of creative drive in him) he realizes that someone has been removed from his life who loved him and whom he needed, but ... So that's one reason why there is this curious hopefulness and a willingness to let the letter go, almost as if he wanted for the letter not to be his. As it really is his absent father's letter—that's all. So the reader thinks: Oh, isn't it ... whatever! The letter was taken away from him and printed up, and then the second time the mother sends it to the dean of the college, and this is terrible. This is awful. It's painfully funny, too. But there is this ambiguous torque or extra strength that the reader is supposed to get.

Right, he is not just a victim ...

The kid is freeing himself in some way that he is not entirely controlling. It's being done *to* him, and he is responding, and I think that's the omni-directional thinking and focus—the aloneness. He's in the past, and maybe the past is to be associated with grief. He's in the future associated with life and hope and action. He's also in the present. But all that has something to do with his trying to cope with the letter, and it has something to do also with action being defined as not only coming from me but from the circumstances, which ... (it's kind of obvious). This is old stuff. Does the will exist? We don't really know. In *Plus*, something happens toward the end, which indicates that there *is* an action and even that there is a growth of body that has something to do with the will and also with a parallel growth of language. But the will is not a simple thing. It's not, "I want to do this, and I'll do it." It's the same in *The*

Letter Left to Me. He's pissed off about the letter but he is himself. He takes action, but it's not unconditional. His will is at every point conditioned by circumstances coming at it. But these circumstances also drive his own power to choose. So I am interested in how we act, decide, choose to run our lives. I think that the mass of this in *Women and Men* becomes no less complex here centered upon one young person in *The Letter Left to Me*. What to do with what you are given and what is taken away. And really, I think that action of any kind—the action of a will—is unpredictably collaborative with circumstances we are in. Was this my homely experiment?

And then there was a long time when I didn't publish a book, years. Well, there were two others getting written, and I was developing all the time like slow film or an abalone building its shell or a bridge—bridge design is one of my interests—getting built. A bridge between two places but weirdly an end in itself.

In your early work, technology and science are predominant and very present in the vocabulary—in the structure, also. More recently, scholarship has paid more attention to not only the science in your work, but also to science as a medium for intimacy, sensual life . . .

Science is supposed to be cold. But its attention is close and clear. There's the bridge to intimacy. Someone looking closely. Touching. I try to find how not to smooth the rhetoric and rhythm of feelings between people, to instead subject them to a kind of realism that's always changing to my ear. I don't find much of that around. Brodkey in a very few early stories sometimes. But not the recent big guns of the novel—my sense of what happens between people. Often, there is a stranger *analysis* that gets into it like a surprise in crisis, as Rilke sees loss one consents to live in, and that has some kinship with the abstracting attention of science or philosophy, which is no less real than what the writing workshops dogmatize as concrete rendering. But often, the transaction between people—the secret *anti*cliché of older man / younger woman in *Actress in the House,* the couple taking a shower on Election Day in *Women and Men*—is full of the unforeseen.

It's as if what could come from an intelligence interested in science (but science found in our habits), has looped partway toward the psychic. I allow myself, as if I were in a lab, to mess with this notion, not unlike what Freud said about the closeness between psychoanalyst and patient (although I am not Freudian): the possibility of two people who are close together seeing the future or together being clairvoyant. And so there is a theory that I even give a name to in *Actress in the House,* not with tongue in cheek but not intended with any Jung or Freud or other professional announcement of the truth. The suggestion is that a relation between two people—this connects with *Women and Men*—can become a new action in which to penetrate enigmas and even see the future. It's definitely in *Women and Men,* in the presence of the angel voices—angels trying to become humanly limited. Through the villain, Ruley, who really is no villain, there enters the story on a fine electric, potentially betraying, line a notion hardly original—that through a close relation of understanding with another person a joint telepathy and clairvoyance can occur. Insofar as it is clairvoyance and a sight of what could come to pass, this result would be active—marriage, perhaps, friendship, half unknowingly strung upon or constructed of thoughts completed together between the two people.

I'm not a Platonist, though this might sound like Shelley in the *Epipsychidion*—more like experimental commitment quite mysterious between people, usually, I would think, two people: and in the end it's hard to know if you see something come true before you will make it come true, or the other way around. Great dangerous troubles the cost of these depths possible between people. The ruinous is in there, too, and I skirted it in *Women and Men* and will come closer in *Fathers Untold,* which I began in 1948–49 and have worked on since then and will finally have the courage to complete along with a nonfiction water book this year (and in *Voir Dire,* which is about the justice of appeals). But in *Actress,* I think I went further with that than I had before. Maybe it's more mature, I don't know. It's worked out in scenes. It's partly two people at a distance spinning slowly around the thing they're becoming. At this closer range, a joined thought begins to occur.

Not doctrine or anything. I guess I did not know how it was going to come out at the end. I knew what I wanted to do, but I did not know how it was going to come out. So I guess you could say it was an experiment.

Do you mean experiment as in experimental writing?

In these remarks I'm going to make in Paris next Friday [June 10, 2006] about risk, I try to make a distinction between what's called experimental writing, which too often to me seems to put the stress on technical overlay or interruption or imposition (as sometimes in our esteemed Sorrentino), metaphor imposed *on* narrative, all certainly reflecting an activity of mind and body, I grant. On the other hand, experiment is an organic risk between people tested by something not well known together and not knowing how it's going to come out.

There's a science vocabulary that flickers through *Actress in the House* and is organic to its thought, and there's an embedded natural calculus named or not in my novel *Cannonball*. I have said this: science provides occasions for finding metaphors in the metaphor field, and as a habit of measure, courage, intuition. I think science is being in the world, observed, questioned. And so I don't see science as being opposed to life. Not technology either, except in our uses of it. Some uses lethal, but the same for amorous passion and stale thought. Easy to forget all that technology lets us do: heal, think together across distances, save. So as for science, which is seen by so many people (especially in this education-poor but system-addicted country) as difficult and fussy and remote, I find it rich and interesting and a source of lenses that we can put upon our life in order to see it. Two examples: Proust, insects and flowers; Nabokov, insects like flowers. Both think with science not only to unveil, unfold, surprise, compare (the known next to the unknown) but to look closer at strange relations, at value, how people are and look, and how things look. And also, in my opinion, both Nabokov and Proust (but maybe more Proust) use the sciences in order to show connection between all the things in the world and that the sex between two people isn't just similar to flowers being visited with and for pollen (or whatever is going on at the beginning of the fourth volume of Proust), not just similar but all part of the same thing. So science I see as connective in what its study shows and connective as an action constructing something. . . . It's not as overt in my last couple of books. Yet calculus, in *Cannonball*, somehow in the physical motions that wait for it to measure—there before the word for it or the book.

I wanted to go back to language, its acquisition in "Night Soul" and in Plus, *for example. Why is it so important to you?*

In Imp Plus, I'm seeing the growth or partly remembering of words, names, statements, hinges of the whole person, and that goes right along with having him grow a body, which seemed inevitable and sensible. In "Night Soul," the sound, which the father listens to in the middle of the night, is seen as the child's growth as well as a sign of it. One growth must surely be parallel to the other—sounds assembling toward a language, just as in *Plus*. So in "Night Soul" there is a darkness between one voice and another or between one person and another. It is not that cliché that's been going around but a true darkness lurking. Ground wants to control Imp Plus and his increasing capacity of words and thoughts, which gives him a power to answer Ground so as to bypass the automatic that's been programmed into him. So the coming of that greater power speaks from the growth of body.

And there's a distant link to "Night Soul": it has its comedy, a profound kind, not a loud kind but idyllic. The father listens three consecutive nights. He comes to a kind of rationale for the infant's differentiated sounds—a language. And he thinks that he's got it, which does not mean that he's in control of his child, but he's learned the language. A friend mentioned Coleridge's "Frost at Midnight," my favorite poem of his, so maybe it was in my thinking. But the trick here is the three days, magical in lots of stories but long enough for a kind of arc of development. As soon as the father has a handle on the night language, the infant's language begins to change, which, I think, is pretty good. Could it happen like that? Maybe. It would take a pretty imaginative father. But it is from his point of view that the story is told. That's very important, too. I mean, imagine telling that story from the point of view of the baby. It would make a sentimental hash of it or an acoustic experiment with findings. Or it would be like Imp Plus becomes the baby or something.

And we also don't know if the baby is awake all the time—the element of sleeping and waking important. Pascal asks how we know all the time that we are awake, how do we know we are not sleeping? We don't know much about ourselves. We are lost in our little corner of the universe and therefore we should believe in God and so forth, which is not my point in "Night Soul." But the development of sounds *toward* words is implicit in the story—the development of sounds and words toward some kind of communication, which is seen primarily in terms of the father understanding something, believing that the kid's sounds are in accordance with some kind of system, which they may be. So it becomes a story about language as growth, language *and* growth, and the development of a kid and of communications with inevitable mysteries between people. The mother continues to sleep, having nursed the baby, though she has her moments when she remembers what her husband said in his sleep.

But in Plus, *the growth is a bit more political. Though politics is even more obvious in some of your other works, such as* Lookout Cartridge. *How do you see your work in relation to political activism?*

Ancient History unfolds the life of a well-known activist, though only in the margins of the novel. Demonstrations, think tanks, late '60s America. A celebrity who has committed some sort of suicide. I had a utopian novel going years ago, which became *Hind's Kidnap*. A utopian community and how it, of course, did not work out (which is also a tired idea). But in the process of that action, I would have found it possible to show people acting out their debates and trying to imagine what would be a just society, which, like betrayal, is the subject of all good novels. The utopia story seemed preachy. The politics is in pressures upon people, not in fictionalized current history. My little Iraq novel, *Cannonball*, forthcoming, speaks more directly but I'm not going to sum it up; and my at-last-almost-finished *Fathers Untold* is marginally about the Hiss period.

Donna Haraway, in her cyborg manifesto, defines a new way for women's resistance that relies on her cyborg. Imp Plus's growth has affinities with the concept of the cyborg. Do you think of Plus *as a feminist text?*

People have asked, "Is Imp Plus expressly masculine?" Indeed, by now I read how the male brain is somewhat different from the female brain. I didn't get into that much but insofar as feminist thought is equality—an emotional equality for men as well as role and marketplace for women. The book has, as well, a female organicist tone to it, to say nothing of gestation—I guess you could say the book is politically correct. I don't think it's a book that the main feminist tradition would find a lot of faults with, unless they dismiss interest in NASA and in biological analysis, embryonic fields in Weiss, and such. I think they would see that the individual here is a man resisting a hierarchical control system, which is easily (too easily) identified as male. And I think I did conceive of the body that is growing—which does not seem especially human at the end, though there are arms (there is something incredible going on)—it doesn't seem especially gender specific. I did not do anything with that, but I don't think it's a new man. I think it's a new human.

You mention thought and body in Women and Men *and the complexities of the individual in relation to biology. In* Plus, *you bring up the regrowing of Imp Plus's body. And there are also the themes of caressing and the contact with surfaces that occur in* Actress in the House, *in particular.*

I think that in the way physical actions occur—the handing of the letter from the mother to the son, physical actions at the beginning of *Lookout Cartridge*—they may suggest that the reality of our life is mind and body in some mysterious way discovering each other and mingled. And that it is not something that we wholly choose.

But breath also is part of it. We have "Breathers" in Women and Men; *Imp Plus mentions his breath. It also penetrates the form of the narrative in many of your fictions.*

Yes, there is a connection, and I don't know that I can sum it up explicitly for you in any way that does not sound obvious or sentimental. Sometimes in one's writing (and I say "one" because I am sure that a million writers have the same experience) you have an instinct to put something down, or to kind of wing it with an inkling that you have. Later, you kind of understand why, but you go ahead and write the fiction, even without understanding why; for example, voice has always been important to me. And I've got a novel about acoustics that I'll do some day. And breath. I don't know where it begins, but it must begin in *A Smuggler's Bible*. When I get to *Women and Men*, I'm aware of trying to connect everything in a more ambitious way than I've ever tried before. And to do that, it helps to have some basic events or habits or reflexes that repeat and give structure to what you are trying to do. So I think of breathing as not only being necessary for life but as associated with intake and outflow, with expansion and contraction, which is my work, my long sentences, which like long passages then contract—long book, shorter book.

When I am feeling more confident with everything, I like to think that this breathing that we do—which keeps the oxygen coming in and is associated with speaking, making sounds—connects us with everything, or at least with everything alive. And, aware of this, and resolved not to make it too heavy in *Women and Men*, I introduced right away a little witticism on the word breather because when we say "a breather," we don't mean someone who is breathing. We mean a rest, a pause. Let's take a breather. And that's sort of light and mundane, even silly sometimes. And of course, it's connected to interruption, and interruption is important in my work. And so the breathing of the world, connected (one hopes) to the breathing of the individual, connected (one hopes) to the voice one person speaks to another person, becomes humorously connected to the most ordinary things that we do. And so when I started with this, I started with the idea that I would entitle certain sections "Breathers," which are supposed to be a pause. And obviously, the breather is never a pause in that book. Not only is it not a pause because very important things happen in the breather, but the breathers tend to be very long. So it turns out not to be a delay between two chapters of the book, which it is, but to become the main thing. And so when a former editor of mine, who was frustrated by some of the problems, for her, of the book, wanted to cut the book approximately in half, it was the breathers she wanted to get rid of. And it would have left the book as a much more conventional narrative about James Mayn and Grace Kimball . . . but it would have done away with the expansions, the contractions. It would have done away with everything important. So the breathers are intimate because they are connected to voice and life, but the breathers are also ambitious and large and connected to the breathing of the universe. The breathing process seems to reach out as far as it can reach.

works cited

McElroy, Joseph. *Actress in the House*. New York: Overlook Press, 2003. Print.

———. *Ancient History: A Paraphase*. Westland: Dzanc Books, 2014. Print.

———. *Anything Can Happen: Interviews with Contemporary American Novelists*. Ed. Tom LeClair and Larry McCaffery. Champaign: U of Illinois P, 1983. 235–51. Print.

———. *Hind's Kidnap: A Pastoral on Familiar Airs*. New York: Harper and Row, 1969. Print.

———. "Joseph McElroy" (author's home page). N.p., n.d. Web. 4 Mar. 2008.

———. *The Letter Left to Me*. New York: Carroll & Graf, 1990. Print.

———. *Lookout Cartridge*. New York: Overlook Press, 2003. Print.

———. *Night Soul and Other Stories*. Normal: Dalkey Archive Press, 2011. Print.

———. *Plus*. New York: Carroll & Graf, 1987. Print.

———. "Plus *Light.*" 2002. TS. Bookmarks Future Letture Conference in Potenza, Italy, 25 May 2002. Address.

———. *Preparations for Search*. New York: Small Anchor Press, 2010. Print.

———. *A Smuggler's Bible*. New York: Overlook Press, 2003. Print.

———. *Women and Men*. Normal: Dalkey Archive Press, 1993. Print.

further works by and on joseph mcelroy

Brooke-Rose, Christine. *A Rhetoric of the Unreal: Studies in Narrative and Structure, Especially of the Fantastic*. Cambridge: Cambridge UP, 1983. Print.

Chevaillier, Flore. *The Body of Writing: An Erotics of Contemporary American Fiction*. Columbus: The Ohio State UP, 2013. Print.

Elkin, Stanley. "Joe McElroy Introduction." *The Review of Contemporary Fiction* 10.1 (1990): 7–8. Print.

Hantke, Steffen. *Conspiracy and Paranoia in Contemporary American Literature: The Works of Don DeLillo and Joseph McElroy*. Frankfurt: European Studies Peter Lang, 1994. Print.

Johnston, John. *Information Multiplicity: American Fiction in the Age of Media Saturation*. Baltimore: The Johns Hopkins UP, 1998. Print.

Kuel, John. *Alternate Worlds: A Study of Postmodern Antirealistic American Fiction*. New York: New York UP, 1989. Print.

Leclair, Thomas. *The Art of Excess*. Urbana: U of Illinois P, 1989. Print.

McElroy, Joseph. *Cannonball*. Westland: Dzanc Books, 2013. Print.

———. "Midcourse Corrections" (autobiographical essay with three interviews conducted by the author). *The Review of Contemporary Fiction* 10.1 (1990): 9–55. Print.

Porush, David. *The Soft Machine: Cybernetic Fiction*. New York: Methuen, 1985. Print.

Pulizzi, James J. "Language after Humans: On the Disembodied Language of Joseph McElroy's *Plus.*" *Science Fiction Studies* 41.2 (2014): 392–409. Print.

Tabbi, Joseph. *Postmodern Sublime: Technology and American Writing from Mailer to Cyberpunk.* Ithaca: Cornell UP, 1995. Print.

Tanner, Tonny. *Scenes of Nature, Signs of Men.* Cambridge: Cambridge UP, 1987. Print.

Walser, Andrew. "A Joseph McElroy Festschrift." *Electronic Book Review.* N.p., 26 Aug. 2004. Web. 30 May 2016.

christina milletti

CHRISTINA MILLETTI IS AN ASSOCIATE PROFESSOR OF ENGLISH AT THE UNIVERSITY AT BUFFALO, STATE UNIVERSITY OF NEW YORK. SHE HAS RECEIVED A HUMANITIES INSTITUTE FACULTY RESEARCH AWARD, MARBLE HOUSE PROJECT RESIDENCY, SEVERAL &NOW AWARDS, AND A MASTERS REVIEW AWARD (ANTHOLOGY IV). SHE IS THE AUTHOR OF *THE RELIGIOUS AND OTHER FICTIONS* (2006).

SINCE I HAVE become familiar with Christina Milletti's fiction, I have envisioned my brain's activity, while reading her work, as stretched in two opposed directions: one explores everyday situations, perhaps, sometimes, even banal activities; the other disrupts the former by allowing the intrusion of impossible scenarios and outcomes in the midst of the mundane. The tension between these two directions results in a back-and-forth between trust in the narrator, setting, and plot structure and a puzzlement about what seemed to fit, to make sense, to be effortless. In a snap, a story can overturn and leave the reader both excited and troubled. In "The Smallest Apartment," one thousand girls live "in a single room," "sw[ing] 2000 slippered feet onto the floor," and eat "from a single bowl with a single spoon" (*The Religious* 43). In "Parcel Post," a woman and the deliverer of a parcel leave each other notes to arrange the delivery. While the delivery is delayed for months, notes accumulate to create Post-it-yellow paper doors stuck to the walls of the protagonist's house, "and through them, she would often come and go" (*The Religious* 99). In "Amelia Earhart's Last Transmission," a mother's whim is granted when she disappears at the kitchen sink: "There was a pop! Then she was gone" (*The Religious* 175).

Often, the first few pages of Milletti's short stories immerse the reader in a world where details seem to fit well: all strikes us as real, normal, even easy to relate to and to project ourselves into. The fact that we took this world for granted and cozied up so quickly in its familiarity is thrown back at us when this "real" world—the world the characters and readers seem to share—crumbles in front of us to question our bearings, beliefs, habits, and goals. In a story like "Where Nööne Is Now," for example, attributing actions to specific characters becomes more and more challenging as the story progresses. This is particularly unsettling because the point of the story—to find the location of a vanished sister—seems to call for a detective-like activity of tracking and deduction. As the story goes on, it becomes clear that the disappearance may or may not have occurred, as the sister may not have existed. "Where Nööne Is Now" and many stories in *The Religious and Other Fictions* (2006) show Milletti negotiating questions of identity, reflecting on a sense of place, stressing the unnatural in the natural, inquiring about the notion of truth, and exploring our relationship to the past and to remembrance.

She also questions her writing medium: *The Religious and Other Fictions* highlights writing's boundaries when it defamiliarizes the ways in which short stories are shaped and received. In reconsidering what we took for granted in the life of Milletti's characters, we are forced to reconsider how, as readers, we are eager to settle comfortably in the realms of these characters, to be soothed by the beauty of her language, to pick up on what makes sense, or to follow clues about the advancement of the plot. When this plot is disturbed, we have to face the limitations of our reading techniques, consider what they hide from us and how they may not be as illuminating as we assume they are. When the limits between fable and realism become porous, a new kind of logic irrupts, making us realize that our traditional categories need to be more pliant—boundaries between literary genres, between truth and lies, between reality and myth, and between genders become permeable.

I interviewed Christina Milletti from 2009 to 2012 via e-mail. Our electronic discussion elaborates on recurrent themes in her fiction—language, identity, truth, imagination, normalcy, control, power, paradox, mystery, illusion, and time. We also engaged in conversation about humor, women's writing, the physical attributes of writing, the avant-garde, and the politics of innovative writing. Much like her fiction, Milletti's answers to my questions are thought provoking, honest, and captivating.

•

In your essay, "Innovative Fiction and the Poetics of Power," you write that "language [. . .] represents a framework that constitutes both the 'doing' and the 'doer' alike: the subject always exists in a condition of relation *to language that implicates the person using it, as much as the addressee" (22). Your insistence on the "doing" and "doer" and "relation" leads me to think of writing and reading as active and physical productions. For you, such productions resist social and linguistic conventions through formal manipulations. Does the physical aspect of writing and reading I draw from your essay also take part in such resistance?*

Your question is central to the essay . . . and to a larger series of questions about the nature of fiction that continues to drive my critical work, namely: how does language act in fiction? What does language do differently in fiction than in other forms of writing? What kinds of forces are at work? To what end(s)?

My insistence on the word "doing" arises in part from a theoretical body of writing—from Judith Butler particularly—which I discuss at length in the essay. Her work (to generalize enormously) suggests that language is a very real matrix that shapes identity in significant ways. If that's so, then I can't help but wonder how fiction in particular impacts its readers . . . and my aim has been to examine what fiction does to us—whether we like it or not.

Perhaps due to its historical bondage to issues of representation, fiction has traditionally been perceived as corrupt, a service genre with populist leanings, a fantasy wholly separate from daily life. Readers look to fiction for entertainment, as a safety valve from daily ennui. We want to get wrapped up in the stories we're told. "You can always count on a murderer for a fancy prose style," Humbert Humbert reflects in the first pages of *Lolita* . . . before Nabokov goes on to seduce us with acts of high-wire linguistic playfulness. It's no surprise the reader almost forgets the novel is about pedophilia as much as the power of words to shape meaning—which is to say, to shape the reader's perception of meaning. Something more than a story is being experienced in a story like that, isn't it? What precisely has it done to us? What kinds of acts have taken place?

Getting to the bottom of questions like these *now*—at this precise sociopolitical moment—is uniquely important. Never before has "fiction" been deployed so skillfully on the (inter)national stage. Whether you call it "spin" or "truthi-ness," both terms suggest that the fictive is suddenly in the spotlight. I can't help but wonder: what have political operatives begun to take note of that many fiction writers themselves have not? What are the conditions of relation at work? Is the nature of fiction changing? Or is fiction beginning to reveal operations in its own construction that have simply always been there?

My essay in *Fiction's Present* takes a look at two writers—Gertrude Stein and Christine Brooke-Rose—whose unusual formal innovations take advantage of subtle linguistic operations. Stein's insistence on the term *insistence*— as opposed to repetition—speaks volumes about her sense of how language operates, how words regularly shift their own meanings about. Brooke-Rose, meanwhile, offers a more postmodern gloss with her notion of "recycled" language. Both writers, however, work at length to demonstrate that focusing on the constraints of fictional language offers their readers insight into how powerful normalizing social forces arise and, more importantly, how their often rigored meaning can be challenged. Put a different way, their fictions suggest how language enables, as well as obstructs, resistance to institutional forces. Or to use another rubric: power.

In other words, for me, fiction isn't simply bound by a page. It's doing a very real—sometimes dangerous—kind of work on the reader. And it's that work that I'd like to examine further.

You mention the importance of the "resistance to institutional forces." Can you expand on how your fictions work toward a resistance to these forces?

Let me clarify my idea of "work" a bit since I don't mean to suggest a Sartre-like notion of "social commitment"—that writing, in particular prose, must directly engage the domain of corrupt worldly endeavor and act against it—which tends, paradoxically enough, to prop up the status quo. Writers do in fact regularly resist (work against) limits put upon them. The Oulipo (*Ouvroir de littérature potentielle*) and its inheritors, for instance, showcase precisely how strategies put in place before a project begins (say, Georges Perec's famous *A Void*, which eschews the letter *e* for almost three hundred pages of smart, rip-roaring storytelling) effectively obstruct the historical relationship between nature/experience and art. What Oulipo writers highlight is the role of language in the mix: that what a writer tries to "work at" is never quite what ends up being written. So I use the term "work" with the understanding that a thorny brew of intention, liveliness, chance, and misdirection is always in play in any fiction.

In my own fiction, generally speaking, I often propose patently impossible scenarios and see where that takes me. The results vary. Sometimes the situation is normalized. Sometimes it becomes increasingly fantastic. But it's never wholly one or the other: the real is integrally rooted in the imaginary and the imaginary bends to its source in the real. For me, the simple fact that the impossible can find easy footing in our daily lives suggests that the border between these two realms isn't anywhere as opaque as we'd like to think. And that fiction, as it unerringly moves between them, offers a point of penetration in seemingly static systems, forces that we (often unwittingly) allow to control us.

Fiction has a unique ability to address difficult subjects even as it dismantles the language that constitutes them. A good story can show us just how rootless we really are; that it's only language that, quite unexpectedly, really holds us fast.

I am curious about the "patently impossible scenarios" that you propose "and see where that takes [you]." I am not sure whether you refer here to the ways in which you approach your writing process, by starting stories with such scenarios. Could you say more about this process?

I recall once reading that John Hawkes started his novel *Blood Oranges* with an image in mind, children carrying a coffin with a dead dog inside. I'm sure that wasn't his only influence though. There are many different beginnings to any work of fiction: the ones that get you started are as important as the ones that keep you going. It's never a one-dimensional process but more of a constellation of habits, stutters, tics. A kind of obstinate antinomy. I personally tend to gravitate toward "if-then" scenarios, an impossible problem, a paradox, that needs solving. The trick, of course, is making an unbelievable proposition seem possible to the reader. In my first collection, there was a story about a light bulb salesman with a massive head ("Retrofit"), a lost woman with an unpronounceable name ("Where Nööne is Now"), and a mother who disappears at the kitchen sink ("Amelia Earhart's Last Transmission"). I suppose you might say that I'm interested in exploring how we cope with impossible events in our lives. Which we all do. Every day. Beckett's "I can't go on. I'll go on" isn't just a key premise of postmodern being. He's thinking about the inscrutable, improbable pulse of each moment. How we go on living with internal conflicts and external obstacles, when it would be so much easier to just climb back in bed, hide under the covers. The fact that we continue to move at all each day is fantastic and courageous—it would be much more sensible to just give up—and we rarely see the humor in our wholly illogical behavior. I guess you might say, my fiction tries to explore how the stories we tell ourselves, at times consciously, at others much less so, give us a reason to keep on going.

The humor that you mention in our illogical behaviors also occurs at the level of language in these stories. Sometimes, I felt like I had read too fast and had to reread a sentence to make sure I got it right. There was humor in that playful process.

If Einstein's definition of insanity is doing the same thing over and over and expecting a different result, then there's no doubt my characters are on the mad end of the spectrum, "preferring" to reject their so-called reality in order to believe something else, something frankly unbelievable. The way they get there—justifying the unjustifiable—is by scrutinizing the language that describes the truth, worrying it, wearing it thin until it tears just a bit, yields a version of the truth that suits them better. In other words, it's a question of language more than event, of pricking phrases that describe reality until they let their air out. Just a bit. Just enough.

That sounds morose: reality as a kind of deflated balloon. But you can do a lot with a deflated balloon that you can't with a bit of overstretched, overfilled latex. An inflated balloon pops if you sit on it, sails out of reach if you let it go. But a leathery, half-filled balloon, well, you can reshape it, use it as a pillow if you'd like. It will rest contentedly by you. Always giving a bit so you can coexist in the same space. That's a mild, ridiculous, whoopee-cushion kind of happiness, and it's always haunted by the threat of a misstep. Maybe I'm just a voyeur. . . . I like to see what happens when that misstep occurs, explore the comedy of the flatulent gaffe. How hard we work to return to order. Yet it's just a rhetorical sham. A game.

The way you have been discussing language so far evokes works by philosophers of language. Wittgenstein and Derrida come to mind, for instance, but others might have influenced you.

It seems to me theory always has a place in fiction. Which is to say, if you go by the maxim that there are no new stories, just new ways to tell them, then good fiction exploits its own language: its secret rooms, hidden corners, trapdoors in the floor. So, sure, that means I'm influenced by theorists who study how language works, its hidden aporias and overlooked operations. Derrida is a fine place to start, as well as feminist theorists like Luce Irigaray, Hélène Cixous, and Judith Butler, who are all interested (in their various, differing ways) in how language shapes reality, our identities: how, for instance, our ideas about gender and sexuality are really a lived space of language, as much as a lived space of the body, and that it's our use of language that shapes how we think about ourselves and the world we live in. Since a good deal of my fiction centers around women who are struggling with the (often unforeseen) roles into which they've been cast, it's no real surprise, I suppose, that I'm as interested in telling stories inasmuch as exploring how language shapes those stories—and can change them—by working the language out. I try to find a door, a fracture in the glass, in (for instance) the turn of a phrase, the unexplored etymology of a word, an altered use of syntax. Language is power. But not a weapon. So it often works slowly. Unpredictably. Though it's got a hell of a kick when the time is right.

Your mention of feminist theorists reminded me of your introduction to the American Book Review on Innovative Fiction by International Women. *In your essay, you note that there are two ways to think of women's writing: one that stresses the experimental qualities of feminine writing—"i.e., a fluidity of prose, the nonlinearity of narrative elements, a decentered or nonhierarchical plot structure"—and the other that is "more hesitant to connect gender with a writing techne" (3). How do you envision your own work in this context?*

First, there are surely more than two ways of thinking about women's writing. My "Introduction" to that special *ABR* issue was looking closely at the prevailing perception that experimental writing by women takes aesthetic direction from women's bodies—that women's writing is fluid, resists closure, is multivalent as opposed to linear, and so on—which, as I argue there (and elsewhere), in fact fails to do justice not only to the many ways women writers write but also the less-discussed strategies women writers often deploy to critique representations of the feminine and our concept of gender itself.

There's a distinct tradition of women's writing that revels in the oddities of language, its operations, the ironies and misalignments of poetic and fictive forms. Emily Dickinson. Gertrude Stein. Virginia Woolf. Djuna Barnes. Nathalie Sarraute. Anaïs Nin. Angela Carter. Clarice Lispector. Janet Frame. Christine Brooke-Rose. Carole Maso. Lydia Davis. Shelley Jackson. My goodness, I could go on and on. Their writing—in very different ways—attends to language as the lens that shapes women's roles, much like women's bodies, and, as such, resists reductive descriptions of the feminine. Gender is an even murkier terrain than we've begun to acknowledge. And their work explores its limn and pith. Makes the feminine—and identity in a larger sense—a far more freewheeling space.

In my new novel, *Choke Box*—finished between the last question and this one in our ongoing exchange—one woman tries to come to grips with her husband's "disappearance" by writing a memoir for her children (as she's been incarcerated for his murder). It's not particularly clear what really happened to him (or to her). Nor is it necessary to really know, since what's "real" is part of the problem of the memoir form itself. What can be said is that all her relationships are tenuous: her bond to her husband, to her own mother and children, to her lawyer and her therapist. They're bound only by the words of the memoir, by her point of view, by the way she represents them. Which the reader eventually (I hope) will come to realize is not unlike how we live our lives. There are failures in understanding, in apprehension. And we go on. Working to change what we can. And sweep what we can't . . . under the carpet for another day.

Congratulation on finishing your novel! You have shared with me that the title, Choke Box, *has anatomical origins. Could you say more about that?*

Thanks so much. The title is a trope on "voice box." Humans, it turns out, are virtually the only species on the planet that can choke to death on food—and it's the larynx that's to blame, it turns out. Because of our evolving need for speech—or perhaps our evolution *because* of speech—humans have a peculiarly "descended" larynx (it's low in the throat compared to other species) and it can get us into trouble.

When we eat, the epiglottis flaps shut to prevent food going down the windpipe, past the larynx, into our lungs. But if we talk and swallow, it flaps open and bad things happen. Turns out, talking and eating is more than bad manners. It's dangerous stuff. Hard anatomical evidence that language is deadly.

Sticks and stones may break my bones, kids sing, *but words can never hurt me.* Of course, by the time you're older, you realize just how wrong that rhyme is. The right word, at the right time, can do you in.

I have to admit when I discovered this "fun fact" I was wholly captivated. Who knew that the very characteristic that makes us most human—our capacity to articulate the world around us—is the very thing that can kill us too. Irony is fundamental to the human condition and it endlessly reveals itself . . . just in case we haven't noticed the peculiarity of being alive.

The narrator of *Choke Box* is a wife and mother who has discovered after years of marriage that her husband isn't quite who he seems. No surprise there, really. No one really is. For her, though, the problems start when he gives up his job as a real estate attorney to be a writer—a memoirist, in fact. Instead of pinning their lives in place, however, his book makes her come unglued—to the point that she claims that he's not only fully disappeared but that he's begun to *control* her, hurt her and their kids, with his words. Of course, her assertion is unbelievable. Yet there's enough that is believable in her "counter-memoir" that makes giving her perception of the world a second chance. When do words hurt us? How do they hurt us? When do they make us choke on, choke *up,* everything we thought we could count on? Everything we thought was the truth?

I am looking forward to reading the novel! The kind of questions it addresses brings to mind the idea of deception and self-deception, which we often consider bad. In your fictions, though, this negative assumption is often questioned.

It's true: I start with the premise that we're all living in a state of ongoing self-deception . . . and that it's nothing short of our incredible, unjustifiable, even foolhardy belief in ourselves—our talents, ambitions, the whole monkey mess of us we carry strapped on our backs—that gets us through each day. Why not look inside that unruly baggage? Unpack it. See if all the contents fit. Usually they don't.

Yet my characters are rarely sinister. They may be disingenuous. Sometimes intentionally naïve. But their occasional fibs—to themselves and to others—are a perceived path to something like truth. So, you might say, I'm rethinking both what deception is and what truth is too. I'm not convinced we have a good idea of either.

Liars, by contrast, are boring, think they know what truth is, and that they're evading it. They don't see the simple deceit all around them, against which more obvious fabrications lack complexity, are dwarfed. Just watch the prime-time news.

In The Religious and Other Fictions, *and from what you mentioned in* Choke Box *as well, searching for someone or something seems to be a recurring theme. Why?*

I'm still figuring that out, working with that trend in my fiction—though, in the next novel, all the characters are exceptionally stationary, have lived in the same room for forty years—but that doesn't mean they won't also be searching: searching for meaning, at a moment when meaning itself is transitional. That it's always changing, as we are. I guess I'm interested in exploring how we make meaning for ourselves and how we live with the results of our unleavened imaginations, particularly when our own conclusions don't buck up against the reality of others.

The "search," as a leitmotif, however, also presents metafictive opportunities: the evident search in the plot (even when it's a red herring) drives and challenges the narrator's more "searching" tendencies so that, at the end of a story like "Amelia Earhart's Last Transmission" or "Where Nööne is Now," it's not clear any longer whether the narrators have found what they're looking for or simply prefer to rest in an ongoing state of "searchfulness" so they can defer the answer to their personal mysteries . . . whose answer they (likely) actually knew before the story ever began.

The much shorter answer? A good mystery always sucks a reader in . . . and once you've got a reader hooked, you can attend to more thorny philosophical questions while you continue to hang the crooked carrot out as bait. Sometimes you end up giving it to your readers and they don't even notice. That's when the story is working just right.

So do you consciously envision your reader as you craft your work?

No. And yes. Which is to say, my primary mode is to figure out what the heck I'm writing about first. Fiction, for me, is always an act of discovery. And the writer perseveres along that journey until the itch is satisfied. At that point, I take a hard look at what's there and make difficult decisions about how the book can best perform itself. And that is, perhaps, the moment my reader steps up to the plate. But that reader is me. No one else. So I want to satisfy my writer and my reader . . . and hope that the other readers out there agree with them. Or at least share some interest in the inquiry that's unveiled itself. Aside from that, it's a real mystery what goes over well with readers other than yourself. That's always a surprise.

Borges talks about the complications of writerly identity (in a related way) in "Borges and I" when he reflects that there are two Borges: the one who makes the work (the writer), and the one who is written about (the author). In the final line of that astonishingly incisive and complex essay—one page in length—he notes that he's not sure which Borges wrote the piece. Because, in effect, there was the one who put the words on the page, the one who read them, revised them. The one to whom it's attributed. But they are interrelated, not autonomous entities, when all is said and done.

You might say that any writer's identity is a vector of several performative poses and that the best writers also have very good readers working for them.

In your short stories, reality, memory, illusion, and imagination are often difficult to distinguish partly because of the "impossible scenarios" that you have mentioned but also because of unreliable narrative voices. Would you care to comment on that aspect of your work?

There's a brilliant moment in Alain Robbe-Grillet's "nouveau roman" novel *Jealousy* in which his narrator imagines a scene in a hotel room where his wife and her lover are possibly staying. In the room, there are several realist paintings that depict seaside life. As the narrator's imaginary gaze surveys (or remembers) the hotel room, it also "sees" the painting of the birds flying over the ocean. The narrator's eye makes no distinction between these different surfaces—between the imagination of the room, his real wife and her potential lover, and an imagined picture hung on a wall—between the similar planes of memory and fantasy and visual art. All of these coalesce in a complex tapestry within the mind's eye that Robbe-Grillet's readers must unravel.

My fiction is nothing like Robbe-Grillet's. But I have learned from it, much as I have learned from Julio Cortázar's work that the difference between reality and fantasy can rest on the slippery placement of a conjunction to make a story turn in on, even undo, itself. I guess that's what fascinates me as a reader and what drives my own work. Stories can do much more than go forward or backward in time: narrative isn't just a chronological experience and the reader's eye isn't merely a camera. Robbe-Grillet's attention to surfaces, conversely, teaches us that.

The experience of language is also vertical. It has an unforeseen depth and scope that is fully resistant to the psychological portraiture found in realist work and is localized around the chasm between what a word *is* and what it might *mean*. From that landscape, plenty of humor and plot can arise. It's the place where all lost socks go.

The great illusion of realist stories is that its readers are moving "forward" through their storylines, that their characters are as "real" as neighbors next door. As a writer, I gravitate toward that illusion because the exposure of it tends to make the reader dizzy, turns them about, until they lose their center—can no longer pin the plastic tail on the cardboard donkey—because the center was an illusion itself.

My interest in illusion and memory resides in the way words fail to describe—usefully—the differences between these states of being. We know this and just ignore it: our complicity with our imprecision, in fact, is embedded in the familiar ways we describe experience. *Reality is just an illusion* is a common enough adage after all. The move from reality to fantasy is just an adverb away.

That "shift" isn't always desirable of course. For instance, Clarice Lispector's *The Hour of the Star* ends when a fortune-teller predicts that the story's main character, Macabea, will meet the man of her dreams imminently. She does—moments later—when (spoiler alert) he runs her over with his big yellow car. Macabea dies right there in the street.

I am interested in your comment on chronology: could you elaborate on your treatment of time in writing?

It's nothing new to note that, in fiction, time is an effect of narrative. Not the other way around. But it's awfully rare for writers to make their readers acknowledge that we experience time at many different tempos, as different shapes. Yet fictions that consider time, how the present is embedded by the past and the future at any given moment, are all the richer for it. The one thousand pages of *Ulysses* take place over the course of a single day. Woolf glossed ten years in twenty pages in the middle of *To the Lighthouse* (a section called "Time Passes") during which she killed off several important characters in trivial ways in order to showcase human insignificance with respect to time. Robert Coover tries an oppositional tactic in his short story "The Pedestrian Accident," with its infinite, ongoing destruction of a young man's body: "How much longer must this go on?" Paul asks, hopelessly, to our ghoulish amusement as he, paralyzed and abandoned by a carnival of rubberneckers, hears hungry dogs approaching. And then there's John Barth's "Frame-Tale," which, once cut from the book and taped together, forms the shape of a Möbius strip, an endless text that reads: "Once upon a time there was a story that began / once upon a time there was a story that began . . ." *Hour of the Star* (which I just mentioned above) begins with the Big Bang. And ends with the protagonist's death. Yet Lispector's novel, about the universe of language and one impoverished woman's life in it, is (merely) seventy-five pages of finely wrought prose in length.

Time doesn't move straight ahead: it's silly that most novels do. But reality has often had a strange relationship to fictional forms.

If you survey the past hundred years of novel writing—roughly from the advent of realism and naturalism at the end of the nineteenth century to the present articulation of the postmodern—there are two clear threads of writing *techne,* or authorial ethos, that run parallel to one another. One thread—let's call it a "realist" thread—tends to propose through its representative prowess "a" reality that "we" share; the other thread—let's call it an "arealist" thread—questions the ethos of that dominant shared reality and the way it wires readers to think about their world. Kathy Acker said it best:

> If I'm going to tell you what the real is by mirroring it, by telling you a story that expresses reality, I'm attempting to tell you how things are. By letting you see through my own eyes, I give you viewpoints, moral and political. In other words, realism is simply a control method. Realism doesn't want to negotiate, open into, chaos or the body or death, because those who practice realism want to limit their readers' perceptions, want to limit perceptions to a centric—which in this society is always a phallocentric—reality. . . . In other words, behind every literary or cultural issue lies the political, the realm of political power. And whenever we talk about narration, narrative structure, we're talking about political power. ("The Killers" 17–18)

Her work, often shocking at first glance, is designed to make her readers encounter the social mores, the political antennae, they've been fitted with. It's hard to break out of that room. Acker is a good tool to pick the lock.

What's been of great interest to me lately, what's significant about this *time* as a writer (to maneuver the terms of your question just a bit), is that the notion of that shared reality has, in just the past few years, begun to shift dramatically. Now, news programs actively engage political propaganda with spin room segments. Televised ads lie and go uncorrected. Politicians so consistently misrepresent the truth that a sizeable portion of their constituency tends to doubt everything they say (to our national detriment), while another sizeable portion believes everything they say with a fervor that forgoes the possibility of doubt (to our national detriment). Meanwhile, in 2011, DARPA (the Defense Advanced Research Projects Agency, basically the research wing of the U.S. military) announced a call for work so they could better understand the role narrative pays "in security domains." The media, politicians, even the military, seem to have all noticed that fiction is leaking across the porous border of the real. What will happen next?

Fiction has always been measured by its relation, or divergence, from reality. It's "believability," as it were. Reality has never been measured by its relation to fiction. Now, I'd like to propose that conditions have changed. Specifically, our expectations of reality have changed, and, therefore, the role of fiction with respect to the real has altered too. That doesn't change the world of fiction. But it does change how we've begun to present material conditions in language.

Take Brock Clarke's *An Arsonist's Guide to Writers' Homes in New England*. Or Shelley Jackson's *Half Life*. By their final pages, the reader can't say with any confidence whether (with respect to the former) the book was a memoir or a fiction or (with respect to the latter) *who* the novel's narrator was. The truth, increasingly, is moving out of reach in fiction. Sounds like the lives we're now living.

There has been much discussion about how to label the kinds of texts you like to write and read. I believe that you prefer the term innovative *to* experimental *or* avant-garde. *What motivates your preference?*

Raymond Federman once reflected that "fiction is called experimental out of despair" ("Surfiction" 7). Christine Brooke-Rose gave the problem her own spin: "It seems to me that the combination of woman + artist + experimental means so much hard work and heartbreak and isolation that there must be little time or energy for crying out loud" ("Illiterations" 55–56). Part of the problem is the issue of "difficulty." Another, that the label "experimental" can refer to a whole range of (sometimes wholly oppositional) stylistic endeavors (the surrealists and the Oulipo could not be farther apart). I think it's pretty fair to say that most writers don't care what their work is called. They just want someone to read it.

Ben Marcus—in the dustup with Jonathan Franzen in *The New Yorker* a few years back—noted (for some, controversially) that the reading brain is a muscle that needs to be trained. As an educator, it's my work to teach students how to look at each fiction on its own merits, to eschew labels and resist the fight-or-flight instinct, to consider writers' strategies they might find initially obstructive (because the sentences are too long or too short or the plot is superlayered or there is no plot at all or the characters are flat or there is no punctuation, too much punctuation, too much white space, too little resolution, I could go on). How, precisely, does the story / page / prose resist familiar patterns? What are the obstructions the author is asking the reader to engage? Most importantly: why?

Historically speaking, modernist writers such as Joyce, Woolf, and Faulkner were initially described as "new realists." Their efforts to portray a subjective view of events in a stylized interior language presented a personal view of reality intended to be more "real" than nineteenth-century fictions that covered a similar terrain. That tendency remains with us. You could make a persuasive argument that twentieth-century fiction is characterized by its ongoing effort to pin down the question of the real with exquisite intensity. Robert Coover's *The Public Burning*, for instance, is as accurate and persuasive an account of American presidents and their power as Kathy Acker's *Empire of the Senseless*. It's our idea of truth and the real that has changed.

In this sense, realism is the most nostalgic of all literary endeavors.

Innovative fictions have been described as academic or insular. What do you think they teach their readers?

Wrestling with words on a page—words we think we know or are familiar with but which are presented in unfamiliar shapes—produces a reader tuned to different kinds of questions. An active reader. A defensive reader. You might say, innovative fictions keep you on your toes, make you deploy a slightly different tool set each time you read them.

That kind of active reading—that kind of *activism*, I don't think the word is too strong—can spin out into daily life where we're regularly bombarded with news programs called "Spin Rooms," political slogans, advertising campaigns. We sorely need more active readers, readers who are willing to interrupt the(ir) programming. I like to think my sentences do that kind of work on a fundamental level, turning themselves inside out before they get to the end of the line. I like to think my seminars do that kind of work, turning my students inside out by the end of the semester. Does that make innovative literature only sound like work? I hope not. Anyone who has read Raymond Queneau, Italo Calvino, Thomas Bernhard, Mark Leyner, or Arno Schmidt knows that fictions that toy with language aren't just thought provoking . . . but downright funny as well.

Often, we think of these texts as alternative, oppositional, defiant, subversive, transgressive, or resistant. I don't disagree with this reading of innovative texts, but I also think that it does not do justice to the positive aesthetic of innovative literature. I am guessing that you think of your and other writers' works not just in privative terms. Can you address the affirmative engagement with literature that your work (or innovative works that you enjoy) calls for?

I can still remember when I was a girl walking into Barnes & Noble—the only real bookstore in town at that time—and trying to find a book that called out to me. The various genres were fun (when I was young I would consume mysteries, sci-fi novels, and thrillers at an alarming, fast food pace) but I was searching for a contemporary fiction that could light me up the way the classics did. Surrounded by shelves of novels, the hush and clang of registers, children playing hide-and-seek in a forest of processed trees, I was at a complete loss. Bereft. I read family dramas until I couldn't digest one more. Wasn't there anything else? My own students now often say the same thing.

And then Nabokov turned my world upside down. Gabriel García Márquez. Italo Calvino. Marguerite Duras. My first alphabet. I've been hanging that way ever since.

"Much fiction is like mustard spread over the belly, take it or leave it, who cares," Paul West writes. "Some fiction has intentions on the reader and wants to inflict grievous bodily harm. . . . They create disturbances in the well-tempered harmony of everyday life" ("A Conversation with Paul West").

Good fiction makes us pause, think, makes us account for ourselves. It doesn't leave us the same way twice.

So, sure, it's resistant. Subversive. It's also elated, adventurous, rip-roaring fun. It's a generative, convulsive, rollicking horse fiction that revels in its own pandemonium and simple joy. It's larger than life. Mindful of paradox. Attentive, weird. It's unapologetic and will fuck you up. It's idiosyncratic and earnest, much too smart. Its intelligence is undemocratic, completely generous, and lathered up by secret hope.

Thank our lucky stars.

works cited

Acker, Kathy. "The Killers." *Biting the Error: Writers Explore Narrative.* Ed. Mary Burger. Toronto: Coach House Books, 2004. 14–18. Print.

Brooke-Rose, Christine. "*Illiterations.*" *Breaking the Sequence: Women's Experimental Fiction.* Eds. Ellen G. Friedman and Miriam Fuchs. Princeton: Princeton UP, 1989. 55–71. Print.

Federman, Raymond. "Surfiction: Four Proposition in Form of an Introduction." *Surfiction Now . . . and Tomorrow.* Chicago: Swallow Press, 1975. 5–15. Print.

Milletti, Christina. "Innovative Fiction and the Poetics of Power: Gertrude Stein and Christine Brooke-Rose 'Do' Language." *Fiction's Present: Situating Narrative Innovation.* Ed. R. M. Berry and Jeffrey Di Leo. Albany: State U of New York P, 2007. 12–17. Print.

———, ed. "Introduction to Focus: Everything Begins with a Yes." *Innovative Fiction by International Women.* Spec. issue of *American Book Review* 30.6 (2009): 3. Print.

———. *The Religious and Other Fictions.* Pittsburgh: Carnegie Mellon UP, 2006. Print.

West, Paul. "A Conversation with Paul West By David W. Madden." Dalkey Archive Press. N.p. Web. Jan. 14 2017.

further works by christina milletti

Milletti, Christina. "Dr. Kirkbride's Moral Treatment Plan." *Buffalo Noir.* Ed. Ed Park and Brigid Hughes. Brooklyn: Akashic Books, 2015. 21–37. Print.

———. "Violent Acts, Volatile Words: Kathy Acker's Terrorist Aesthetic." *Studies in the Novel* 36.3 (2004): 352–73. Print.

lance olsen

LANCE OLSEN IS A PROFESSOR OF ENGLISH AT THE UNIVERSITY OF UTAH. SINCE 2002, HE HAS SERVED AS CHAIR OF THE BOARD OF DIRECTORS AT FICTION COLLECTIVE TWO (FC2). HE RECEIVED AN ARTIST-IN-BERLIN GRANT, THE PIONEER AWARD FROM THE SCIENCE FICTION RESEARCH ASSOCIATION, AND FELLOWSHIPS FROM THE MARY ELLEN VON DER HEYDEN BERLIN PRIZE IN FICTION, THE GUGGENHEIM, THE TANNER HUMANITIES CENTER, AND THE NATIONAL ENDOWMENT FOR THE ARTS. HE WAS ALSO THE WINNER OF A PUSHCART PRIZE IN 1998. HE IS THE AUTHOR OF *CALENDAR OF REGRETS* (2010), *ANXIOUS PLEASURES: A NOVEL AFTER KAFKA* (2007), *NIETZSCHE'S KISSES* (2006), AND *GIRL IMAGINED BY CHANCE* (2002).

LANCE OLSEN'S FICTIONS and critical works point out somewhat of a confusion about the aims of experimental literature. These aims are commonly "seen through a pessimistic optic that emphasizes its destructive, nihilistic, depressing qualities," but, to Olsen, postmodern innovation also enables "a joy taken in the destruction because of the possibility it creates for regeneration" ("Deconstructing" 49–50). His novels, critical studies, short-story collections, poetry, and hypermedia texts undertake this regeneration.

To this end, his avant-pop fictions provide "a positive response to [. . .] constricting [. . .] and despairing relativistic visions" ("Stand By to Crash" 55). His interest in creating "positive" productions evolved into "critifictions" that break down the boundaries between fiction and criticism in order to allow fiction and theory to regain subversive powers "by pirating and deconstructing the spectacle from within" ("Omniphage" 41). This mode of deconstruction "from within" enables a reenvisioning of the notions of cultural production and textual authority. *Girl Imagined by Chance* (2002), for instance, evokes the logic of manufactured capitalist representations. As Olsen explains in the following interview, the novel layers photographs and the life of a couple who invents an imagined daughter to cope with the social pressures on childless families. *Girl Imagined by Chance* asks questions about the boundaries between reality and fiction and the ways in which daily life involves counterfeited reality.

In *Nietzsche's Kisses* (2006), the relationship between fiction and reality takes the form of an exploration of Nietzsche's journey on his last night. His fragmented thoughts illuminate his affair with Lou Andreas-Salomé, his relationship with Richard Wagner, and his relationship with his sister Lisbeth. The novel includes first-person descriptions of the sanitarium, third-person flashbacks, and second-person stream of consciousness about our conception of memory, representation, family, and identity. *Anxious Pleasures: A Novel after Kafka* (2007) addresses parallel themes, paired with a reflection on unwriting and unreading, as well as rewriting and rereading. The novel relates the contemporary story of Margaret, a young woman reading Kafka's *Metamorphosis*, and that of the Samsas and their downstairs neighbor.

Olsen further explores the fragmentary nature of character, time, and voice in *Head in Flames* (2009), which weaves an unusual harmony between fonts, times, and spaces to question the relationship between past and present. He juxtaposes the voice of Vincent van Gogh on the day of his suicide, of Theo van Gogh (the brother of Vincent's great-grandson) on the day of his assassination in Amsterdam in 2004, and of Mohammed Bouyeri, Theo's murderer, who stands against Theo's denunciation in an experimental short film of Muslim treatment of women. Here, Olsen's exploration of textual materiality is predominant. Such explorations come up in the interview that follows, which was developed over the course of an e-mail exchange from November 2009 to April 2010.

As our discussion reveals, Olsen's ability to express clearly matters that are challenging and complex is commendable. He expands on the issues of genre, aesthetic philosophies, dominant linguistic expressions, cultural trends, and the literary canon; his synthetic treatment of such issues stresses their practical ramifications, especially in today's political environment. As the current chair of the board of directors at FC2, he also addresses the state of the current publishing industry and the ways in which it impacts formally innovative writing.

When I met Lance in October 2009 at the &Now Festival of Innovative Writing and the Literary Arts, he was enthusiastic about this project and offered many great suggestions. Throughout the interview process, his interest in collaboration was stimulating and enriching. This collaboration and other modes of collaborating are part of the themes discussed here.

•

In your essay, "Fourteen Notes Toward the Musicality of Creative Disjunction, or Fiction by Collage," you observe the increasing production of "critifictions," or texts that break down the distinctions between criticism and fiction. Could you explain why you find this mode of writing particularly valuable in the context of fiction's present (185)?

I'm not sure I'm interested in the question of "value" with respect to fiction's present. I'm not even sure I quite understand the use of such a word when discussing aesthetic issues, since it houses within it connotations of commerce, of monetary or material worth. The sort of fictions about which I care these days aren't concerned with such matters or perhaps are actively working against them.

So, at least in this context, it might be useful to replace "valuable" with "significant." If we do that, if we ask why the increasing production of critifictions is particularly significant in the context of fiction's present, my answer would take some form of the following observation: the kind of fiction I've been responding to most over the last few decades, the kind that has been referred to as "innovative," "experimental," "alternative," "avant-garde," "postmodern" (all, granted, overdetermined, troubled, and troubling terms), has been inextricably linked with a certain critical or, better, theoretical consciousness. From one perspective, of course, all narrativity save for those most acutely cookie-cutter varieties (Harlequin romance, pulp science fiction, potboiler porn, and so forth) is "experimental" in that it involves countless acts of exploration and discovery on the part of the author and the reader. From another, however, such a statement is devoid of nuance, a sense of the larger conversation across time and space called literary history, and an understanding of the (ir)realities concerning the pragmatics of the contemporary American publishing industry. Maybe closer to the point would be some provisional statement along the lines that "experimental" narrativity—or "innovative," "avant-garde," or whatever other term we might choose to employ in this situation—is that which asks such questions as: What is narrative? What are its assumptions? What are its politics? What are its limits? How does narrative engage with the issue of representation? Of identity? In other words, perhaps another way of approaching a tentative definition of "experimental" narrativity might be to suggest that it is the sort that embodies a self-reflective awareness of and engagement with theoretical inquiry, concerns, obsessions, forms. By its very presence, in other words, it evinces a self-reflective awareness concerning the problematics of language and writing.

What's significant about the proliferation of such postgenre, postcritical prose—this collapse of criticism into its object, the ongoing rich complication of the accepted difference between privileged and subordinate discourses—is the varieties of extraordinary forms, aesthetic and political critiques, and play to which it gives rise: The Difficult Imagination, we could call it, the sort that challenges what we want to take for granted about texts (the world being one text among others).

How does the collapse of theory and fiction affect your own writing?

For better or worse, I guess, my fiction is contaminated with a theoretical awareness, my criticism a fictive one. And once you've left the Edenic garden of narrative innocence, well, there's no turning back, no return ticket. I've been interested for decades, as I say, in what Raymond Federman called critifiction, but, in many ways because of my training in the academy, I tried to keep my criticism and fiction separate for a very long time, like two misbehaving children—until 1999 or so, when I began working on my novel *Girl Imagined by Chance*, a story about a childfree couple who invent a little one to appease the culture committed to being fruitful and multiplying, and everything changed for me.

One of the principles that governs *Girl*, at least in my mind, is that of "hovering"—a certain refusal, in other words, to settle that occurs at different strata in the text. Obviously there's that hovering between a certain theoretical imagination and a certain creative one (Baudrillard is a strong presence in the book, for example), between nonfiction and fiction, between fiction and poetry, even between words and image (in many ways, *Girl* is ultimately a text about the difficulties inherent in the idea of representation that employs photography as its dominant metaphor). There is also the hovering at the stratum of plot concerning the invented girl's physicality. Given the narrator's slightly unhinged mind, it's not surprising that his prose also exhibits a kind of hovering, a jitteriness, a failure to stick with any idea or feeling for more than a few arrhythmic heartbeats, thereby giving rise to an aesthetics of uncertainty.

Behind that aesthetics floats Wittgenstein's ghost. What I've always loved about him is how, toward the end of his life, he became more and more possessed with trying to say what we might be able to know about the world with anything like conviction. The more possessed he became with the problem, however, the less he could be sure about. Something analogous seems true to me about any photograph: the more you study and contemplate one, the less you know about it. What can you say with anything like conviction about what's going on in it? Who took it? When it was taken? What its relationship is to "reality"? How much has been "staged"? How much is "authentic"?

And one form of hovering that engaged me a great deal in *Girl* was between autobiography and fiction. *Girl* is particularly intrigued by how much our memories of ourselves, our pasts, those events we think of when we set out to construct who we are, carry a deeply fictive charge and how we compensate for our lives being a series of distinct photographic instants in a sea of forgetfulness by generating narrative links, by turning discrete shots into filmic (and forever disputable) narrative.

That critifictional frame of mind has followed me through my last several books and is especially ascendant in *Anxious Pleasures,* a retelling of Kafka's *Metamorphosis* that fractures the original (which, it turns out, wasn't strictly original to begin with) into a number of different points of view, some of which masquerade as (and some of which in fact quote) scholarly engagements with Kafka's text. The idea in certain ways was no more complicated than showing a novella that had had a profound effect on me that I cared about it, but doing so brought me full force into the critifictional moment.

Currently I'm working on a novel that in good part is infused with the earthwork artist Robert Smithson's theoretical writings about "entropology," a neologism Smithson borrowed from Lévi-Strauss that holds within it both the words *entropy* and *anthropology*. Entropology, Lévi-Strauss asserts in *World on Wane*, "should be the word for the discipline that devotes itself to the study of [the] process of disintegration in its most highly evolved forms." For Smithson, entropology embodied "structures in a state of disintegration"—but not in a negative sense, not with a sense of sadness and loss. Rather, for him *entropology* embodied the astonishing beauty inherent in the process of wearing down, of wearing out, of undoing, of continuous de-creative metamorphosis at the level, not only of geology and thermodynamics, but also of civilizations, of earthworks like his Spiral Jetty and, ultimately, of the individuals—like you, like me.

History is also central to your work. Can you say more about the relationship between fiction and history in your novels?

I'm drawn to artists and thinkers out of step with their times, those who tend to proceed through paralogy rather than homology toward creation, who believe, as Lyotard once pointed out, that "invention is always born of dissension" (*Postmodern Condition* 25). Now I'm not sure how much, if anything, my Kafka, or my Nietzsche, or my van Goghs have to do with the flesh-and-blood people who once shared those names. The relationship of fiction to yesterday in writing is nothing if not mind-bogglingly tricky. Rather, those characters remain, despite the research I've done on them, constructs for contemplating the role of the artist or philosopher in our culture, as well as troublings incarnate (and I use the word loosely) of what we think about when we think about selfhood and how it's scripted. That is, through their fictional iterations, my characters ask in what sense all selfhood is full-on fiction, all history and biography and memoir subsets of storytelling, what the connection might be between subjects acting in "the world" and "subjects" translated into syllables and sibilants.

My novel *Calendar of Regrets* is arguably more obsessed with these questions than most of my work. The text takes the shape of twelve interconnected narratives, one for each month of the year, all having to do with notions of travel—through space, through narrative, through (or perhaps nearly so) death itself, and, of most consequence to this conversation, through history. For the first half, each of the first eleven narratives breaks off midway through, at which point the next narrative commences. For the second half of the text, each of the first eleven narratives concludes inconclusively, but in reverse order. Hieronymus Bosch inhabits one storyline, Dan Rather another, Iphigenia another, a journalist in Burma in 1976 another, and so forth. Each of its narratives is connected to the others, not through plot events but rather through a musical structure of recurring metaphors and images, transpositions of the same scenes and/or phrases, and temporally transmuted characters. The result, I like to hope, is a multiple narrative about narrativity itself, the human passion for trying to make sense through storytelling, how we tell ourselves and our cosmoses again and again in an attempt to stabilize them, but *Calendar* is also an exploration about the relationship of past to prose.

It's endlessly fascinating to me, these concerns we've been thinking about at least as far back as Hayden White's *Metahistory: The Historical Imagination in the Nineteenth Century*: how historians don't simply find history but actively shape it by arranging events in a certain order; by striving to answer questions (i.e., to narrativize) about what happened, when, how, and why; by deciding which events to include and exclude (i.e., to edit); by stressing this moment and subordinating that (i.e., by purposefully ideologizing)—which is to say, by making a kind of fiction out of sixteenth-century's Hertogenbosch or last week's Topeka or whenever and wherever.

But writing that imagines itself to be history creates the illusion of endeavoring to get every bloodless fact right, whereas writing that imagines itself to be fiction can do something shockingly different: it can allow a reader to experience an experience from inside out, from within a player's consciousness, from multiple subjective perspectives, can release the scent of diesel into the air, the background sounds of trams clanking on the streets bordering Oosterpark in Amsterdam, the way the light falls on a field of wheat at twilight after a hot day in Auvers-sur-Oise, the imagined cadences of a fanatic's voice. That's what really engages me: the complexities of a moment felt.

From that point of view, the point of view Linda Hutcheon calls historiographic metafiction, whereby texts express both intense self-reflexivity about their own processes *and* (incommensurately) "historical" "events" and "personages," such a fraught aesthetic and ontological gesture, is definitional, I suppose, of the postmodern mode of consciousness, if we still want to use that adjective.

You mention the "(ir)realities concerning the pragmatics of the contemporary American publishing industry." Could you say more about such pragmatics, both as a writer and as the chair of the board of directors at Fiction Collective Two?

If we checked in on American publishing in New York in the early sixties, we would find more than a hundred thriving houses bringing out a plethora of innovative writers: Coover, Pynchon, Gass, Ishmael Reed, John Barth, Donald Barthelme. All that began to change with the recession brought on by the 1973 oil crisis. Attention in the publishing industry shifted increasingly and inextricably from daring artistic investigations to the bottom line. Great editors were laid off. Publishers went under or were absorbed by other publishers. What we've seen over the fifty years or so, then, is what one might call the McDonaldization of U.S. publishing. (We're back, I'm afraid, to my ongoing analogy between culture and fast food franchises.)

In a sense, then, the worst has already happened in the world of books. By and large they have come to seem over the last four or five decades an increasingly conservative, market-driven form of communication. In addition to the publishing situation in Manhattan, even bestsellers now exist in a secondary position in our culture to the spectacles of film, television, the web, the Xbox, the iPod, the iPhone, the iPad. Currently not a hundred thriving houses but three behemoth media corporations dominate commercial publishing while employing the print arms of their swollen conglomerates as tax write-offs. They consider low sales figures and small audiences tantamount to failure. That is, they view their products exactly the same way executives at McDonald's view theirs. More disheartening still, many independent presses have decided to mimic in miniature this preposterous paradigm rather than trying to subvert, reimagine, or otherwise stand in opposition to it.

That isn't to suggest, of course, that Manhattan isn't bringing out some vibrant and surprising work (one need think no farther than José Saramago, David Mitchell, Don DeLillo, Lydia Davis, and Mark Danielewski), but it is to suggest that Manhattan is bringing out less of it—much less of it—than it once did. Nor would I want to suggest that alternative presses don't bring out some embarrassingly bland, simple, sloppy work. Still, those alternative presses by and large remain sites of energizing aesthetic, political, and philosophical resistance. They remind us that our fiction, and hence our lives, can always be other than they are. They exist as possibility spaces where everything can and should be thought and attempted, where the work of such corporate authors as Dan Brown, John Grisham, or Danielle Steel simply isn't seen as enlightening, let alone engaging.

It's as though next to the universe of commercial publishing there has come to exist an alternate one, à la one of Borges's stories, composed of (often innovative) authors who live a completely different existence with completely different aims and ethics. They bring out each other's work, read and review it, teach it at colleges and universities across the country, study it in critical essays, urge others to start up journals and presses to help get the word out about the fiction they love, fiction that takes the act of exploratory, frequently demanding writing earnestly—all that, and those people write their own fiction, too. I think of them, with the greatest respect and admiration, as literary activists—people like Lidia Yuknavitch at Chiasmus Press, Ted Pelton at Starcherone, Steve Gillis at Dzanc.

If it's the case that the early twenty-first century is the worst of times for American fiction because of those market pressures that favor novels and short story collections that want to be films when they grow up, it's also the best of times because of these sorts of people. Competition in their universe has been replaced with collaboration. Corporate paradigms have been replaced with collective ones.

FC2's story in particular, which now forms part of our country's past, points as well to one future of American publishing by offering a successful model based on alliance and partnership, a production paradigm run by and for authors, the idea that it is less important to make a profit than it is to disseminate significant experimental projects. The result is to remind ourselves with every book printed in this universe that there are exciting options that stand against the commercial milieu's structuring, functioning, and ambitions. There are ways of caring about innovative fiction that Manhattan, to put it bluntly, can't begin to begin to fathom. If executives there exhibit a McDonaldization Effect on publishing, the small, independent presses that have been proliferating joyously across the States over the last two or three decades offer the equivalent of an amazing mom-and-pop Vietnamese restaurant down the block.

The one constant for Fiction Collective, and now Fiction Collective Two, is that there have been no constants except a commitment to our mission statement: "to publish books of high quality and exceptional ambition whose style, subject matter, or form push the limits of American publishing and reshape our literary culture." The Collective has always stood against, as one of its founders, Peter Spielberg (others, by the way, included Jonathan Baumbach, Steve Katz, and Ronald Sukenick), pointed out in 1974, its first year in existence, "books designed by cereal packagers, marketed by used-car salesmen . . . and ruled or overruled by accountants." That's more the case now than ever before, I'm happy to say. The Collective fashioned itself as an adaptable, flexible entity, and here we are more than thirty-five years later (originally the idea was to put together a literary experiment that might last two or three, tops), with the help of such leaders as Curtis White, R. M. Berry, and Cris Mazza, having brought out some of the finest and most diverse innovative writers of the second half of the twentieth century and first decade of the twenty-first: Brian Evenson, Toby Olson, Leslie Scalapino, Steve Tomasula, Raymond Federman, Lidia Yuknavitch, Harold Jaffe, Stephen Graham Jones, Kate Bernheimer, Noy Holland, Doug Rice, Samuel R. Delany, Michael Martone, Clarence Major, Vanessa Place, Melanie Rae Thon, and so on. In addition, we established two contests to help identify and celebrate innovative writers not yet published by the Collective: the Sukenick, which comes with $1000 and publication by FC2, and the Doctorow, which comes with $15,000 and publication by FC2.

You also teach at the University of Utah. How does your understanding of formally innovative writing's current state and goals affect your teaching and translate into the institutional setting of the university?

It's pretty easy, unfortunately, to write merely competent fiction—the kind cranked out in most of the 350 or so creative writing programs across the United States: so-called well-crafted domestic realism where character is plump and Freudian, style is transparent, plot is pleasantly arced, and adversity always gives way to luminous moments of human connection and insight. My own approach to teaching writing is to short-circuit that approach, become self-conscious about it, invite my students to conceive of fiction writing as an opportunity to explore, question, and rethink narrativity and its assumptions—all in workshops that are the opposite of therapy sessions. I continuously urge my students to remain curious and realize it's only at the brink of failure that liberating, illuminating breakthroughs occur. I continuously urge them to keep in mind, while they're composing, Beckett's lines in *Worstward Ho*: "Try again. Fail again. Fail better" (81).

At their best, I think, creative writing programs can be special, energizing zones of mutual support, mutual challenge, and personal-aesthetic growth by means of exposure to a multiplicity of challenging voices and approaches, both "creative" and "theoretical," both contemporary and historical. (In my workshops, we're as likely to spend time discussing an essay by Bataille or Barthes, a novel by Ourednik or Pavíc, a story collection by Gary Lutz or Lucy Corin, a poetry collection by Susan Howe or Stephanie Strickland, a hypermedia project by Steve Tomasula or Young-Hae Chang, as discussing student work.) At their worst, creative writing programs can be stultifying assembly lines that spit out flat, faded, predictable well-made products in order to fill classrooms and make money for deans. But in either case—and perhaps this is their greatest contribution to our culture—workshops generate careful readers, thoughtful readers, close readers, self-reflective readers at a time when many literature courses teach how to think in sweeping ideological terms while employing texts in quite general terms as symptoms or samples of this position or that.

When talking about them, it's useful to keep in mind that creative writing programs usually exist within English departments that usually exist within some form of humanities divisions that exist within the larger institution of the college or university that is in ongoing crisis due to recent budget cuts in the wake of the economic collapse but, more profoundly, due to the corporatization of higher education. Just yesterday I came across a story emblematic of this trend in, of all places, *USA Today*. A biology professor at Louisiana State University, Dominique G. Homberger, was removed from her teaching position midsemester for refusing to artificially inflate her grades. Apparently her transgressions, according to those in power, included giving quizzes at the beginning of each class, both to check on attendance and encourage students to keep up with reading, and failing to grade her tests on a curve (believing "students must achieve mastery of the subject matter, not just achieve more mastery than the worst students in the course" (Jaschik). Not only was she yanked from the classroom, but the administration also raised her students' grades after Homberger left—a gesture that brings up all sorts of questions about grade ballooning and professor autonomy but also one that suggests just how much our institutions of higher learning are becoming the equivalent of (once again) fast food franchises that value customer satisfaction over something like real intellectual complexity and learning.

Put that together with continuously smaller numbers of full-time faculty, greater numbers of lecturers and graduate assistants behind the desk at the front of the room, more work for less pay, fewer raises, overcrowded classes, necessarily less face time between professor and student, necessarily shorter comments on papers and stories and tests as a result, the proliferation of online courses that sabotage human interaction and Socratic pedagogical models, more emphasis on silly national rankings that privilege quantity over quality, more emphasis on "outcomes assessment" rather than thought, and a departmental atmosphere virtually everywhere shot through with a sense of being continuously under the gun (which invariably leads to greater tension and petty squabbles), and I wonder how many of us will be able to recognize what higher learning has become in another five or seven years.

All of which is also to say my relationship to the academy is conflicted at best. The thing that keeps me here now is the extraordinary zone, even in its currently decadent form, called the classroom. It's a zone that exists nowhere else in our culture, and when a conversation is firing beautifully there—well, for me it gets no better. But I'm not at all clear on how long, given the above situation, that environment will last in any meaningful way.

For you, formal innovation allows aesthetic and political developments. Can you elaborate on the ways in which the aesthetic and the political coincide in your work?

A few years ago, you may remember, the National Endowment for the Arts notoriously questioned 17,000 adults about their literary preferences and habits. It defined "literature," I should mention, as "any type of fiction, poetry, and plays [sic] that . . . respondents felt should be included and not just what literary critics might consider literature" (Weigart 21). Consequently, opening one of the 723 novels Barbara Cartland wrote during her lifetime (and which have sold more than a billion copies worldwide) is equivalent to opening *The Unnamable,* say, or *Gravity's Rainbow.* Even so, the survey, which was published under the title *Reading at Risk,* discovered that since 1982 there has been a loss of roughly twenty million readers in the United States (a number representing a ten percent drop in readership) and that reading rates are declining among all demographic groups regardless of gender, ethnicity, education, age, or income level, with the steepest drop in the youngest groups—that is, those between eighteen to twenty-four and twenty-five to thirty-four, respectively. Although annual sales for all types of books were predicted to top $44 billion by 2008, up 58 percent from the year before, only 46.7 percent of adults say they are reading "literature" (remember what passes for same), compared with 56.9 percent two decades ago. Of those surveyed, 95.7 percent said they preferred watching television to reading, 60 percent attending a movie, and 55 percent lifting weights. "At the current rate of loss," the NEA concluded, "literary reading as a leisure activity will virtually disappear in half a century."

The survey points to the rise of electronic media—especially television, movies, and the Internet—as the primary culprits for drawing our culture's attention away from fiction, poetry, and drama. Yet the problem is not simply that people are reading less. It is also that they are reading easier, more naïvely, less rigorously.

In addition, we're talking about the nature of the narratives people experience daily—both inside and outside books. In *The Middle Mind,* Curtis White contends that the stories generated and sustained by the American political system, entertainment industry, and academic trade have helped teach us over the last half century or so by their insidious simplicity, plainness, and ubiquity how not to think for ourselves. I doubt much needs to be said about how recent political narratives of the United States have led to the "starkest and most deadly" poverty of imagination, nor about how, "on the whole, our entertainment . . . is a testament to our ability and willingness to endure boredom . . . and pay for it." A little probably should be said, though, about White's take on the consequences of this dissemination of corporate consciousness throughout academia. For him, the contemporary university "shares with the entertainment industry its simple institutional inertia"; "so-called dominant 'critical paradigms' tend to stabilize in much the same way that assumptions about 'consumer demand' make television programming predictable" (White). If, in other words, our student-shoppers want to talk about Spider-Man, Stephen King, and hip-hop in the classroom, well, that's what they're going to get to talk about since that's how English departments fill seats, and filling seats is how they make money, and making money is what it's all about . . . isn't it? Who needs Wallace Stevens or New Criticism? J. M. Coetzee, Shelley Jackson, or Carole Maso?

Unfortunately, the result—particularly in the wake of cultural studies—has been the impulse to eschew close, meticulous engagement with the page; to search texts "for symptoms supporting the sociopolitical or theoretical template of the critic"; to flatten out distinctions between, say, the value of studying James Joyce or Kathy Acker or Ben Marcus, on the one hand, and Britney Spears or Bart Simpson or that cute, feisty gang from South Park, on the other, and therefore unknowingly to embrace and maintain the very globalized corporate culture that cultural studies claims to critique.

What we are left with, then, is the death or at least the dying, as I mentioned earlier, of Difficult Imagination—one that often comes coupled with the charge of exclusiveness, snobbery, and elitism leveled by frustrated, faintly anxious readers at disruptive, transgressive, nuanced, intricate texts dedicated in myriad ways to confronting, complicating, interrogating, and even perhaps for brief periods of time short-circuiting the bird-brained, user-friendly narratives produced by our dominant cultures that would like to see such narratives told and retold until they begin to pass for something like truths about the human condition.

I'm not at all sure, when discussing the question of the avant-garde (or whatever we decide to call it) and accessibility, what we really mean by the latter term since *accessibility* is one of those highly subjective words that, as Nabokov claimed of *reality*, should always appear between quotation marks. Nor am I clear about to whom a work should be "accessible"—an MFA student, a bus driver, an associate professor of biology, a rancher, a river guide? Nor do I understand why many people seem to believe texts in general should be more than less "accessible." But what I want to suggest is that, whatever we may think of when we use that word, texts in general should be just the opposite. They should demand greater labor on the part of readers, even a good degree of uneasiness, rather than effortlessness and comfort. Why? Because I want to suggest that texts that make us work, make us think and feel in unusual ways, attempt to wake us in the midst of our dreaming, and dream us in the midst of our waking, are more useful epistemologically, ontologically, and politically than texts that make us feel warm, fuzzy, and forgetful.

So when I speak of renewing writing of the Difficult Imagination, I am not referring to the renewal of a series of vanguard theoretical constraints, doctrines, or trends so much as the renewal of a narratological possibility space. What is important about its products is that they come into being often and widely, because in them we discover the perpetual manifestation of Nietzsche's notion of the unconditional, Derrida's of a privileged instability, Viktor Shklovsky's ambition for art, and Martin Heidegger's for philosophy: the return, as Curtis White writes, through complexity and challenge (not predictability and ease) to perception and contemplation.

Because of its natureless nature, writing of the Difficult Imagination will always make you feel a little foolish, a little tongue-tied, a little excluded, before an example of it. That's a good thing. You will find yourself standing there in a kind of baffled wonder that will insist upon a slightly new mode of perceiving, a slightly new way of speaking, to capture what it is you just experienced. I began in the late eighties writing fairly conventional, if faintly magical-realist, fiction. By the midnineties, that had changed—in part because I simply lost interest in my earlier works' familiarity. After my novel *Burnt*, the architecture of my sentences and narrative became increasingly more intricate, deliberately resistant to default reading methods. Emblematic of this impulse is my novel *Head in Flames*, a collage text composed of chips of sensation, observation, memory, and quotation shaped into a series of narraticules told by three alternating voices, each inhabiting a different font and aesthetic/political/existential space. The first belongs to Vincent van Gogh on the day he shot himself in Auvers in July 1890. The second to Theo van Gogh (Vincent's brother's great-grandson) on the day he was assassinated in Amsterdam in November 2004. The third to Mohammed Bouyeri, Theo's murderer, outraged by the filmmaker's collaboration with controversial politician Ayaan Hirsi Ali on a ten-minute experimental short critiquing Muslim mistreatment of women. In the film—it's called *Submission,* the translation of the Arabic word *Islam*—four Muslim women narrate how they were abused; their naked bodies are veiled with semitransparent shrouds as they kneel in prayer and Qur'anic verses advocating the subjugation of women are projected onto their flesh. My intention is that the aggregate unfurls into an exploration of art's purpose, religion's increasingly dominant role as engine of politics and passion, the involvedness of foreignness and assimilation, and, ultimately, the limits of tolerance.

Writing from the Difficult Imagination reminds us, then, that language, ideas, and experience are profoundly complicated things. But such talk may seem to beg the question: can the Difficult Imagination's project ever hope for something resembling "victory," however we may define it? The answer is absolutely not. And maybe. Staging the inaccessible is an always-already futile project. And an indispensable one. Its purpose is never a change but a changing—an unending profiting from the impossible, from using our marginal status as innovationists to find an optic through which we can reinvolve ourselves with history and technique, present ourselves as a constant (if, admittedly, embarrassingly minor) prompt that things can always be different than they are. Any such changing will occur—if it occurs at all—locally. That is, such writing will never generate a macrorevolution but a necklace of micro ones: nearly imperceptible, nearly ahistorical clicks in consciousness that come when you meet a startling, illuminating, tough fictive thought experiment. Then again, what else could any of us possibly ask for from a narrative?

You suggest that "texts that make us work, make us think and feel in unusual ways, attempt to wake us in the midst of our dreaming, and dream us in the midst of our waking, are more useful" than others that do the opposite. Yet, some think that when this "work" does not come from a direct response to current pressures in the content of fiction, it cannot be political. Are you implying that texts can resist, or at least question, the cultural developments you mention without addressing them directly in their content?

I mean to suggest that texts can critique dominant cultures, not only through their content, but also through their structure, through their use of language, through their difficulty, through the ergodic process one must learn to negotiate them.

I tend to be fairly uninterested in texts whose politics—whatever those politics may be—are situated primarily in their content and are primarily effortless and obvious rather than involved and nuanced. I'm left blank before a novel like, say, Toni Morrison's *Beloved*, which wears its predictable politics on its sleeve, despite some absolutely beautiful language. (I'm afraid I find it overrated.) I remember Marjorie Perloff once asking me, with reference to it, whether there were really still any readers out there who might come into contact with the book who would need convincing that slavery and slavery's ghost were bad things. Morrison's novel, that is, is telling us what we already know in ways we already know it. I simply don't find that a particularly appealing reading experience. I'm not suggesting novels invested unsubtly in identity or leftist or conservative or other politics shouldn't be read. I'm just suggesting I'm not going to be their most ideal reader.

Rather, I'm interested in the opportunities inherent in, for instance, Mark Danielewski's *House of Leaves*, or even in any individual sentence written by Ben Marcus or Joe Wenderoth—writing that seems, at least on the face of it, at least in terms of its content, nearly apolitical much of the time. Such writing's formalistics—different as they will surely be from example to example—are (as Samuel R. Delany once said of science fiction) tools to help us think. *House of Leaves*, for instance, challenges us through its narratological, epistemological, and ontological complexities to contemplate how we narrativize and why; reminds us that at root the word *narration* is related to the Proto-Indo-European word *gno*—to know. Every Marcus or Wenderoth sentence asks us what a sentence is, how it functions, how language languages, what its relationship is to the things of the universe, how it is always already manipulated and asks us by each sentence's very presence on the page to consider by whom and to what end. Again, such writing, by its otherness, tells us to remember variety and change at an existential level, which strikes me as an immensely significant political act.

Limit Texts, I suppose you could call instances of this strain of writing (varieties, Lydia Davis might say, of disturbance)—those that take various elements of narrativity to their brink so we can never think of them in quite the same ways again. To the brink, and then over. Perhaps *Grenztexte*, after Karl Jaspers's notion of *Grenzsituationen*—moments, that is, accompanied by anxiety, in which the human mind confronts the restrictions of its existing forms; moments that allow us to abandon, fleetingly, the securities of our limitedness and enter new realms of self-consciousness. They're the sorts of texts that, once you've taken them down off the shelf, you can't put back up again.

By being in the world, they ask us to embrace a politics of thought, freedom, radical skepticism. I imagine which texts comprise such a category will be different for each of us, depending on who we are, and where, and whence we've come. For me, they include such weirdly sundry texts as Kathy Acker's *Blood and Guts in High School*, Michael Joyce's *Afternoon: A Story*, Robbe-Grillet's *Jealousy*, Steve Tomasula's *VAS*, Jen Bervin's *The Desert*, Stuart Moulthrop's *Reagan Library*.

So I guess what I'm ultimately suggesting is that meaning carries meaning, but structuration carries meaning as well.

When reading Head in Flames, *I found myself wondering about which font of the story attracted me the most on each page, which one seduced me when I did not focus on processing the words only. I thought about what called my attention, and I asked myself: do I usually look at fonts in prose this way? To me, this is an example of the structuration and formalistics you mention here. Could you expand on your use of font and pagination in* Head in Flames *or in other novels and perhaps of other explorations of structuration and formalistics in your work?*

The fonts are precisely emblematic of this notion of structuration-as-meaning. In a sense, every novel's form is also a politics. "Our satisfaction with the completeness of plot," Fredric Jameson once noted, is "a kind of satisfaction with society as well" (12). One could say much the same is the case with our satisfaction with undemanding style, character construction, subject matter, et cetera.

From that perspective, I've been interested in disruptive linguistic and architectonic structures since *Tonguing the Zeitgeist*, the avant-pop novel I wrote in the early nineties about the commodification of the body. In it, Ben Tendo, an unassuming clerk at a porn supplier, Beautiful Mutants, Ltd., is kidnapped by a music corporation, forcibly addicted, implanted with a new voice box, and otherwise manufactured into the next big thing. The book marked a kind of breakthrough for me, a movement into syntactic complexity and energy, as well as into structural perversions (frequent jump cuts, rapid point-of-view shifts, foregrounding detail over scene, deliberately hazing key plot points), which led me away from the relatively conventional shapings I was doing in *Live from Earth* and toward textual openings—toward an understanding, to paraphrase Charles Bernstein, that fiction can be the possibility of possibility.

From the early nineties on, my partner, Andi, and I also began collaborating on text-image collages. Right now we're working on a series of fake diseases for her ongoing installation project, *Freak Show*. Once we began working closely together, the page began to lose its invisibility for me. It became real, a conscious element in the authorship of any text. Recently, Andi and I collaborated on an entire text-image collage chapter in *Calendar of Regrets*.

Another important moment for me with respect to this idea of structuration-as-meaning occurred when I was writing *Girl Imagined by Chance*. Its first draft, although slanted in content (a young couple creates a make-believe daughter and make-believe existence for her in order to appease our culture of reproduction), was quite conventional in form, which didn't feel at all right to me, although I couldn't have articulated why at first. Shortly after finishing the first pass, I traveled to Finland on a Fulbright for half a year and rediscovered those stunning pared-down lines, not of northern European literature but of northern European architecture—the sort imagined by Alvar Aalto, the so-called father of modern Nordic design, himself intrigued by the cubist and collage impulses in artists like Braque and Picasso. I worked on *Girl* almost every morning while in Turku, a town about an hour north of Helsinki by train, where Andi and I lived and where I taught, and by the third month there I noticed the sentences in my rewrite of the novel had changed dramatically, become leaner, more compact, something like more lyrical. The movement from one to the next worked less by conventional transition than by collage-like juxtaposition. I also became increasingly aware of white space—how the reduced, purified sentences floated in it on the page in ways that struck me as beautiful and somehow sad. I'm sure it was an easy step from the emphasis on the visual and notions of reproduction in the appropriated and manipulated photographs that introduced each chapter.

I obviously returned to that notion of white space as Nordic formalistics in *Head in Flames*, and, as you noticed, also became interested in how font itself influences how we read, how we think of the text before us, how we (usually unconsciously) process it. I suppose for me there's some weird synesthesia at play. Early on in the writing process, my imagination came to associate a gentle, graceful Times font with Vincent Van Gogh. The brash bold version of that font seemed quintessentially Theo, a type of Michael Moore figure (only more so) in the Netherlands. And a font from an entirely different universe—elementary, brutal, even—felt right for Mohammed: a Courier for the courier delivering a message that the western world doesn't want to hear; one can't see that font, I think, without hearing the loud, unsettling clacks of the manual typewriter.

So the page has become increasingly part of the stage in my writing, affording, I like to think, its own contribution to the dynamics of the text, its own awareness of the author's role in the production of the text's materiality, how a text *matters*. I can't imagine that having happened without books like

Federman's *Double or Nothing* being in the world. To know they exist, at least for me, is to always already be influenced by them.

I notice that you use the words white space *instead of* blank space, *a term often used to describe books like* Head in Flames *or* Girl. *I've always found the word* blank *inadequate to talk about the pages of such books because it implies that the text is lacking something in its whiteness. I am, however, interested in the notion of white space, and I suspect that, for you, it does not express a void or a lack. Could you say more about how you consider the white space, its materiality, its role?*

White space is never blank space, never void, in writing. It is always something else, even in the most conventional short story or novel, where it functions as a visual announcement that a modification in time, space, or point of view is in the process of occurring. In innovative fiction, that function widens a good deal, often becoming something close to graphic metaphor. In Carole Maso's *Ava*, for instance, the wash of whiteness on the page suggests the wash of death itself that is infecting the protagonist through the course of the novel. In Mark Danielewski's *House of Leaves*, white space is emblematic of the not-knowing that pervades the text, the Nothing at the text's and the house's heart. In Beckett's *How It Is*, it's a kind of musical notation: the breaths the protagonist takes on his crawl through the mud. There's that startling splash of it following the final period of the nine-page syntactic erasure that "concludes" his *Unnamable* as well: a torrent of white silence that gestures toward what self and text have become, present absence and absent presence, the trace of all that's there that isn't there. In *Girl Imagined by Chance*, white space functions in an architectural capacity, as I say, while in *Head in Flames* it functions in several roles at once: as metaphor for the absolute distances separating the voices and visions of Vincent, Theo, and Mohammed, each a kind of artist manifesting an aesthetic position unconditionally inconsistent with the others; as cubist design principle reminiscent of the one at work in *Girl*; as the silences that refuse to be silenced in our culture, and yet are, and yet aren't, as first Vincent's voice, then Theo's, and finally Mohammed's flicker out of existence during the course of the last third of the book. *Calendar of Regrets* couldn't exist in its present form without my growing consciousness of what is simultaneously materially present and unpresent on every page.

You mentioned your use of photography in Girl, *which is another way to approach textual materiality. Because you've also experimented with visual texts before* Girl, *I wonder if your approach to them might have changed from your earlier projects to your later explorations.*

I suppose the *kinds* of visual arenas I've explored have changed. When Andi and I first started playing around with text-image collages in the late eighties, the process involved literally cutting and pasting—creating text-images by scissoring found visuals and gluing them on a page, then adding words, then photocopying or scanning. The process was much more tactile back then, which I confess I miss a little these days. When Andi moved completely to the computer, all sorts of new prospects opened up, of course, including the illusion of seamlessness in the finished product, which illusion, interestingly, can generate a stronger sense of the uncanny in the reader/viewer—you know, something so perfectly perfect that it actually unsettles. One image in our fake diseases project, by way of illustration, shows an elderly woman with her mouth sutured shut. Andi digitally manipulated the photograph of sutures she had on her own leg (the result—long story—of a chainsaw accident she suffered several years ago) and, as it were, grafted those onto that woman's face, which was appropriated from, I believe, a medical textbook. The consequence is so realistic as to be doubly, deeply strange, other and not other and not not other simultaneously. With the photographs in *Girl,* and those in *Calendar,* the manipulations are subtler, but the consequence is the same: a trompe l'oeil that produces what we hope are disconcerting effects on the viewer, a sense of defamiliarization, a rupture of habitual perception. Andi and I are also exploring, in another chapter in *Calendar,* as I mentioned, the idea of layout, and, in another, I'm exploring words *as* images, words as having a very real visual component to them.

I guess, speaking of which, I've always been a weirdly visual being. Living with Andi's remarkable sense of sight for the last thirty years has brought that out in spades. And I've always been attracted to highly visual writers like Laird Hunt, Guy Davenport, and (oddly, perhaps, considering his blandly suburban plots and characters and forms) John Updike; always been attracted to page manipulators like Federman and Tomasula; always been attracted to painters, sculptors, new-media artists, filmmakers; always been fascinated by how the purely visual can usually do a lot more work a lot more quickly than can the purely linguistic (think, for instance, of any four square inches of a polyptych by Bosch, or dense panel in Gibbons and Moore's *The Watchmen,* and recall how many narratives are at play there, how many intimations) but also by how (to echo N. Katherine Hayles's notion of MSA, or Media Specific Analysis) the visual performs in remarkably different ways in different media, that each medium rethinks what the visual is and can do and how it can do it.

Once you begin thinking about visual elements on a page, it's very hard *not* to think about visual elements on a page, *not* to think about every page as more than a vehicle for words marching like so many black ants down from the upper left-hand corner to the lower right-hand with the only impediment in front of them being the occasional punctuation mark or new paragraph indentation.

You mention your collaboration with Andi, and you have explored collaboration throughout your career. Our discussion is a different mode of collaboration, one that involves a weaving of ideas through our written exchange. Would you care to comment on your views concerning the interview form?

These are the strangest things for me, these written interviews that take their course over a period of months and yet give the illusion of unedited spontaneity, improvisation, facility . . . while in reality taking the form of carefully constructed artifacts—fictions (like memoir, like history), perhaps we could call them, that masquerade as nonfiction, as unmediated structures of communication, even as they meticulously stage voice, character (which should never feel like character), plot, rhythm, you name it. I'm reminded how, later in life, Nabokov refused to give real-time ones because he was keenly self-conscious about how stuttery and stupid he could sound in them. Even for those he did participate in that impersonated face-to-face ones, Nabokov would, as I recall (and, needless to say, I could be inventing a fiction as I write this), sit up in his room at the Montreux Palace Hotel in Switzerland and have the interviewer sit down in the lobby. The interviewer would then write a question on a card, which he would send up. Nabokov would write out his response, which he would send down. Such a process allowed them, as our interview does us, to think in slow motion. I wouldn't have it any other way. Who in the world wants to watch an interviewer and writer think in real time? The consequence, at best, would usually be the same as art speeded up and flattened out: entertainment rather than illumination, heat rather than light. At worst, it would be all muddle. I'm grateful for the opportunity here to shape what amounts to a kind of (to return to one of our touch points during our conversation) collage of mini-essays, and, although, looking back, I hear silence after silence among what we've said that could have been filled with interesting sound, we've covered some wonderfully productive, suggestive ground. I greatly appreciate it; greatly appreciate your sharp questions, Flore, that have taken us both into spaces we didn't know we were heading.

And, of course, what we've generated has underscored performatively the sense that collaboration is the basic mode of most writing, most creation, although our culture usually likes to repress that fact by embracing the washed-out Romantic myth of the solitary artist creating in the solitary mind in the solitary room. All published stories and novels are collaborative projects that involve an author, other texts with which he or she is in dialogue (either consciously or unconsciously), various ghosts in the machine, editor or editors, publisher, printer, reviewers, bloggers, teachers, critics, people who set up reading series, and on and on.

The only thing we're doing here that most writers aren't is acknowledging the obvious: we're producing something neither of us could have produced alone and have thereby taken ourselves to destinations we couldn't have imagined before beginning our journey and most likely not even then.

works cited

Beckett, Samuel. *Company, Ill Seen Ill Said, Worstward Ho, Stirrings Still.* Ed. Dirk Van Hulle. London: Faber, 2009. Print.

Jameson, Fredric. *Marxism and Form: Twentieth Century Dialectical Theories of Literature.* Princeton: Princeton UP, 1971. Print.

Jaschik, Scott. "Who really Failed?" *Inside Higher Ed.* 15 Apr. 2010. Web. 15 Jan. 2017.

Lyotard, Jean-François. *The Postmodern Condition: A Report on Knowledge.* Manchester UP, 1984. Print.

Olsen, Lance. *Anxious Pleasures: A Novel after Kafka.* Emeryville: Shoemaker & Hoard, 2007. Print.

———. *Calendar of Regrets.* Tuscaloosa: Fiction Collective Two, 2010. Print.

———. "Deconstructing the Balzacian Mode: Postmodern Fantasy." *Extrapolation* 28.1 (1987): 45–51. Print.

———. "Fourteen Notes Toward the Musicality of Creative Disjunction, or Fiction by Collage." *Fiction's Present: Situating Narrative Innovation.* Ed. R. M. Berry and Jeffrey Di Leo. Albany: State U of New York P, 2007. 185–90. Print.

———. *Girl Imagined by Chance.* Tallahassee: Fiction Collective Two, 2002. Print.

———. *Head in Flames.* Portland: Chiasmus Press, 2009. Print.

———. *Nietzsche's Kisses.* Tallahassee: Fiction Collective Two, 2006. Print.

———. "Omniphage: Rock 'n' Roll and Avant-Pop Science Fiction." *Edging into the Future: Science Fiction and Contemporary Cultural Transformation.* Ed. Veronica Hollinger and Joan Gordon. Philadelphia: U of Pennsylvania P, 2002. 30–56. Print.

———. "Stand By to Crash! Avant-Pop, Hypertextuality, and Postmodern Comic Vision in Coover's *The Public Burning.*" *Critique: Studies in Contemporary Fiction* 42.1 (2000): 51–68. Print.

———. *Tonguing the Zeitgeist.* San Francisco: Permeable Press, 1994. Print.

Weigart, Pauline. *Teaching and Education: 21st Century Issues and Challenges.* New York: Nova Science, 2008. Print.

White, Curtis. *Curtis's Short Blog.* N.p. Web. <https://curtissshortblog.wordpress.com/author/curtissshortblog/>.

further works by and on lance olsen

Bell, Alice. "Schema Theory, Hypertext Fiction and Links." *Style: A Quarterly Journal of Aesthetics, Poetics, Stylistics, and Literary Criticism* 48.2 (2014): 140–61. Print.

Burnett, Fred W. "Postmodern Fantasy and Postmodern Biblical Studies: A (Science) Fictive Review of Lance Olsen and Samuel Delany." *Journal of the Fantastic in the Arts* 8.2 (1997): 244–74. Print.

Lackey, Michael. "The Uses of History in the Biographical Novel: A Conversation With Jay Parini, Bruce Duffy, and Lance Olsen." *Conversations with Jay Parini*. Ed. Michael Lackey. Jackson: UP of Mississippi, 2014. 125–48. Print.

Olsen, Lance. *10:01*. Portland: Chiasmus Press, 2005. Print.

———. *10:01* (hypermedia). *Iowa Review*. N.p., November 2005. Web.

———. *Architectures of Possibility: After Innovative Writing*. Washington: Raw Dog Screaming Press, 2012. Print.

———. *Burnt*. La Grande: Wordcraft, 1996. Print.

———. *Circus of the Mind in Motion: Postmodernism and the Comic Vision*. Detroit: Wayne State UP, 1990. Print.

———. *Ellipse of Uncertainty: An Introduction to Postmodern Fantasy*. Westport: Greenwood Press, 1987. Print.

———. *Freaknest*. La Grande: Wordcraft, 2000. Print.

———. *Hideous Beauties*. Portland: Eraserhead, 2003. Print.

———. *How to Unfeel the Dead: New & Selected Fictions*. Toronto: Teksteditions, 2014. Print.

———. *Live from Earth*. New York: Available Press/Ballantine Books, 1991. Print

———. *Lolita: A Janus Text*. New York: Twayne, 1995. Print.

———. *My Dates with Franz*. Amherst: Bluestone Press, 1993. Print.

———. *Rebel Yell: Writing Fiction*. San Jose: Cambrian Press, 1998. Print.

———. *Sewing Shut My Eyes*. Normal: Fiction Collective Two, 2000. Print.

———. *Scherzi, I Believe*. La Grande: Wordcraft, 1994. Print.

———, ed. *Surfing Tomorrow: Essays on the Future of American Fiction*. Prairie Village: Potpourri, 1995. Print.

———. *Theories of Forgetting*. Tuscaloosa: Fiction Collective Two, 2014. Print.

———. *[[there.]]*. Fort Wayne: Anti-Oedipus Press, 2014. Print.

———. *Time Famine*. San Francisco: Permeable Press, 1996. Print.

———. *William Gibson*. Mercer Island: Starmont House, 1992. Print.

Olsen, Lance, and Mark Amerika, eds. *In Memoriam to Postmodernism: Essays on the Avant-Pop*. San Diego: San Diego UP, 1995. Print.

Petrovic, Paul. "Between Visibility and Invisibility: Baudrillard, Jean-Luc Marion, and Lance Olsen's *Girl Imagined by Chance*." *Extrapolation: A Journal of Science Fiction and Fantasy* 46.2 (2005): 249–58. Print.

alan singer

ALAN SINGER IS A PROFESSOR OF ENGLISH AT TEMPLE UNIVERSITY. HE HAS PUBLISHED FOUR CRITICAL BOOKS: *THE SELF-DECEIVING MUSE: NOTICE AND KNOWLEDGE IN THE WORK OF ART* (2010), *AESTHETIC REASON: ARTWORKS AND THE DELIBERATIVE ETHOS* (2003), *THE SUBJECT AS ACTION: TRANSFORMATION AND TOTALITY IN NARRATIVE AESTHETICS* (1994), AND *A METAPHORICS OF FICTION: DISCONTINUITY AND DISCOURSE IN THE MODERN NOVEL* (1984). HE HAS ALSO AUTHORED FOUR WORKS OF FICTION: *THE INQUISITOR'S TONGUE* (2012), *DIRTMOUTH* (2004), *THE CHARNEL IMP* (1998), AND *MEMORY WAX* (1996).

"**SHALL I BE** the regurgitation of the meal you cannot stomach, husband of my life?" asks Delta Tells, the protagonist of Alan Singer's 1996 *Memory Wax* (11). Delta's question, provoked by her husband's unfaithful behavior and full of anger and calculated determination, is an example of *Memory Wax*'s tone, which, like its characters, ventures into the extremes. In many ways, the text resembles a verbal assault testing the limits of humanity: Delta's bloody thoughts and actions present us with unthinkable physical and psychological scenarios where receiving and inflicting pain takes extraordinary proportions.

The body, at the center of *Memory Wax*'s physical, sexual, emotional, and intellectual explorations, is essential to Singer's other fictions. *The Inquisitor's Tongue* (2012), set during the Spanish Inquisition, investigates spiritual and physical acts of violence. The narrative's treatment of the horrors of the Inquisition asks questions about truth and identity, as the confession of Osvaldo Alonzo de Zamora, a converso, is read aloud by a priest of the Inquisition to a suspected sinner. In reading sentences such as, "I was my twin brother's image of myself," we realize that manipulations of body and identity are matched by Singer's linguistic transfigurations (29). A sentence such as the one cited above might slow down the reader in processing the novel's information. Formal experimentations such as these constitute a vital aspect of Singer's research in poetic language and grammar. *Charnel Imp* (1987) exhibits such research:

the narrator of the novel, "a ventriloquist for love," tells us, in labyrinthine ways, of the lives surrounding a slaughterhouse (189). The unreal situations and conflicting voices of the novel highlight the unreliability of the narrative and ask questions about self-understanding and self-deception. Commenting on the sentences of *Dirtmouth* (2004), Singer explains, in the following interview, that his prose strives "toward the lapidary, the small scale adjustment of one's attention to emerging aspects of the artifact" to match "the excavation of bog people" that takes place in the book. The forensic investigation involves a number of contradicting voices that transform the nature of the detective activity of the novel, thereby asking questions about how we access "truth."

In his critical work, Singer addresses matters parallel to those explored in his fiction: *A Metaphorics of Fiction: Discontinuity and Discourse in the Modern Novel* (1984) considers formal experiments in the modern novel. In *The Subject as Action: Transformation and Totality in Narrative Aesthetics* (1993), he examines human agency in relation to literary innovations in the works of Thomas Nashe, Laurence Sterne, Henry James, Maurice Blanchot, William Gaddis, and John Ashbery, among others. In *Aesthetic Reason: Artworks and Deliberative Ethos* (2003), Singer demonstrates that the aesthetic is not distinct from sociopolitical changes. *The Self-Deceiving Muse: Notice and Knowledge in the Work of Art* (2010) rethinks the relationship between self-deception and reason, thereby illuminating the relationship between life and art. As Singer explains in the following discussion, the ideas that he investigates in his theoretical work have affinities with his artistic production, but his novels are not applications or examples of his philosophical and literary research. Yet, they are created side by side and thus inform each other organically.

The conversation that follows took place at the Association for the Study of the Arts of the Present conference in October 2011. The centerpiece of the conversation is Singer's recent book, *The Inquisitor's Tongue*, and themes and preoccupations dear to the author—the body, the structure of his sentences and narrations, humor, film, literary theory, and the state of experimental writing.

●

One of the things that, I think, people will quite obviously remember about your work is that you address shocking subject matters—the forbidden or taboos, such as cannibalism or familicide. Where does that come from?

Well, cannibalism in *Memory Wax* is really only a rumor, a bit of a red herring. Though I must admit that, in all of my novels, I am very interested in the limits of the body, in the vulnerability of the body and the ways in which we have reimagined ourselves at these limits. For me, affect is always a kind of physical effect. I have always been interested in thinking about the way perception determines personality and identity. The malleability of identity—its situational and improvisational nature—is the central preoccupation of my new novel, *The Inquisitor's Tongue*. This book is predicated on the history of conversos who were licensed to convert, and yet they knew that conversion was a theatrical effect. So there is a tension between the idea of necessity—the necessity to convert—and the theatricality that the conversos then have to become physically the masters of. One of my characters hides his converso nature and the other admits it. But the one who admits it is the more conflicted. He knows that one thing that those "tolerant" Catholic authorities who endow a theatricalized identity cannot abide is that their creations reveal the artifice. For this is to reveal the hypocrisy of those who pretend to be tolerant, making them no less theatrical characters in their own world. So identity is a form of acting out, not an indwelling nature, despite our long-standing romance with this belief.

I want to go back to The Inquisitor's Tongue, *but I'm also interested in talking more about the body. What is interesting in your work is that the body is presented sensually in the sexual sections of your fictions, but most of the time bodies are seen more viscerally.*

Along these lines I am trying to put together a new theoretical book project, *Posing Sex: Towards a Perceptual Ethics for Literature and Visual Art*. It is a book about ethics that roots ethics in perception. I am focusing on visual art depicting the sex act, and the question is: "What do you see?" My touchstones for this are artists like Francis Bacon, John Currin and Lisa Yuskavage—I gave a paper on Currin at the Association for the Study of the Arts of the Present conference in 2009. The work of someone like John Currin promotes a curious rearticulation of the mind-body relation. We are typically anthropomorphic in our view of the world, and so we see, in physical objects that are not animate, human features and affects. But in looking at Currin's porn images—or we call them porn images—there is a kind of reversed anthropomorphism that takes hold. We are induced to become all body, ideally a body without a mind. The paradoxical effect of that temptation is that the viewer becomes more mindful of the fact that consciousness is an obstacle to identity. And yet this very anxiety becomes a self-perpetuating métier. Well, we really don't have time to go into it, but briefly I want to acknowledge that the effect I'm interested in here connects directly with Spinoza and the way in which the subject's self-perpetuating existence depends not exactly on a reciprocity between the mind and the body but on continuity between mind and body. You know Spinoza's famous phrase, "the order and connection of ideas follows the order and connection of things" (*Ethics*). Everything that we experience, everything that we know through the senses, strengthens the substance of mind and gives mind its trajectory and gives mind its resources for reflection. So, one of the things that you can tell here is that I'm still working this thing out. I published a version of this argument a few years ago in which I use John Currin again to make the point. In any case, this kind of thinking is shot through my fiction.

In your fiction, do you envision a different kind of reading to respond to this mind/body relationship?

Yes. And I hope this is manifest in my syntax, which is typically extended and complicated. I don't want to give the reader an opportunity to break away from the sensory surface of his or her attentiveness to the world. So there is a kind of physical momentum in the language that makes conceptual abstraction difficult, that makes the impulse to indulge in deep character analysis difficult, and that brings everything to the surface of the experience of the moment. And, to me, experience always begins with the body. So that's my way of explaining the syntax in all of my books. I want to believe that there are readers who enjoy the quality of attention or attentiveness that I am demanding. It is the kind of thing that I enjoy, and I have written a lot about the qualities of human attention in my last book, *The Self-Deceiving Muse*. This book is very specifically about the ways in which self-deception and the rationalization of self-deception is an elaboration of our resources for attentiveness to the world. And the more attentive we are, obviously, the more of the world there is. This is not simply a presupposition that the world is big. Rather, it is an inducement to exercise the kind of tenacity and doggedness of attentive mind that expands the range of possibilities for our experience of the world. Where the world stretches to accommodate that resource of attentiveness is where things get interesting for me, in both the critical work and especially in my fiction. From my first novel, *The Ox-Breadth*, to *The Inquisitor's Tongue*, I'm striving to use language as a "stretcher" for a wider and wider canvassing of the world.

In Dirtmouth, *there is something forensic or surgical in the structures of sentences.*

Forensic is a good word, in that context especially. Maybe one way of describing my sentences is to think about them in terms of forensic tasks like excavation, which in *Dirtmouth* is the excavation of bog people. My sentences strive toward the lapidary, the small-scale adjustment of one's attention to emerging aspects of the artifact—the world of my characters. Your focus on one thing depends upon its imbrication in a matrix. One thing connected to another induces a response to what else there is to notice. There is a kind of continuity of experience that matters to me in the density of this matrix. This doesn't appeal to every reader, and it's not always storytelling in the quick way that readers often want to be able to process their experience. Sometimes readers think there are no characters in my books because they bleed into their worlds. I am of course interested in creating character, but in my books we must acquaint ourselves with them in a different way than we are used to, in a way that permits us to keep faith with human nature if we accept that character is a kind of improvisational enterprise. Self-perpetuation is possible because of change, not because of repetition.

To respond to some of what you have said from the perspective of a reader, especially when I read the excerpt from The Inquisitor's Tongue *in* Golden Handcuff's Review, *I thought about proprioception.*

Oh, really.

Yes, I thought about what we do as our ligaments adjust to surfaces and are able to make us function, but we don't exactly know or think about it when we walk, unless we go through an injury and therapy. I kept thinking about that because of the treatment of the leg in the excerpt. I thought: is this proprioceptive writing, or does it invite for proprioceptive reading, and what would that be?

I like that you are thinking of it as proprioceptive writing because it is very much the modality of experience that counts for me with respect to engaging the world. I do think that some readers find it exhausting, even off-putting. But the alternative, I think, is a cheapening of experience, a minimizing of the possibilities of experience.

Well, in this excerpt, but also in other novels of yours, it is also very funny.

I'm delighted to hear this. I think the books are quite funny.

Could you talk more about humor in your work?

There is a lot of comedy in my fiction. For example, my characters are forever unwittingly exposing the secrets they think they are disguising so well by an elaborate theatricality. In this respect, I think of comedy not as a limit experience but as a kind of threshold of self-renewing and self-understanding. Wherever there is laughter, there is always an occasion to be self-reflective in a way that is unpredictable. Those experiences of self-reflection are authentic ones, more so than the contrived pseudoscientific or psychological states that are associated with so-called dramatizations of intellectual seriousness. So I'm hoping that the comedy in my fiction works very much toward the same end: orchestrating ever-more scrupulous occasions for self-reflection.

And you've talked about characters in that regard, but narration—the construction of the narration and of the narrator's voice, or voices since they are sometimes very diverse—is also part of this self-reflective process in your fiction. Could you talk about that aspect as well?

It's pretty fair to say that my narrators are somewhat oppressive because they are always insisting on a kind of absolutism both perceptually and conceptually. They are, in a way, monomaniacs who interest me for their powers of rationalization, which I take to be always a form of creativity. Nevertheless, and especially in my last two books, I've been drifting in the direction of multivocal forms, toward drama, to try to break the spell of authority cast by the first person. But I don't in any way reject the first-person voice. When I think about the earlier novels, and specifically the first-person narratives where those narrators do seem to be especially tyrannical and maniacal, I nonetheless think all of that is undercut by comedy. In any case, I've always been interested in theatre, so I've been resorting to multiple voices, multiple narrations—contrapuntal ones—so that however much a single voice is dominating it gets inflected with something alien to its nature. I am actually writing a novel now that, in effect, has a play within it. It's about an experimental playwright director and his relation with his heart surgeon, who thinks of himself as a kind of theatrical director in his own right in the operating theater.

I was actually curious about whether you've seen your work change or if you have envisioned it differently. You've mentioned the change in the way you've used voice. Is there anything else that you can trace in roughly the last twenty years?

I think this movement toward multiple voices and toward a quasi-theatrical mode of presentation is a kind of concession to my critics about the authoritarianism of the voices in the earlier books, though, for me, they are not really authoritative characters: they never succeed, they don't have mastery, but the desire for that kind of mastery is, for me, related to pathos and not something to be intimidated by. So my use of more dialogically torqued narrative voice is a way to explore the delusions of self-possession and the liabilities of professing self-mastery.

And even in your theoretical work, you have written about errors and self-deception and that goes on in the fiction, so that the narrators are undermined, or . . .

Well, my narrators are not destroyed, but they are changed. For me the key feature of a successful fiction is change, and one of the threads that runs through all of my books is that metamorphosis prevails. I'm deeply committed to change because I'm committed to the idea that character is essentially circumstantial and improvisational. For a reader, character is worth investing in, in so far as we reckon with the contingencies of character formation. The lure of personality types invites us to act in error without the knowledge that we act in error—which is to know that there are other ways of acting. Character in my books is always a self-consciously hedged proposition: to believe in character is to be interested in what character does not yet know itself capable of.

So, when you start a project, does it start with those more abstract ideas?

Never with an abstraction. It almost always starts with some action or some perception, instead of some thematic setup that, in all likelihood, will preempt serious wonder about what we will see, what we will think, what could happen that has not already been thought out. My fiction is often described as philosophical, and I resist that presumption. It sounds as if my compositions are frontloaded with the conceptual, and they are not at all (which is not to say that I'm not and that I don't expect my reader to be philosophically minded—I do). But the kind of fiction I like to read is the fiction that makes it impossible to conceptualize, except in the act of reading, in the act of paying attention, in the ways in which our attentiveness to our environment is an elaboration of our existence—back to Spinoza. That's why I like Joe McElroy's work and writers like John Hawkes, Cormac McCarthy, or Djuna Barnes, writers who've been important to me, especially Djuna Barnes early on. When I read *Nightwood* for the first time, I immediately felt a rapport with not just the book but the possibility of the world in which such a book can be read and valued for its experience of mental and emotional complication that is wholly original. The book has now paradoxically become a kind of cult item, a museum piece, which has the effect of blunting its originality perhaps.

I think I would agree. . . . Beckett is also in the background of your work.

Yes, Beckett also, especially the plays; especially the short plays and the short last novels.

It's obvious in How It Is.

Beginning with *How It Is* and all the way through the last trilogy. Beckett makes a demand upon the reader that he or she accept the world as its appearance. Appearance is a mandate that a reader adapts to the constraints of the text. The imperative of the reader's adaptation to those presentations of the fictional world entails a kind of hope. The very prospect of adaptation, however ruthlessly forced by the author, is important to me. I do believe that this kind of ruthlessness entails an optimism about the possibilities for development. Development obviously is the wrong word if it implies a predictable destination, but change matters.

When exploring your work, including the theory, it's tempting to find connections between your theoretical and fictional books. Do you actually have a theoretical project in the works while you also do your fiction?

Yes, that's right. It's not deliberate on my part. I'm almost always working simultaneously on both a critical work and a novel. But I don't see these as divergent paths. I see them as just extensions of one another. The same problems that come up in the fiction seem to come up in the criticism or critical writing and vice versa. It's not that one takes priority over the other and one follows the other. There are just different registers in which I can work out my interest in these problems or experiences, the métier of thinking through error, for example.

Do you do research for your fictions?

No.

I thought maybe you did for the slaughterhouse in Charnel Imp.

Everybody tells me that. I've never been to a slaughterhouse. Someone told me that they'd been to a slaughterhouse, and what I described in *Charnel Imp* could have been a documentary or a report on slaughterhouses. This is fine, but the particulars of my setting are anchored in the imaginative necessities of my desire to contrive a worldliness for my characters. I do check myself, after the fact of composition, just to be sure I haven't lost all rapport with the conditions of practical experience. With *The Inquisitor's Tongue,* I didn't do exactly research, but I wanted to be sure that my characters possessed familiarity with the artifacts of the historical period that I was co-opting for my own plot purposes. I never thought I'd write a historical novel—no doubt some readers will call it that—but the history of the Spanish Inquisition is not the only air that my characters can breathe. *The Inquisitor's Tongue* is not really a book about the Inquisition, but the métier of inquisition; it's a book about the burdens and follies of identity. It turned out to be a book that is set in Spain because I was interested in the predicament of people who know that they were sanctioned to lie about their identity, to become conversos. As I've already said, the lie makes them safe but all the more fearful of the society that sanctions the lie and hates the liar even more passionately for the knowledge he possesses of society's hypocrisy. This is the psychological drama that drives one of the main characters. It's bad enough that society would tolerate, even put you up to your charade, but they will not tolerate you making the charade transparent. It's actually a very theatrical thing: everyone must play his or her part. The church sanctions the conversos; the conversos play along, until the self-consciousness of "playing" becomes an unbearable humiliation of the secret identity they are harboring as their own. Of course, in my mind there is an affinity here with the reader, who is always "playing" along at the expense of whomever he or she will never be able to admit themselves to be in the act of reading.

I look forward to reading it. I had a question about Memory Wax: *Is it a feminist book?*

I really resist speaking of it that way. It is too ideological. I suppose that all of my texts are feminist in the sense that I am interested in characters' facility for change, a facility of adaptation to surprising circumstances, challenging novelty. There is certainly a strand of feminist literary theory, as a gender position, that highlights this possibility. But this is precisely what blurs the line between genders. And in fact, one of the things that I like to do in my fiction is to give male characters qualities of the other gender and vice versa. I like to think of character as doubly sexed in a weird way.

Is myth an influence on your writing?

It's not an armature. There is the Medea myth in *Memory Wax,* but it's just another version of the task of imagining an extremity of experience. I traded in the currency of myth only for that reason. In other words, I thought I was just adopting an idiom with cultural currency. I am usually not interested in myths because I am not interested in storytelling that lends itself to conceptual abstraction and renders us passive in the grips of the story. Myth making is another story. Or maybe I should say that I am deeply committed to myth making, with the emphasis on making.

You've talked about the kinds of texts that you like to write and read. How would you call them? Do you feel strongly about categories? I know some writers prefer avant-garde or innovative or experimental . . .

I don't feel strongly about that. The idea of experimental writers brings to mind lab rats, men in white coats. . . . This is something that my students often tell me: "You're the experimentalist. So what are you researching?" Certainly the label "experimental writer" invites this comedy. But I would say that experience, at the pitch of its vitality, is always experimental. So, I don't need to be associated with an avant-grade, and we know that the avant-garde has been a disappointment to itself. If we don't know it, Lyotard will remind us. There is something in Lyotard's notion that the avant-garde wasn't responsible to itself because it turned novelty into capital. I think that he's got a point because the artists never ask, "Do you understand me?" or "Is this good?" The artist is always invested in the question of "What is painting?"; "What is writing?"; "What is thinking?" The questions are the same for all artists.

For you, the kinds of texts that you write and that are sometimes called experimental are the texts that ask, "What am I?"

Or, "What am I doing?" literally. There is an important difference between doing something and knowing what you're doing. In my critical work I've been very focused on that difference, and I'm very suspicious and antagonistic toward theorists who want to license unthinking activity or activity that totally jettisons the enlightenment baggage of conceptuality. I think that's just not interesting. As I said, I never start a fiction frontloaded with some conceptual intention. Nevertheless, my fictions are deeply conceptualizing because experience is a complex of attitudes and perceptions and interactions with other people and other things. Without some resource of conceptual understanding, human experience ceases to be a vital proposition. So I would accept the characterization of my novels as philosophical, as long as we understand that every indulgence of conceptuality is a function of experience, experience that is articulated in the fiction, in the act of writing.

So, would you say that your goals are or your practice as a writer is essentially different from so-called realist novelists?

Sure. When I think of someone like Jonathan Franzen . . . Well, there is too much fiction that is written these days that seems committed only to giving the reader confidence that he or she has ideas and "real" human feelings. What's worse is that these ideas are ones whose currency is already widely acknowledged. It is oddly a presumption of knowledge rather than a deference to experience. Franzen makes it explicit when he says that he sees the significance of fiction as essentially archiving the moment we are living through, so that future generations will know exactly what we are doing right now. I think that's extremely narcissistic and not interesting. I don't really care to record or memorialize what we are doing right now. We are doing it, and consequences will follow in the form of transformative experience. Making snapshots contributes very little to understanding human experience as an ongoing enterprise.

In your criticism of experimental or innovative works, you address their political agency, or you might have a better way to phrase this . . .

Well, I guess fiction is political, but only in the ways that it alters our engagements with the circumstances of everyday life that have to do with making judgments, taking actions, once again knowing what you are doing rather than simply doing. Literary work is political only insofar as it is a specific prompt to take responsibility for oneself by attempting to better understand what the limits of one's experience are. I have no confidence that literary works are political in the sense that they change the world. They change the reader. The reader perhaps changes the world.

But there is this idea that's often thrown around that literary works won't change anything, but as a fiction writer, do you want to respond to these kinds of statements?

Everyone who is alive is participating in something. I'd like to think that strong art makes us more attentive to the world around us. For my money, that is as ambitious as you can be, politically speaking, as a writer or a reader.

Does your commitment to art that makes us more attentive affect your life as a university professor? You've mentioned your students . . . Do you teach creative writing? I know you teach literature . . .

I do both. I teach one fiction workshop a year since we started the MFA program at Temple, about twenty-five years ago. So I've been doing it all that time. I bracket my own aesthetic leanings when I teach a workshop. My concerns as a workshop leader are very pragmatic—to make the student self-conscious about what he or she is doing so that they can, like the good Beckett character, go on. In my workshop experience, I've found that students who want to be writers are tempted to want a template. I try to discourage this orientation.

They want to be taught . . .

Again, what matters is thinking and knowing what you're thinking. This is a kind of cognitive vigilance that the workshop experience can cultivate. I do think that fiction is a kind of métier for enhancing powers of attention to the world. We are not just agents. Rather, we need to be able to give good accounts of ourselves as agents, sharable accounts—which means that we hold ourselves accountable to other people too.

Do you want to talk about your work with Fiction Collective Two?

Sure.

Is The Inquisitor's Tongue *also published with FC2?*

Yes, I've published almost everything with FC2. The press has been a great support for writers like me who don't inhabit obvious market niches. Even more importantly, the single editorial priority at FC2 is the authoritativeness of the act of imaginative invention. There is no kowtowing to ideas of public taste or current events. My friends and colleagues who publish in more commercial presses often complain that they don't have the experience of working with editors and production staff who are engaged with the work itself, the ideas animated within it. They get dictated to a lot about the pressures of the marketplace, especially these days. I used to think I was just an endangered species; now I think that I am a protected endangered species, whereas many people I know who publish with other presses have really taken hits. Either they've been dropped or they've been chided or controlled and redirected by editors and also by public relations people who have a bigger and bigger role in the whole enterprise now.

Do you think that that has an impact on the kind of fiction published in this country?

That FC2 does?

No, I mean the general pragmatics of publishing in the United States. Sometimes critics forget that there is a practical reality to publishing.

No doubt. I don't deny the economic realities. But I think that there is less and less published and less variety in what's published within the mainstream. In a way, filmmakers have suffered more dramatically than writers because filmmakers are prisoners of a more onerous economy. Can you imagine Godard making films like he made in the sixties and seventies today? He is making films actually, but Hollywood is now global, so there is very little out there that gets distribution on big screen. Although I was surprised last summer that the Malick film *The Tree of Life*, which, I think, is a real feat of invention, was in theatre for a really long time. Did you see it?

I missed that. I have an eleven-month-old, so my movie life has been reduced!

I know, I know! It's out in DVD now, but you'd have to get a really big screen for it. It's one of those movies that makes you, like any good work of art, ask the question, "So what is a movie?" I also think fiction writers are striving to pose this question with respect to novels and short stories. But *The Tree of Life* got really wide distribution. I saw it a couple of times with strange audiences. I went once to a suburban mall and went with people between sixty and eighty, and I thought, *they are not going to sit through this*. And they sat through the whole thing, and when the film was over they were absolutely silent. No one was talking. And they really sat in their seats for a while. How did this happen? So maybe this is proof that there is a wider market for art than its purveyors imagine.

Talking about visual arts, you mentioned that you're currently working theoretically on visual arts and you also have in the past.

Yes, in the book on self-deception, there are chapters on painters.

As a fiction writer, would you also want to explore that?

I started out going to film school in UCLA, and then I got really disenchanted in film school, so I started writing fiction.

What about the burst of new technology, new media literature, is this something that changes the ways in which you think of writing?

It probably does. Someone like Peter Greenaway is working now in so many different modes—video, on-site projection, CD-ROM. His last project, which was a multifilm project on both DVD and CD-ROM insists upon unexpected continuities between the visual sense and literary sense-making. I don't think that this insight is necessarily new for writers. But I do think this kind of multimedia project gives some stimulus to those aspects of writing that keep us attuned to the reciprocity that plays between sense experience and self-explanation.

But would you be interested yourself in doing projects like this, or something that does not "look" like a traditional book—especially now that I know you have a film background?

Well, I hope that my work is already inflected with that kind of experimentation. The interest in new perceptual possibilities has always been there for me. Maybe some of it came out of my interest in film and things I saw filmmakers doing in the sixties and seventies but then were lost and are now coming back in the eyes of video artists, painters, people doing computer animation.

works cited

Singer, Alan. *Aesthetic Reason: Artworks and the Deliberative Ethos*. University Park: Penn State P, 2003. Print.

———. *The Charnel Imp*. New York: Fiction Collective Two, 1988. Print.

———. *Dirtmouth*. Tallahassee: Fiction Collective Two, 2004. Print.

———. *The Inquisitor's Tongue*. Tuscaloosa: Fiction Collective Two, 2012. Print.

———. *Memory Wax*. Normal: Fiction Collective Two/Black Ice Books, 1996. Print.

———. *A Metaphorics of Fiction: Discontinuity and Discourse in the Modern Novel*. Tallahassee: Florida State UP, 1984. Print.

———. *The Ox-Breadth*. New York: New Earth Books, 1978. Print.

———. "Reasonable Imaginings: Learning From Imagination." *Symploke: An Interdisciplinary Journal of Theory* 16.1–2 (2009): 227–40. Print.

———. *The Self-Deceiving Muse: Notice and Knowledge in the Work of Art*. University Park: Penn State P, 2010. Print.

———. *The Subject as Action: Transformation and Totality in Narrative Aesthetics*. Ann Arbor: U of Michigan P, 1994. Print.

Spinoza, de Benedict. *Ethics: Part II*. 1677. Print.

further work by alan singer

———. "Fiver Chambered Heart"; "Audience" (Excerpts from *Play,* a novel in progress). *Contemporary Fiction after Literature: New Essays*. Ed. Daniel T. O'Hara and Gina MacKenzie. Evanston: Northwestern UP, forthcoming 2018.

steve tomasula

STEVE TOMASULA IS A PROFESSOR OF ENGLISH AT NOTRE DAME UNIVERSITY. HE IS THE AUTHOR OF *VAS: AN OPERA IN FLATLAND* (2004), *THE BOOK OF PORTRAITURE* (2006), *TOC* (2009), *IN & OZ* (2012), AND *ONCE HUMAN: STORIES* (2014). HE RECEIVED THE MARY SHELLEY AWARD FOR OUTSTANDING FICTIONAL WORK, THE IOWA PRIZE FOR MOST DISTINGUISHED WORK PUBLISHED IN ANY GENRE, AND WAS NAMED A HOWARD FELLOW IN 2010. HE IS THE EDITOR OF *HERE·NOW: THE ANTHOLOGY OF PROSE, POETRY, FOUND, VISUAL, E- & OTHER HYBRID WRITINGS AS CONTEMPORARY, CONCEPTUAL ART* (UNIVERSITY OF ALABAMA PRESS).

IN MARCH 2006, Steve Tomasula was invited to Florida State University to read from his then-recently published novel, *The Book of Portraiture* (2006). At the time, I was both writing on and teaching *VAS: An Opera in Flatland* (2004) to a class of undergraduate students in a contemporary American literature course. Tomasula visited my class and answered students' questions about the novel. In the classroom, as in the interview, he was extremely generous with insights and anecdotes, making the intricate issues of the evolution of the body and writing accessible and fascinating to a group of non-English majors. The centerpieces of the interview, recorded after class, are *VAS* and *The Book of Portraiture* as they relate issues of body representations and modification, which were the focus of my research at the time.

VAS is the result of the collaboration between Tomasula and graphic designer Stephen Farrell. The novel is composed of a collage of documents about eugenics; tables of comparisons of cranial measurements and Miss America measurements since 1921; medical imaging; egg and sperm commercialization websites; IQ tests; biology patents; excerpts from anatomy, history, and natural history books; aesthetic surgery advertisements; newspaper articles; and a twenty-five page reproduction of chromosome 12 code. These documents interrelate with the life of Square, a writer whose wife suggests that he have a vasectomy after she has a miscarriage and an abortion.

As Tomasula reveals in the interview, his research on bodily and writerly materiality has led him to envision the body of books—their physical existence in the world—as a metaphor for the human body. Many of Tomasula's fictions point out that both the body of texts and human bodies are constantly reshaped, modified, and "edited," thereby asking questions about embodiment and materiality in the physical realm of the body and in the intellectual realm of writing and reading. *The Book of Portraiture,* of which *VAS* should have been the last chapter, focuses on such questions while exploring the relationship between textual and visual productions. The novel is "a postmodern epic in writing and images" about how we represent ourselves, thereby shaping the definitions of humanity ("Steve Tomasula"). Both novels reveal that what we fail to acknowledge may be more damaging: they make visible the pagination of fiction, the contexts of publications, the manipulative abilities of media, the reshaping of former media, and the ways in which all of these questions also apply to our lives.

This interest in the media of writing is in line with Tomasula's early experiments with multimedia fiction, such as "Dog" (2000) and "C-U-See-Me" (2000). His essays on genetic art ("Gene(sis)" and "Genetic Art and the Aesthetics of Biology") and on the relationship between image and text in contemporary writing ("Art in the Age of the Individual's Mechanical Reproduction") also illuminate the impact of technology on our lives. Tomasula's new media novel *TOC* (2009) invites readers to reconsider myths about religion, culture, truth, politics, and ethics. The novel presents an assemblage of text, film, music, photography, spoken words, animation, and painting about our conception and experience of time—the invention of the second, the beating of a heart, humans' spiritual and everyday use of time, and the history of their past and future ("Steve Tomasula").

The following interview was recorded during Tomasula's visit in Tallahassee; it takes up issues of gender, bodily representations, social paradigms and biases, control and power, and the ways in which these social matters interrelate with fiction. His comments about the state of the body and the book in the twenty-first century are eye opening and invigorating. The interview was updated via e-mail in 2016, thus offering information on Tomasula's more recent publication, *Once Human* (2014). His continued research on the materiality of the text in a wide range of literary media is fascinating, especially as we see the different steps of this research unravel in the following discussion.

•

Let's start with your working methods. I realize that you do a lot of research for your books, and I was wondering if you start with an idea and then do the research, or if the research is the first step and then you frame it into something you want to do artistically.

A bit of both. In general, the rapture of research becomes more focused as the book takes shape. I got the idea for one chapter in *The Book of Portraiture*, for example, by watching a bank of video screens monitoring the comings and goings in an office building. After a while, you start to see connections between the various people that come in and out of the cameras' field of vision. Sometimes, the connections are real: a woman might be talking to a man as if she's his boss, and it turns out she really is. Sometimes, the connections are only fictions you've made up, maybe based on appearance or body language, maybe without realizing it. It occurred to me that this bank of video monitors was a kind of portrait of the people being videotaped but also of a society that uses technology, here the tools of surveillance, to shape narratives about its people. But a paintbrush is also a technology. So is writing. And a chromosome stain of someone's DNA. And the different ontologies implied by the kinds of portraits that can be made with particular tools become apparent when they are put next to each other. So I began to focus on a range, from the invention of writing to the expression of a person's genetic code. *VAS*, which takes up the latter in more depth, was originally supposed to be the last chapter of *The Book of Portraiture*—so in my mind they are sort of a single novel, a kind of history of representation, especially in terms of the political or philosophical consequences that emerge from the way we represent people and how our representations shape our lives and the lives of others. Across both novels I dip into different moments of history to explore what it means to depict people in video or paint or photography or writing or data. . . . And the way our means of depiction keep changing, and so what gets depicted keeps changing—especially our conceptions of the self.

A poet once told me she envied novelists because they only have to come up with one idea every five years, and I think in my case it was only one idea, period. But it seems to be an idea that's rich enough to keep turning over. When I was writing the psychoanalyst's chapter in *The Book of Portraiture*, I visited a medical library quite a bit because their archives had a great collection of journals from the turn of the century. It was fascinating to read across the years and see how conventions, like citing references, developed and how these citations eventually replaced the anecdotes about patients that doctors used to share in these journals as a way to help each other explain things they were seeing independently in their offices. It was like watching these anecdotes—medical "folk tales," really—evolve into footnotes, and then cross-referencing, and eventually the documentation system journals use today that allow knowledge to come into existence via the creation of its paper trail. How do we know what we know? I realized that I was looking at an epistemology coming into being, and so that became part of the story I was telling in the novel, especially the way one epistemology evolves into another and some assumptions embodied in a way of life rise to dominate while others fade: the notion that women are essentially underdeveloped men, for example, like in the way doctors in these journals depicted "diseases of the nerves": hysteria in women or shell shock in soldiers, that sort of thing. For the contemporary chapters, the research became more "journalistic," like hanging out with people doing corporate surveillance; I spent lots of hours in a lab genetically sequencing flies; the doctors and technicians in another medical research lab let me sit in on experimental surgeries. I thought I'd just be a fly on the wall, you know, an observer, but these places are always understaffed, so they started asking me to do things, like hand them a scalpel, or whatever, and I ended up helping with some of the low-level tasks. One study involved genetically engineering blood vessels that would grow around a blocked artery. As part of the study, the lab technicians were putting stitches in the aortas of rats to simulate strokes, and I got pretty good at sewing the rats back up after their operations. So the research, like the writing, takes a lot of different forms, and morphs as the novels develop.

It's interesting that you mention journalism because you've also written articles on eugenics and art. What is it in your fiction that you're trying to do differently, or how do you differentiate your different projects?

Trying out an idea, or a way to write about it, in a short story or essay is a great way to think through approaches or themes that I'm thinking about exploring in a longer work: body or genetic art, for example, subjects I've written essays on. The constraints of a short story or essay can be a great clarifier. But then, of course, on a larger canvas like a novel you've got a lot more freedom. You can combine types of writing—the journalism, or a comic book, or opera libretto—you can do what the essay can't—express things that are hard, or even impossible, to put in a declarative fashion—to give a sense of something that might lie beyond expression—the millennium of chance events that have led to us having this conversation, for example.

So that one is feeding the other. Readers realize that a book like VAS *is a very informative book, and that might be unusual when dealing with fiction.*

Novels can be many things, of course: theory or entertainment, commercial product or class or ethnic story, personal or cultural memory. . . . Maybe the best novels are all of these. But I think my novels have the most affinity with those that try to understand the world through the languages we use to describe it: poems, songs, comic books, math equations. . . . Each represents an aspect of the world in ways that are inaccessible to the others. I mean, I can represent a circle by drawing it on a blackboard or by using a CAD program, by writing *circle*, or $A = \pi r^2$. Each is a representation but also more than a representation, the way my composer in *IN & OZ* reads music to imagine songs that can't actually be heard: a note so low that it could only be heard by whales. I mean we can naïvely draw circles and use them to build bridges, or we can step back and ask what do we mean by a 'circle'? What's left out? Or assumed? Or said between the lines? To get to this question it's often important to think through the language of science, technology, laws, social customs, or assumptions. . . . I call *VAS* a novel mainly because the novel is that category that's baggy enough to include all these different ways of speaking.

You compare VAS *to a body. Would you differentiate body art from a book like* VAS?

For sure. Body artists like Orlan literally use their bodies as their medium, but I'm only using the body of the book. Besides subject matter, the body, there is an overlap in the way we both consider the materials of our art inherent to the message. I really try to make books that are material objects. I want to write novels that can't be made into a movie without destroying what's primary to the novel: its own medium of language, especially language embodied. I don't mean that too literally because any idea can be translated: a song translated into the visual language of a painting (see Godard's *Goodbye to Language*). But from the start, the body of *VAS* was important to its story. I wanted the book to be a real object in the world just as a body exists in the world. A simple thing to say. But a lot of times we think of novels as a sort of dream that readers inhabit. Entertainment. Or escapism. But our stories have consequences. People get sent to gas chambers because of words, because of fictions. I can't think of anything more real than *that*. But commercial culture tries to make the novel into a form of entertainment. Something less than it can be. Novels should be entertaining—I don't want to make these mutually exclusive categories—but at the same time I'd like my novels to be more than just entertainment, and for me this has always meant taking the body of the book seriously: that is, turning the same kind of attention I try to bring to the narrative to the book carrying this narrative instead of treating it as if it's a crystal goblet, as one designer famously put it, meaning that the layout of a book should be invisible to readers: so unnoticeable that it is transparent as crystal, and into this form the contents of the book will be poured, the way we can pour any story into any Kindle. That is, my own poetics—the attention on narrative as a confluence of discursive objects—necessarily includes the book being used to express it.

I try to use the book as both metaphor *and* material—language as material, of course, but also its embodiment. The role of form is probably even more evident in my novel *TOC* because it's a work of electronic fiction. But to me, even though it was published on DVD (and rereleased on iPad), it always was a book—it just happened to be a book in which words could morph, or sing. The real difference is that *TOC* is a story about time, and so I wanted to use "time" as one of the materials: I tried to use the clock inside the computer along with the language, visuals, music, programming, and other elements as I tried to use the book that is *VAS* as a metaphor for the body and the body as a metaphor for the book. That is, *VAS* is very much about making the metaphor of the "body as a text" literal: we're literally editing the ABCs—the AGCTs—of DNA and creating a type of writing that is an entity in itself and has very real consequences for us and future generations. So I guess the short answer is, in terms of body art and the body *of* the book, I was hoping that readers would start to see the body as a book by being aware of the fact that they were reading a book that has a body.

You write that you are interested in "the materiality of the text: the stuff available for a writer to sculpt into the narrative" ("Narrative + Image"). Does this kind of writing, one that pays attention to the materiality of the text, provoke a different reading? What kind of reading would that be?

A reading that includes materials. That sees "things" as part of the conversation. A reading that can look at a protractor used to measure the slope of a forehead, for example, and see it as both a semiotic object and a scientific instrument: a material poem that embodies a way of life, as does an ancient Greek urn, or a scan sheet used in an IQ test. I hope it's also a reading that sees the novel itself as a material object, maybe one that gathers and reframes these objects, especially discursive objects—words or ideas that are both real entities and the products of narrative. Poets do this all the time. To be a poet you have to think of form, even if it's only where to break a line. Yet I do realize that these books ask people to read in ways they might not have practiced before. Much of *VAS* is lineated prose, and much of its language has affinities with poetic language, and of course the play of different genres and images is important to the story. There is a linear, plot-driven story at its heart, but it's contained within a cloud of other narratives that keep recontextualizing it, or complicating it, or turning it back on itself so that the overall story—what I would think of as the real story—emerges from the interaction of all the other little histories and stories and images that *VAS* contains. It's realism, in other words. It's really not so different from thinking about the "story" of a day by considering one day's newspaper as being made up of hundreds of little stories—the ads and sports reports and celebrity gossip and stock reports and weather and lots of little things that were separate until they were gathered together but also the story of how all these little stories came to be and came to be gathered into the metastory that we call "the news." That's why I've tried to incorporate signposts for how to read. The collages that make up one passage, for example, have big bold headings above them inviting readers to just keep turning pages if they want to. Or, I hope these directions say, it's okay to wander down into the swamp of micronarratives that's at the bottom of the page the way some people read all the footnotes and others skip them or only dip into the notes when something in the body text motivates them. We're living in this sea of information, and trying to make sense of it is a lot closer to what living is like than having it laid out for us in a linear fashion. But I guess I'm trying to have it both ways, or at least give an intimation of this more chaotic, messy sea of information we live within. Readers can wander some of the labyrinths of language I've set up, but they don't have to to enjoy the book or to get what it's about.

Do you consider your work to be a feminist work?

To be honest, I was a little surprised by the number of times critics, or reviewers, or others kept bringing this up. I'm glad it can be read this way, and I can see why: my fiction has a number of female protagonists—a manga artist in "The Color of Flesh"; a biologist creating an embryo as art in "Self Portrait(s)," for example (gathered in *Once Human: Stories*), though the themes aren't as consciously feminist as fiction by Kathy Acker, Carole Maso, or Debra Di Blasi, and others. Still, there's a strong affinity between feminist theory and the philosophical images I was working with. The main narrator of *TOC* is pregnant and so very aware of how time is embodied by her flesh while her husband lies in a coma—a kind of timelessness. The role of the male gaze sort of haunts *The Book Portraiture* in that women are continually misread, or reduced to objects by their depictions, but it's also about how all representation turns its subject into objects: we live under continual pressure to create portraits of each other based on our shopping habits or Yelp check-ins—I'm thinking of data mining here—that is, the male gaze reduces women to objects but it also transforms the gazer into a kind of Medusa—a monster turning others into stone by the way they're looked at. Now replace Medusa with computers running algorithms—turning people into data points. There are no women in the beginning of *The Book of Portraiture* because our history is one in which women were often erased, and the novel points this out since it is as much about the writing of history as it is "historical." In one chapter, Velázquez, the narrator, mentions that he has a wife and slave, two presences that are nowhere else in his narrative though they surely had a profound effect in shaping it. Yet, they're invisible to the reader, and I have him bring them up as a way to suggest the many forces shaping a narrative or life story that aren't acknowledged. Forces that are invisible to not just the readers but to Western society—think of the Western cannon, for example: it's our history of writing that for the longest time seemed to think women authors didn't exist, at least not until feminist critics began writing women back into this story. *The Book of Portraiture* consciously ends with a Middle Eastern point of view: an Arab who is a conglomeration of several Arabs I knew while I lived in the Middle East, people who, with varying degrees of persuasion, could imagine how someone could use their body as a statement by strapping a bomb to it and walking into a crowd of what they saw as oppressors. This story alternates with that of a genetic artist, who is also, not coincidently, a woman. An artist who adopts genes as her medium. That's the arc that I wanted the book to take—that's one of its threads, anyway—where people who are invisible at the start of the novel at least get a say, if not the last word, at the end. Even if they speak by using their bodies, it's sort of an inversion of how their bodies had previously been equated with speech as a way to suppress them. The Freudian misreading of a female patient in the middle chapter is the hinge between the two ends of the narrative: it's the moment when women start to appear in the book. But they appear as "text" to be read or, rather, misread—in a way that I hope comes across as funny because it is absurd, really. It's only as the plot unfolds that they begin to write.

So you see The Book of Portraiture *as an archaeology?*

The colored pages in *The Book of Portraiture* are an effort to imply this. In the first chapter, the tan pages are supposed to evoke the sand that the narrator is writing in with his finger. In the last chapter, the chapter with the genetic artist, the same color is supposed to evoke skin. We (the book designer Robert Sedlack and I) were trying to pick a color that would stand in for different things in different points of the book: an artist sketchbook in one chapter, old faded photographs in another. When the novel is closed, the different shades of tan pages look like strata in an archaeological dig. The lower layers give shape to those that come after, even as those latter layers bury those that come before. I'm very indebted to Foucault, especially his *Archaeology of Knowledge*.

Something that is surprising about VAS *is that, through the different quotes and the different references in the footnotes, the reader feels an ethical urgency, but the ethical statement is never quite there. Were you, as the author, intending to make an ethical statement? Why do you choose to "force" the reader to make connections on his or her own? What does the narrator (or even the author) think? The reader is invited to ponder on many ethical questions, but there is no authorial presence saying, "This is how we should react to the fact that these things are happening right now."*

The Truth! The Truth! Why can't you simply tell the Truth instead of these elaborate fictions? That's the question put to all novels, isn't it? I think that's why there's so much science in my novels: because increasingly scientific objectivity is being equated with the truth—the way to understand the world and ourselves. So scientific studies and results make really great test cases for what we mean by 'the truth.' I'm reminded of your earlier question about information in my novels, and also why science is so successful: because it only takes on questions that can be answered scientifically. Which is another way of saying, why is literature such a perpetual failure? Because it only takes on questions that can't be answered scientifically, that is, objectively or definitively: love, the human condition. . . . The failure of language to provide definitive answers, or even expression, is one of the great themes of literature—and philosophy, for that matter. But of course thinking in terms of success or failure is probably beside the point. For, after we describe, scientifically, how the universe works, then what? That is, there's this continual pressure to describe us "objectively"—through algorithms or metrics: who we are based upon our shopping, income, word-clouds, "friends," their likes. . . . But someone has to write these algorithms; someone has to decide which metrics to gather; someone has to interpret, for example, data like the number of times we attend a church versus a bar versus a shooting range versus a peace rally. . . . In other words, no amount of facts can substitute for the subjective judgments that go into their creation or use. So if there's an argument in the novel, it's along those lines: the failure of language, or the effort to step outside of our moment and understand it and ourselves. We can say that Lincoln, for example, was able to step outside of his moment and rise above slavery. But this also seems like a simplification and also a retrospective, revisionist, view of what his moment was actually like. One thing seems sure: the answer isn't to forsake ambiguity or subjectivity. That's the lesson from Orwell's *1984* or the example of any totalizing narrative, whether it comes from a dictatorship, system of apartheid, or Disneyland. They all try to control interpretation.

The novel has always seemed like one of the ways we have to protect this mental space. I like to begin with some idea that seems loopy to us—like phrenology, for example, or trying to cure hysteria by giving women electric shocks—and then, by degrees, bringing readers around to a point where they have to ask themselves, "Why is this crazy, again?" Burning a heretic might be based on ignorant, naïve, misogynist, or racist premises. But the logic is often tight. And codified as law. Or custom.

Recognizing this allows the past to shed light on the present because a lot of those crazy, outdated ideas extend into our own time, though we often don't recognize them as such because they've evolved into a form that's familiar and so makes sense to us and so is acceptable and so is invisible. To us. The metaphor of archeology or cities built onto older, buried cities applies here. Take phrenology, the belief that a trained scientist could determine a person's intelligence or moral character by reading the bumps on his or her skull. It sounds nuts to us, but essentially what they were saying was that different parts of the brain were responsible for different kinds of thought—an idea that is very much alive in the brain scans read by cognitive scientists. I'm not equating the two, but the mistake of the phrenologists was to give their readings of bumps too literal an interpretation, and I wonder if there isn't a lesson there for cognitive scientists, who, given the hundred years or so that exist between us and phrenologists, will probably seem just as antiquated to future generations. In *The Book of Portraiture,* one narrator uses electricity to stimulate nerves to cure hysteria or shell shock—diseases that seem like screwy fictions to us but show up later in the book as post-traumatic stress disorder.

Anyway, we got sidetracked there. Part of *The Book of Portraiture,* and *VAS,* for that matter, is this recognition that the world is always changing as are our ways of knowing it. We can't help but be postmodern because we live in a world that includes global economies; the logic of cut-paste-and-burn; the thinking of Foucault and jihad—all the ways of thinking that make the world postmodern. Moderns couldn't live in a world that never heard of Freud and Marx, and people at the time couldn't live in a nonmodern world, even if they never heard of these thinkers. After 9/11, lots of commentators declared an end to the age of irony and postmodernism in general: yet, the attack on the World Trade Center was a kind of Pearl Harbor in a postmodern war: it was waged by a group of individuals who were capable of DIY destruction on a level that only nations could have achieved in the past. They did it by manipulating the postmodern infrastructure we've created: the access that cash buys to anything in a capitalist democracy, including 747 flight simulators; global networks allowed it to be funded by transfers from foreign countries to any neighborhood via ATMs; the attack was coordinated over cell phones, and so forth. What followed was a battle over the narrative, and Bush's totalizing propaganda machine won. Every age makes certain things possible, and these possibilities bring about certain assumptions or habits of mind and living (think of the lines at airport security now) while leaving others behind. It's hard to see this, though, while they are still developing around us.

I think that given the outrageous quotes that appear in VAS (and the juxtapositions of some of these quotes), we cannot help but ponder about what's influencing our conclusions and about authorial intent. We wonder why the page is organized in this way, what the role of juxtaposition and pagination is, why the narrator is not *commenting on the shocking content of the book.*

As the painter Diego Velázquez tells the Inquisition in *The Book of Portraiture,* just putting objects into an order is to comment about them. I'm sure it's informed by my own biases and a white, male perspective and all that goes along with being born at a particular time at a particular place. You're completely right; I do want to call attention to the fact that these things are not givens, nor do they grow on trees, that is, are natural. There's a reason we are speaking English instead of French: Napoleon initially didn't want to sell half the continent to the United States. He'd sent an army to defend New Orleans. But malaria wiped them out. So we're speaking English today partly because Napoleon's troops didn't have mosquito nets. I've just made a cartoon, I know, but one with an element of truth I hope comes through in the novels: to call attention to ourselves, our culture, and to consider how it is constructed, or rather emerges out of lots of lower-level actions, and, today, how much of that construction or emergence is being directed, or framed, in the language of very powerful commercial entities. If there's a political stance in *The Book of Portraiture* and *VAS,* it's to ask the reader to step back and recognize the fact that very powerful interests are investing a lot of effort to get us to think of ourselves, our privacy, our bodies in ways that serve their interests; ours, not so much. One of the ideas that circulates through *VAS* is the way that we demonize Hitler, and rightfully so, but the danger in demonizing Hitler is to not recognize how "natural" it was for him to put the extermination of "undesirables" into play. The novel asks us to remember that Germany was only like the eleventh industrialized nation to legalize the elimination of "undesirables"—it took twenty years before the Nazis got around to it. So I put a quote by Hitler next to one by Winston Churchill—both of which basically make the same claim—in the hopes that a third thing will emerge: the commonness of the assumptions that much of the industrialized world was operating under, the banality of it all, the casualness with which entire populations were being discounted via policies as systematic as screening out "inferior" "races" at Ellis Island to those as local and ad hoc as the judging of the "fitness" of families at state fairs, as if they were cattle: a precursor to the Miss America contest....

And that's shocking!

Right, and it's partly because we think it's something that *they* did, not us. Our role gets buried. When the German government was looking for a way to set up a legal system where it could selectively, but legally, get rid of people, they copied an Indiana law. The Germans called it "The Indiana Ideal" because Indiana politicians, social workers, and lawyers had figured out how to say that some people were undesirables and that the state had an obligation to get rid of them. But right away you see how vague that word *undesirable* is: it could be single mothers, alcoholics, homosexuals, sexually promiscuous people, the mentally or physically handicapped—you go down the list. Think about Victorian standards and their definition of what's right and moral and good, and anything that doesn't fit that definition is undesirable and therefore a threat to the gene pool, to society. That was the mindset at the time—and it didn't come from cranks or quacks—rather, it was people doing cutting-edge work in their fields. Dr. Moniz, the inventor of the lobotomy, got the Nobel Prize for this work.

Hitler brings all of this to one conclusion, and rightfully so the world is horrified by the Final Solution. Nevertheless, when you look up these old eugenics journals—medical journals devoted to how to improve the gene pool of a country, both by practices like selective breeding and the sterilization of undesirables—you'll see an interesting thing: right around 1945, when the extent of Hitler's atrocities are being exposed and eugenics suddenly gets a bad name, the titles of the journals change. But eugenics doesn't go away—the journals just change their names: they take on names that have words like "genetic counseling" instead of "eugenics" in their titles but the articles (the practice) essentially continues. It's the whole idea of how we create knowledge again, what comes to be considered "knowledge." And there's a real continuity in this body of knowledge that spans 1945. In no way am I equating what Hitler did to genetic counseling, but it's revealing to note how a line of thought continues living, only evolving into a commercial form. A woman, for example, might be required to have genetic counseling because her insurance company requires women of a certain age to have their fetuses screened—not out of any moral or Victorian concern for the hygiene of a gene pool but simply because accountants calculated that this is a way for insurance companies to maximize profits. The profit motive, instead of "inferior gene pools," is the story motivating our actions and thoughts today. In Bombay, a few years ago, 99 percent of the fetuses aborted were female. That says something about that society's values and assumptions and how a mindset can develop that allows a de facto eugenics program to emerge. The insurance companies I cited are just one node in a web of interests that create this "flatland" for *us,* the state of nature we live in. Is this good or bad? Obviously, medical advances and screening practices have made life better for a lot of people in a lot of ways. I'm just trying to step back and ask, for example, what sort of world are we bringing into existence by trading away privacy for the ease of using mobile phones or charge cards or any of these formations that can be used to portray us as nodes in a network? How has an attitude that sees the body as something that can be manipulated—and collaged and bartered and have artificial parts put in—changed? How has it changed what we now mean when we say "human"? It wasn't until the '70s that blood could be bought and sold, for example. Before that it was considered a "gift of life" that could be given but was illegal to sell. Now it's a billion-dollar industry, so obviously there's been a sea change in the way we think about our bodies, our selves. Some of the characters in *VAS,* and also in *The Book of Portraiture* and *Once Human,* recognize that the body isn't fate anymore, at least not in the way it would have been for their parents' generation. The idea of the posthuman has a lot of resonance for them. Being freed from the genetic destiny we were born with is very appealing—just ask anyone with a heart condition—but what do we begin to see when we look in the mirror? Or at others? Spare parts?

I think of Thomas Kuhn on this point: Galileo discovers moons orbiting Jupiter and realizes that the earth isn't the center of the universe. But Galileo's critics were at least partly right for refusing to look through his telescope to "see for themselves." Not because they were afraid of what they would see; rather, they were right to recognize that looking through a gadget to settle an ontological question would be a surrender. An admission that observation could trump faith. Not only that, to them, *Earth* meant "fixed center of the universe." Galileo was also asking them to cast aside the way the word *Earth* had been used for centuries, even if doing so meant that a way of life would also become passé, including the church, the center of culture, the political power that held empires together. If we think of it that way we can see how hard it would be for them to get their minds around the idea of earth being simply another planet. Similarly, that word *human* used to mean one thing to our fathers and mothers, but it can't mean the same thing to us, living as we do in a world where a child can be created from the sperm of one person, an egg from another, and developed in the womb of a third, rented by a fourth who contributed none of the other components.

You've been alluding to the fact that people in VAS—*and in your other books perhaps—are in this flatland, and you compare that to any society that isn't aware of its own constructions, the things that societies see as natural. In your books, you bring up these problems—the way we understand "human-ness," for example. On the other hand, we cannot be out of the flatland. So all literature can do is make us aware that that is happening; is that the intent?*

At least partly so, but isn't that a lot? In *Flatland,* Edwin Abbott has his character Square wonder what the phrase "Upward but not Northward" could mean. Remember, his Square (like mine) is a two-dimensional character: a figure drawn on a flat sheet of paper so he can't get his mind around the idea of a third dimension. This seemed like a perfect metaphor for the difficulty we have in imaging a world built on assumptions other than those that are so familiar that they seem natural. The sorts of existential crisis that moments like this can create have happened before: Galileo and his machine displace earth from the center of the universe; Darwin displaces humans from the center of the earth. And now the posthuman turn is causing us to reframe the individual. . . . Or less abstractly, think how war has almost become a state of nature for us in the United States and how it is baked into our economy; or consider how we talk on phones whose manufacture depends on virtual slaves, civil wars waged by child soldiers over conflict minerals and all the rest while we wonder how Germans could have gone along with things they knew were wrong. But who can really say what they would have done in the same position? Say it's for the good of the state? It's for the good of society? Not my problem? This war that's going on right now—the British medical journal *Lancet* reported something like 600,000 Iraqi civilians have been killed so far—in our name—so why are we talking about literature instead of rioting in the streets? It is what we should be doing, but we're not; we think it's somebody else's problem, or not my job. . . . We look the other way.

Or, what can you do?

Yeah, what can you do? Maybe be aware of how constructed everything we take for granted really is? In *IN & OZ,* the main character, Mechanic, is lying in sludge under a car, repairing a transmission, something he's done a thousand times before. But this time he sees how his life is reflected by the mesh of the transmission's gears. That is, he has this existential awaking in which he sees that the only reason he's a mechanic is because his father was a mechanic; a way of life that had once seemed so natural to him now suddenly appears to be completely arbitrary, an accident of birth, and I have to admit that at the time I was writing the novel I was thinking of my own neighborhood during the Vietnam War. Houses up and down our street had those pennants the military gave to the parents of soldiers (I think they have to buy them now). Some pennants had more than one star, meaning that the house had more than one kid in the military. If one of the kids got killed, their parents would get a gold star to paste onto the pennant. At the time, I assumed the whole country was full of houses with those flags. It was only much later, after going off to college and coming into contact with other people—wealthier kids—that I realized that the war was just something on TV for them. And it was a shock. I felt so stupid to not have realized this earlier. It was like having my eyes opened to the fact that whole classes of people are used as fodder to support the lifestyles of others—in wars, on factory floors, in mines, in lots of different ways that seem "normal" to the people who don't know any differently—which seems like an even greater example of mental blindness given the history of slavery in the United States and the case for reparations. I once saw a color-coded map that showed the distribution of diseases in America; that Southside of Chicago / Northwest, industrial corner of Indiana—where *IN & OZ* is set—had so many cancers that the colors just formed one black smudge on the map. Yet growing up there, the fact that we could tell which direction the wind was blowing by which oil refinery, soap factory, or steel mill it smelled like seemed normal to us.

I guess a hope of mine for *VAS, The Book of Portraiture, Once Human, IN & OZ, TOC,* and literature in general is that they can help teach people how to "see," that is, how to read. And by read I mean read narrative as a poet might read, to see what is really being said or the multiple things that are said by explanations and arguments that are really meant to sell or manipulate us. Every time I hear one of these simple-minded explanations for going to war or to vote against healthcare or any of the things people want us to do that are really not in the interests of being human, I think that one of the things reading literature can do is to teach us how to be aware of the ways rhetoric is used against us. *IN & OZ*—really all my novels—are partly about this relation between art and life—and by art I mean artifice, even if it's only a form of meditation, an attempt at self-awareness in the writing of the work and hopefully in the reading too. One book probably won't change anyone's life, but maybe together they might make someone ask why so much of Fox News's coverage of the war resembles the plot of a Rambo movie. Whose interests are being served by depicting this war as an action film with good guys (always us) and evildoers who rush to blow themselves up because they "hate freedom." If you can read, you can see. If you can't read, you can't see; but it helps if we make the creation of our stories visible.

works cited

Tomasula, Steve. "Art in the Age of the Individual's Mechanical Reproduction." *The New Art Examiner* 25.7 (1998): 18–23. Print.

———. *The Book of Portraiture: A Novel.* Design by Robert Sedlack. Tallahassee: Fiction Collective Two, 2006. Print.

———. "C-U-See-Me." "Steve Tomasula" N. p. 2000. Web. 3 Apr. 2016.

———. "Dog." "Steve Tomasula" N. p. 2000. Web. 3 Apr. 2016.

———. "Gene(sis)." *Data Made Flesh: Embodying Information.* Ed. Robert Mitchell and Phillip Thurtle. New York: Routledge, 2003. 249–57. Print.

———. "Genetic Art and the Aesthetics of Biology." *Leonardo* 35.2 (2002): 137–44. Reprinted in *Meta-Life: Biotechnologies, Synthetic Biology, ALife and the Arts.* Ed. Annick Bureaud and Roger Malina. Cambridge: Leonardo/ISAST and MIT Press, 2014. Print.

———. *IN & OZ.* Chicago: U of Chicago P, 2012. Print.

———. "Narrative + Image = Two Languages (in One Work) x Multiple Meanings [A Rationale for an Issue]." *Electronic Book Review.* N.p., Summer 1998. Web. 18 Feb. 2016.

———. *Once Human: Stories.* Design by Robert Sedlack and others. Tuscaloosa: Fiction Collective Two, 2014. Print.

———. "Steve Tomasula" (author's homepage). N.p., n.d. Web. 20 Feb. 2008.

———. *TOC: A New-Media Novel.* Design by Stephen Farrell. Animation by Matt Lavoy. Programing by Christian Jara. Tuscaloosa: Fiction Collective Two, 2009. DVD. Apple App Store. Vers. 1.1. 17 Apr. 2014. <https://itunes.apple.com/us/app/toc-a-new-media-novel/id547077664?mt=8>.

———. *VAS: An Opera in Flatland.* Design by Stephen Farrell. Chicago: U of Chicago P, 2004. Print.

further works by and on steve tomasula

Banash, David. *Collage Culture: Readymades, Meaning, and the Age of Consumption.* New York: Rodopi, 2013. Print.

———, ed. *Steve Tomasula: The Art and Science of New Media Fiction.* New York: Bloomsbury, 2015. Print.

Bauer, Sylvie. "Poets and Language Whores in *IN & OZ*, by Steve Tomasula." *Golden Handcuffs Review* 17 (Fall–Winter 2013–14): 193–204. Print.

Bettencourt, Sandra. "The Novel as Multimedia, Networked Book: An Interview with Steve Tomasula." *MATLIT: Revista do Programma de Doutoramento em Materialidades da Literature* 4.1 (2016). Web. 9 Mar. 2016.

Chevaillier, Flore. *The Body of Writing: An Erotics of Contemporary American Fiction.* Columbus: The Ohio State UP, 2013. Print.

Ciccoricco, David. "The Materialities of Close Reading: 1942, 1959, 2009." *Digital Humanities Quarterly* 1 (June 2012). Web. 9 Mar. 2016.

Elias, Amy J. "The Dialogical Avant-Garde: Relational Aesthetics and Time Ecologies in *Only Revolutions* and *TOC*." *Contemporary Literature* 53.4 (2012): 738–78. Print.

Ghosh, Shoba Venkatesh. "The Archeology of Representation in Steve Tomasula's *The Book of Portraiture*." *Electronic Book Review*. N.p., 1 Dec. 2013. Web. 9 Mar. 2016.

Gibbon, Alison. *Multimodality, Cognition, and Experimental Literature.* New York: Routledge, 2012. Print.

Gruszewska-Blaim, Ludmiła. "A (post-)novel?: 'VAS: An Opera in Flatland' by Steve Tomasula." *Canon Unbound*. Ed. Jadwiga Węgrodzka. Koszalin: Wydawnictwo Uczelniane Politechniki Koszalinskiej, 2011. 63–83. Print.

Have, J. "An Interview with Steve Tomasula." *Electronic Book Review*. N.p., 23 Aug. 2012. Web. 9 Mar. 2016.

Hayles, N. Katherine. *How We Think: Digital Media and Contemporary Technogenesis.* Chicago: U of Chicago P, 2012. Print.

Holland, Mary. *Succeeding Postmodernism: Signifying Families in Late Twentieth and Twenty-First Century American Fiction.* New York: Bloomsbury, 2013. Print.

Iuli, Cristina. "Playing with Codes: Steve Tomasula's *Vas, an Opera in Flatland*." *Writing Technologies: Representational and Literary Futures: American Writing in the New Millennium*. Ed. Tatiani G. Rapatzikou and Arthur Redding. Spec. issue of *Writing Technologies* 3 (2010): 64–85. Print.

Maziarczyk, Grzegorz. "Print Strikes Back: Typographic Experimentation in Contemporary Fiction as a Contribution to the Metareferential Turn." *The Metareferential Turn in Contemporary Arts and Media: Forms, Functions, Attempts at Explanation*. Ed. Werner Wolf. New York: Rodopi, 2011. 169–93. Print.

Pellegrin, Jean-Yves. "Tactics against Tic-Toc: Browsing Steve Tomasula's New Media Novel." *Études anglaises: Revue du monde Anglophone* 62.2 (2010): 174–90. Print.

Pérez, Emily. "Between the Looking Glasses: Self-Representation and the Represented Self." *American Letters & Commentary* 19 (2008): 136–41. Print.

Szilak, Illy. "Steve Tomasula's Brilliant Literary Time Machine." *The Huffington Post*. 14 Feb. 2014. Web. 9 Mar. 2016.

Tissut, Ann-Laure. "Signs of Time: VAS, A Story of Languages." *Science and American Literature in the 20th and 21st Centuries, from Henry Adams to John Adams*. Ed. Claire Maniez, Ronan Ludot-Vlasak, and Frédéric Dumas. Newcastle upon Tyne: Cambridge Scholars, 2012. 147–58. Print.

Tomasula, Steve. "Ars [telomeres] longa, vita [telomeres] brevis: Edunia & The Natural History of an Enigma." *The Association for the Study of the Arts of the Present Journal* 1.3 (2016): 289–311. Print.

———. "Code and New-Media Literature." *The Routledge Companion to Experimental Literature.* New York: Routledge, 2012. 483–96. Print.

———. "Emergence and Posthuman Narrative." *Flusser Studies: A Multilingual Journal for Cultural and Media Theory* (Spring 2010): n. pag. Web. 12 Mar. 2016.

———. "Information Design, Emergent Culture, and Experimental Form in the Novel." *The Routledge Companion to Experimental Literature*. Ed. Joe Bray, Alison Gibbons, and Brian McHale. New York: Routledge, 2012. 435–51. Print.

———. "Many Makers Make Baby Post: 40 Years of Reading 'The Babysitter.'" *The Review of Contemporary Fiction* 32.1 (2012): 219–34. Print.

———. "Nodes for a Posthuman Reading." *Théorie, Littérature, Epistémologie* 30 (2014): 11–25. Print.

———. "Our Tools Make Us (And Our Literature) Post." *Transatlantica*. Université Paris-Sorbonne. 30 Dec. 2014. Web. 3 Mar. 2016.

———. "Three Axioms for Projecting a Line or The Future of the Postmodern Novel." *The Review of Contemporary Fiction* 26.1 (1996): 100–108. Print.

———. *VAS: An Opera in Flatland, Cyborg Edition* (limited edition book, audio CD, and slipcase). Design by Stephen Farrell. Perf. Steve Tomasula, Christian Jara, Maria Tomasula, Paul Johnson, Paul Appleby, and Alloy Orchestra. Portland: Chiasmus Press, 2004. Print and CD.

———. "Visualization, Scale, and the Emergence of Posthuman Narrative." *Sillages critiques: Exposition/Surexposition* 17. Ed. Monica Michlin and Françoise Sammarcelli. Université Paris-Sorbonne. Dec. 2013. Web. 12 Mar. 2016.

Vanderborg, Susan. "Of Men and Mutations: The Art of Reproduction in Flatland." *Journal of Artist Books* 24 (2008): 4–11. Print.

Vincler, John M. "The Monstrous Book and the Manufactured Body in the Late Age of Print: Material Strategies for Innovative Fiction in Shelley Jackson's *Patchwork Girl* and Steve Tomasula's *VAS: An Opera in Flatland*." *Dichtung-Digital: A Journal of Art and Culture in Digital Media*. N.p., spring 2011. Web. 9 Mar. 2016.

afterword

IN THE INTRODUCTION to this book, I stressed authors' divergent views on the current status of innovative fiction. Yet, it becomes quite obvious, at the end of this interviewing process, that there are significant convergences in these authors' paths, choices, and interpretation of literary experimentation today. Therefore, I wish to focus on these convergences in conclusion to the discussions presented in *Divergent Trajectories*. The contributors to this volume question the nature of the book, and although each does so in his or her own way, the modes of experimentation displayed in the works of R. M. Berry, Debra Di Blasi, Percival Everett, Thalia Field, Renee Gladman, Bhanu Kapil, Michael Martone, Carole Maso, Joseph McElroy, Christina Milletti, Lance Olsen, Alan Singer, and Steve Tomasula delineate an aesthetic portrait of today's literary research. A thread between the interviews lies in the importance of the material medium of the book. The white page of Berry's *Frank*, Everett's *Walk to the Distance*, Field's *Point and Line*, Maso's *AVA*, and Olsen's *Head in Flames* comes to the forefront of what each books is, becoming part of the narration and of the questioning process of its own nature. The images in Di Blasi's *Skin of the Sun*, Everett's *The Water Cure*, Olsen's *Girl Imagined by Chance*, as well as in Tomasula's *VAS: The Book of Portraiture* and *TOC* are not mere illustrations; they unravel instead the materiality of the text, asking readers to (re)examine what fictions are made of and how books deliver these fictions. Thus, the old content versus form debate is revisited to shed light on the nature of the fictional medium itself. This overlapping concern for materiality among writers offers a new awareness of the problems of language as a medium.

This shared preoccupation for the question of mediation often correlates with a reflection on time and its treatment in narratives. In Tomasula's *TOC*, Everett's *The Water Cure*, and Maso's *AVA*, the exploration of time pushes the linearity of writing to an extreme limit. Kapil's experiment with the winterization of her manuscript impacts the form of the book that will ultimately end the process of its creation. Berry's research in a writing of the here and now sheds light on what literature of the present might be. Finally, the historical novels of Singer and Olsen reinvigorate the debates on the correlation between history and fiction.

These explorations of time often prompt writers to branch into various disciplines and media. The fictions of Olsen, Field, Kapil, and Singer engage in reflections on time and history, calling into question the notion of truth, authenticity, discourse, and fiction. Milletti's short stories pursue philosophical matters involving reality, truth, and logic. The books of McElroy and Tomasula explore the relationship between literature and science, weaving technical and fictional realms. The fictions of Di Blasi, Everett, Olsen, and Martone engage visual media, questioning the role of images, typefaces, and artistic designs in fiction. Di Blasi, Olsen, Martone, and Tomasula have also produced new media texts; for these writers, while literary innovation does not necessarily involve the meeting of new technologies and written texts, it can be part of the reflection on what the literary medium is. In other words, reading a new media book may reveal what a book has always been.

The body of the book, of the characters, and of the authors, comes into play in the questioning of this medium. Tomasula's body-texts are obvious examples of moments when the skin of the text and the skin of the body permeate. Gladman's exploration of the Ravic "language," which relies on the body's ability to communicate—physically—the messages to be conveyed, invites us to rethink the role of the body in verbal communications. Kapil's investigation of the inside and outside, the boundary between what is body and what is not, positions the text as a form of geographical or physical marker, a mode of verbal scarring. Likewise, Singer notes that he is interested in "the limits of the body, in the vulnerability of the body." The examination of these limits leads to an introspection of the reader's own body and its access and relationship to the words on the page. In Maso's work, the breathing body of Ava that punctuates her interrupted thoughts implies that the text, like the character, breathes in between our hands. The hybrid body of the scientist who became a machine in McElroy's *Plus* defamiliarizes our access to language. These bodily questions prompt a reflection on the nature of reading and writing; they are also often untangled with reflections on authorship.

The limits of authorship and of originality come into question in many of the works discussed in the volume. Di Blasi's experiments with Jirí's publications, all part of her production but published under Jirí or his associates' names, inquire about the confines of authorship. Field notes that she wrote a play using "a collage of [her] own writing, found text, and prompted collaboration with the actors," which implied that "authorship remained unglued from any single point, reusing information and forms in strange ways." Martone is known for playfully writing under aliases and even publishes under the names of current publishing authors. His use of disguises, alter egos, and pseudonyms mocks the notion of original authorship. These authorial experiments bring into question the parameters of writing and publishing, unsettling what we take for granted about writing, the author, and the materials that create a text.

In addition, while not all works presented in *Divergent Trajectories* make recent politics their central focus, many of the discussions presented here comment on the attacks of 9/11 and/or the wars and events that followed it; others wrote fictions that respond directly or indirectly to these events. In that sense, I would not classify the works of Berry, Di Blasi, Everett, Field, Gladman, Kapil, Martone, Maso, McElroy, Milletti, Olsen, Singer, and Tomasula as fictional reactions to the 9/11 attacks, but these authors seem to converge in their exploration of recent political decisions that, while not the motor of their writing, have been in the background of their artistic endeavors. The interviews of Tomasula and Maso address this matter more directly because they were initiated in 2006. Everett's character in *The Water Cure* comments virulently on the wrongs of the decisions made during the Bush presidency. Berry's interview also engages in this matter, referencing *Forms at War*'s contestation of "the false present of the Bush years": "*Forms at War* brings back what never went away. Its writing is the work we are" (back cover). In many ways, the exploration of what these works are is addressed implicitly in the interviews collected in this volume.

Thus, the authors presented here unite in a political engagement as it relates to the literature. They do not always contest past or current political endeavors, but their aesthetic experiments take a political stance. Field mentions that her writing is "political in that it relates to the affairs of groups." Maso notes that her writing is political "on a certain level, although not in the way one might conventionally define 'political.' It imagines a place of freedom, where one is not constricted by those models of selves and by already accepted versions of what one can be and what one should think and who one should listen to." Olsen writes: "My intention is that the aggregate unfurls into an exploration of art's purpose, religion's increasingly dominant role as engine of politics and passion, the involvedness of foreignness and assimilation, and, ultimately, the limits of tolerance." As these excerpts show, Field, Maso, and Olsen's relationship to the political and its definition may be different, but their writing is a form of aesthetic and political contest.

Clearly, Berry, Di Blasi, Everett, Field, Gladman, Kapil, Martone, Maso, McElroy, Milletti, Olsen, Singer, and Tomasula have diverse approaches to these political implications. Each work has its own texture, tone, theme, and formal concerns. Thus, my goal is not to imply that each writer's viewpoint, motivations, and literary productions are similar. After reading the thirteen discussions, it is interesting to note, however, some common threads that are emblematic of the persisting concerns of recent literary experimentations. Consequently, as I started insisting on the divergent trajectories of these authors, I end insisting on their convergent trajectories. In other words, while each interview has individual merit, read next to each other, these individual discussions shape an answer to the question "what is writing?" in the twenty-first century. The ways these authors conceive of their answer to this question in relation to each other also helps chart and define the evolution of innovative writing.

index

&NOW, 23, 144, 161
[[there.]] (Olsen), 181
[prompts], 56, 59

10:01 (Olsen), 181
1984 (Orwell), 206
9/11, 38, 206, 217

Aalto, Alvar, 176
Abbott, Edwin, 210
abstract, 12, 28, 50, 73, 78, 101, 105, 109–10, 119, 123, 131, 136, 185, 188, 191
Abstraktion und Einfühlung (Everett), 54
absurd, 6, 7, 71, 73, 121, 204
academia, 6, 20, 26, 39, 60, 88, 100, 121, 157, 163, 170, 171
Acker, Kathy, 62, 155–57, 159, 171, 175, 203
activist, 89, 132, 139, 167
Activist (Gladman), 79
Actress in the House (McElroy), 131–32, 135, 136, 138, 140, 142
Aeschylus, 62, 65
aesthetic, 1, 2, 14, 19, 29, 33, 38, 42, 100, 150, 158, 161–63, 166, 167, 169, 170, 173, 177, 193, 197, 215, 217, 218
Aesthetic Reason: Artworks and the Deliberative Ethos (Singer), 182–83, 195
Afternoon: A Story (Joyce, Michael), 175
agency, 49, 131, 183, 192, 193
agon, 62–63
AIDS, 82, 114
Alexie, Sherman, 51

Ali, Ayaan Hirsi, 173
Alice through the Looking Glass (Carroll), 90
alienation, 5, 12, 70
Alive and Dead in Indiana (Martone), 97, 108, 111
alternative modes of writing, 3, 19, 20, 87, 158, 162, 167
ambiguity, 10, 30, 127, 135, 206
American Desert (Everett), 54
American Woman in the Chinese Hat, The (Maso), 114–15, 125, 128
Ana Patova Crosses a Bridge (Gladman), 70, 72, 74, 77–78
Ancient History: A Paraphase (McElroy), 130, 132, 133, 139, 142
Andreas-Salomé, Lou, 161
animal, 32, 67–68
animation, 107, 195, 198
anthropology, 6, 91, 164
anticolonial, 82, 84, 85. *See also* colonial
Anxious Pleasures: A Novel after Kafka (Olsen), 160, 161, 164, 180
Anything Now Gone (Di Blasi), 25, 27
appropriation, 4, 31, 38, 176, 178
arab, 173, 204
archeology, 65, 206
architecture, 25, 27–29, 56, 66, 71–73, 77, 92, 172, 176–77
Architectures of Possibility: After Innovative Writing (Olsen), 181
Aristophanes, 65
Arlem (Gladman), 79

219

art, 2–3, 19, 23–26, 39, 41, 49, 58, 60, 65, 66, 68, 93, 98, 105, 106, 114, 122, 128, 147, 172–73, 179, 183, 192, 194, 198, 211–12, 218; abstract, 109; body, 200–203; book, 3, 56, 116; earth, 86, 164; visual, 1, 2, 3, 23–26, 122, 154, 184, 194
Art Lover, The (Maso), 114, 122–23, 128, 129
artifact, 38, 57, 80, 103, 179, 183, 186, 190
artist, 3, 23, 29, 35, 59, 64, 66–68, 96, 111, 117, 122, 156, 164–65, 176–78, 180, 184, 191, 195, 201, 203–4
Ashbery, John, 183
Ashley, Robert, 59
Association for the Study of the Arts of the Present, 183–84
Assumption (Everett), 41, 53
audio, 3, 25, 38, 39, 100
Aureole: An Erotic Sequence (Maso), 115, 124, 128
author, 2–4, 7, 11, 26, 48, 57, 62–64, 68, 75, 81, 97–98, 107–8, 110, 131, 153, 157, 162, 167, 176, 183, 189, 204–5, 215–18; death of, 98. See also authorship
authorship, 4, 23, 24, 66, 98, 107–8, 176, 217
AVA (Maso), 114–15, 117–20, 122–23, 125, 128–29
avant-garde, 4, 20, 21, 41, 145, 156, 162, 172, 191, 213
avant-pop, 160, 175, 180

Bacon, Francis, 184
Bakhtin, 65–66
Balzac, Honoré de, 44, 180
Barnes, Djuna, 150, 188
Barth, John, 155, 166
Barthelme, Donald, 100, 166
Barthes, Roland, 44–45, 169
Bataille, Georges, 169
Bauer, Sylvie, 51, 54, 212
Baumbach, Jonathan, 168
beauty, 19, 26, 37, 49, 67, 107, 117, 119, 123, 145, 164, 174, 176
Beauty Is Convulsive: The Passion of Frida Kahlo (Maso), 115, 128
Beckett, Samuel, 6, 10, 18, 64, 74, 125, 148, 168, 177, 180, 189, 193
Beloved (Morrison), 174
Benjamin, Walter, 66
Bernhard, Thomas, 158

Bernheimer, Kate, 40, 168
Bernstein, Charles, 175
Berry, R. M., 1–4, 5–22, 54, 129, 159, 168, 180, 215–18
Bervin, Jen, 175
Big Picture (Everett), 54, 55
biography, 57, 61, 98, 165; auto, 91, 93, 164
biology, 58, 67, 85, 88, 130, 140, 169, 172, 197, 198, 203
Bird Lovers, Backyard (Field), 56, 59, 62–69
Blake, William, 66
Blanchot, Maurice, 183
blog, 24, 30, 94, 180
Blood and Guts in High School (Acker), 175
Blue Guide to Indiana, The (Martone), 95, 97, 111
body, 10, 11, 21, 28, 32, 38, 56, 59, 60, 67, 71, 73, 75, 76–77, 80–84, 86, 89, 90, 92–94, 115–17, 119, 133–35, 137–38, 140, 149, 155, 175, 182–85, 197, 199, 204, 209, 216; of the book, 107–8, 120, 198, 201, 202–3, 216
Body of Martin Aquilera, The (Everett), 54
Bolter, David, 99
Boltzmann, 51
book, 1, 3, 6, 9–10, 17–19, 26, 28, 30, 32, 37–39, 45–53, 57–60, 62–64, 66, 68, 72, 74, 75, 77–78, 80–81, 84, 87–94, 98, 101, 105–8, 111, 114–28, 132–34, 136–38, 140–41, 151, 153, 155, 156, 158, 163, 164, 166, 167, 168, 170, 171, 174, 175–77, 183–90, 194–95, 197, 198, 199–204, 206, 207, 210–12; children's, 41; comic, 200, 201; interactive, 23, 38; and materiality, 11–12, 24, 97, 201–2
Book of Portraiture: A Novel, The (Tomasula), 3, 197–99, 204, 206, 207, 209, 211–13, 215
border, 83, 85, 86, 147, 156
Borges, 153, 167
Bosch, 165, 178
Bouyeri, Mohammed, 161, 173
Bowers, Neal, 98, 107
Braque, 176
Bravo, Manuel Álvarez, 92
Break Every Rule: Essays on Language, Longing, and Moments of Desire (Maso), 114, 116, 124, 128
breather, 140–41
Brecht, Bertolt, 62, 64–66, 68
Brodkey, Harold, 136

Brooke-Rose, Christine, 142, 146, 150, 156, 159
Brown, Dan, 167
Burnt (Olsen), 172, 181
Bush, George, 46, 47, 207, 217
Butler, Judith, 146, 149

Cain, Amina, 84
Caldwell, Christine, 83
Calendar of Regrets (Olsen), 160, 165, 176, 177, 180
Calvino, Italo, 158
Campbell, Laura, 84
cannibalism, 183
Cannonball (McElroy), 138, 140, 142
canon, 2, 161
canvas, 12, 49, 70, 200
capitalism, 4, 7, 30, 160, 191, 207
Carmody, Teresa, 78, 84
Carse, James, 65
Carter, Angela, 150
Cartland, Barbara, 170
Cavell, Stanley, 5, 14, 21
Cěch, Jiří, 24, 30, 31, 33, 34, 40, 217
cell phone, 20, 96, 106, 207
Cézanne, Paul, 11
Chang, Young-Hae, 169
chaos, 38, 58, 130, 155
character, 1, 13, 30, 31, 41, 42, 46–48, 52, 57, 61–63, 65, 66, 70–72, 76, 94, 105, 108, 109, 114–15, 118–19, 121, 131, 134, 145, 149, 152, 154–55, 157, 161, 164–65, 168, 175, 178–79, 182, 184–90, 193, 206, 209–10, 216–17
Charnel Imp, The (Singer), 182, 189, 195
Chekhov, Anton, 64, 100
chiasmus, 13
Chiasmus Press, 21, 167, 180–81, 214
choreography, 59, 71, 77, 116, 119, 122
chronology, 97, 124, 154
Churchill, Winston, 208
Circus of the Mind in Motion: Postmodernism and the Comic Vision (Olsen), 181
city, 60, 62, 71, 74, 78, 85, 88, 109, 110, 114, 131, 132
Cixous, Hélène, 83, 116–17, 149
Clarke, Brock, 156
cliché, 12, 107, 136, 138
Clinton, Bill, 37

closure, 56, 57, 115, 150
clown, 58, 64, 65
Coetzee, J. M., 171
Coleridge, 139
collaboration, 3, 4, 19, 23, 24, 56–57, 59, 60, 66, 77, 98, 102, 110, 122, 130–31, 136, 161, 167, 173, 175–76, 179–80, 197, 217
Collette, 124
colonialism, 47, 85, 87, 91–92. *See also* anticolonial
comedy, 61, 139, 141, 186, 187, 191
commercialism, 2, 26, 42, 166–67, 193, 197, 201, 207–8
computer, 12, 48, 58, 92, 100, 107, 110–11, 116, 178, 195, 202, 204
consciousness, 17, 18, 29, 31, 35, 38, 73, 87, 116, 161, 162, 165, 166, 171, 173, 177, 184
conservatism, 2, 31, 166, 174
contemporary, 1, 2, 3, 6, 7, 9, 29, 48, 72, 84–85, 89, 130, 132, 158, 161–62, 166, 169, 171, 197–98, 200
content, 2, 3, 8, 17, 24, 50, 58, 66, 67, 71, 80, 97, 107–8, 116, 121, 123, 126, 152, 173, 174, 176, 202, 207, 216
context, 3, 4, 12, 13, 16–18, 45, 57, 60, 71, 73, 76, 88, 96, 97, 99, 105, 108, 130, 150, 162, 185, 198
contributor's notes, 97, 107
convention, 1, 2, 5, 11–12, 20, 42, 46, 58, 88, 107, 115, 121, 141, 146, 172, 175–77, 199, 217
Cooper, Mark, 13
Coover, Robert, 5, 130, 155, 157, 166
Corin, Lucy, 169
correspondence, 3, 82, 96
Cortázar, Julio, 154
country, 44, 68, 71, 87, 127, 132, 138, 167, 193, 208, 211
creative writing, 26, 29, 80, 168, 169, 192
crisis, 9, 72, 77, 78, 136, 166, 169, 210
critical theory, 1
critifiction, 3, 160, 162, 163, 164
culture, 1, 2, 4, 7, 31, 38, 41, 45, 47, 48, 53, 61, 63, 67, 70, 73, 76, 80, 84–86, 88–90, 94, 99, 155, 160–61, 163, 165–66, 168–69, 170–73, 176–77, 180, 191, 198, 201, 207, 209
Currin, John, 184–85
Cutting Lisa (Everett), 54
cyborg, 81, 91–94, 140

Damned If I Do (Everett), 54
dance, 56, 59, 71, 119
Danielewski, Mark, 166, 174, 177
Darwin, 210
Davenport, Guy, 178
Davis, Lydia, 150, 166, 174
death, 24, 27, 30, 32, 35, 41, 68, 81, 86, 115, 123, 134, 151, 155, 165, 171, 177
deception, 34–35, 152. See also self-deception
deconstruction, 44, 110, 160
defamiliarization, 4, 65–66, 71, 145, 178, 217
Defiance (Maso), 114, 121–23, 128, 129
Delany, Samuel R., 168, 174, 181
DeLillo, Don, 142, 166
Derrida, Jacques, 14, 44, 45, 98, 149, 172
Desert, The (Bervin, Jen), 175
design, 29, 36, 100, 108, 136, 168, 176–77, 216. See also designer
designer, 107, 197, 202, 204. See also design
desire, 45, 49, 60, 73, 74, 83, 94, 99, 115, 117, 119, 188, 189
dialogue, 3, 45, 62–63, 71, 180, 188
diaspora, 80, 85, 87
Di Blasi, Debra, 1, 3, 23–40, 203, 215–18
Dickinson, Emily, 150
Dictionary of Modern Anguish (Berry), 6, 10, 11, 16, 18, 21
Difficult Imagination, 163, 171–73
digital, 1, 3, 25, 107, 111, 178
Di Leo, Jeffrey, 4, 7, 8, 21, 54, 129, 159, 180
Dirtmouth (Singer), 182, 183, 185, 195
discharge, 84, 86, 89
discourse, 10, 42, 46, 47, 51, 56, 62, 64–66, 93, 163, 216
DJ Spooky, 23
documentary, 93, 124, 189
Donne, John, 88, 90
Dos Passos, John, 62
Double or Nothing (Federman), 177
Double-wide (Martone), 112
draft, 48, 80, 83, 176
drawing, 23, 26, 32, 38, 39, 49, 72, 73, 116, 201, 210
Drought and Say What You Like (Di Blasi), 23, 24, 39
Drucker, Johanna, 58
Duras, Marguerite, 158
Dzanc, 142, 167

ecology, 57, 67, 130
economy, 8, 34, 36, 38, 87, 169, 194, 206, 210
editor, 19, 39, 51, 70, 100, 107, 134, 141, 166, 180, 193, 197
ekphrasis, 66
electronic, 4, 7, 10, 82, 145, 171; literature, 202
Electronic Book Review, 5, 21, 143, 212, 213
Eliot, George, 18
Ellipse of Uncertainty: An Introduction to Postmodern Fantasy (Olsen), 181
Ellison, Ralph, 64
Ellsworth, Michelle, 60
e-mail, 5, 7, 53, 57, 72, 82, 92, 96, 98, 99, 100, 106–8, 110, 145, 161, 198
embodiment, 24, 63, 94, 115, 131, 134, 164, 198, 200–3
entertainment, 8, 146, 171, 179, 201
entropology, 164
environment, 8, 17, 25, 29, 32, 61, 71, 89, 161, 170, 188
epic, 66, 88, 90, 94, 198
epigraph, 72
epistemology, 74, 130, 172, 174, 200
epistolary novel, 6, 41
Erasure (Everett), 41, 44–45, 47, 53–55
Erotic, 56, 115
essay, 5, 7, 8, 10, 18, 20, 42, 43, 46, 47, 56, 57, 70, 75, 91, 96, 110, 114, 116, 117, 123–24, 145–46, 150, 153, 162, 167, 169, 179, 198, 200; experimental, 24
essence, 32, 49
ethics, 1, 57, 64, 65, 167, 184–85, 198, 205
etymology, 25, 150
Evenson, Brian, 168
Event Factory (Gladman), 70, 71, 73–76, 78
Everett, Percival, 1, 2, 4, 20, 41–55, 215–18
exile, 125
Experimental Animals (A Reality Fiction) (Field), 68
experimental writing, 2, 3, 20, 21, 26, 46, 86, 90, 100, 130, 137, 150, 156–57, 160, 162, 183, 191–92. See also experimentation; innovative writing
experimentation, 2, 3, 4, 7, 12, 24–26, 29, 30, 38, 42, 46, 47, 50–51, 57–58, 67, 80, 86, 89, 94, 98, 107, 126, 134, 136–37, 139, 150, 167–68, 173, 177, 182, 187, 195, 198, 215–18. See also experimental writing

Extreme Fiction: Fabulists and Formalists (Martone), 112

fable, 145
family, 27, 35, 41, 82, 106, 114, 115, 126, 131, 133, 134, 158, 161
fanaticism, 63, 166
fantasy, 58, 63, 72, 115, 134, 146, 154
Farrell, Stephen, 197, 212, 214
father, 36, 87, 92, 111, 119, 131, 134, 135, 138, 139, 176, 210, 211
Faulkner, William, 157
Federman, Raymond, 120, 156, 159, 163, 168, 177, 178
Fellini, 64
feminism, 114–15, 140, 149–50, 190, 203–4
fiction, 3, 4, 6, 9, 12, 16, 18, 19, 20, 25, 26, 28, 29, 31, 37, 39, 42, 43–46, 56–59, 63, 64, 67, 90, 96–101, 104, 105, 108, 110, 115, 116, 119, 121, 130–31, 133, 140, 141, 144–49, 152–58, 160–68, 170–75, 177, 179, 182–94, 198–206, 215–17; contemporary, 1, 2, 7, 8, 10, 130, 157–58, 162, 167, 177, 197; electronic, 202; science, 162, 174
Fiction Collective Two (FC2), 3, 5, 19, 20–22, 40, 112, 160–61, 166–68, 180, 181, 193, 195, 212
Fiction's Present: Situating Contemporary Narrative Innovation (Di Leo and Berry), 4, 7, 8, 20–21, 54, 98, 129, 146, 159, 162, 180
Field, Thalia, 1, 56–69, 215–18
film, 12, 13, 23, 56, 57, 59, 66, 82, 89, 91, 99, 123, 131, 133, 136, 161, 164, 166–67, 173, 178, 183, 194–95, 198, 212. *See also* movie
flatland, 209–10
Flatland (Abbot, Edwin), 210
Flatness and Other Landscapes, The (Martone), 112
Flaubert, Gustave, 62
font, 9, 11, 25, 28, 66, 100, 161, 172, 175–76
footnote, 10, 31, 200, 203, 205
foreigner, 65, 71, 73–75, 115, 124, 173, 207, 218
For Her Dark Skin (Everett), 54
form, 2–4, 8, 13, 17–19, 24, 25, 28, 37, 41, 42, 52, 57, 58, 60, 66, 71, 78, 80, 84, 89–91, 93, 97, 99, 100, 107, 109, 114, 116, 120–23, 125–26, 131–32, 140, 146, 150, 162–64, 168, 174–76, 178–79, 183, 187, 200, 202, 206, 208, 216–18
formalism, 65, 66, 106, 174–76

formally innovative writing, 1, 3, 4, 8, 20, 161, 168. *See also* innovation
Forms at War: FC2 1999-2009 (Berry), 8, 21, 217
formula, 20, 120, 121
Fort Wayne Is Seventh on Hitler's List (Martone), 97, 112
Foucault, Michel, 205, 206
Four for a Quarter: Fictions (Martone), 96–98, 105, 110, 112
FOX News, 53, 211
fragment, 37, 47, 71, 73, 74, 80, 85, 91, 114–16, 118–20, 126–27, 132, 161
frame, 17, 39, 42, 52, 60, 61, 66, 81–82, 86, 97, 101–4, 108, 164, 199
Frame, Janet, 150
Frank (Berry), 6, 11, 13, 15, 21, 215
Frankenstein, 6, 13
Franzen, Jonathon, 157, 192
Freaknest (Olsen), 181
freedom, 60, 117–18, 121, 175, 200, 212, 217
french theory, 44
Frenzy (Everett), 54
Freud, Sigmund, 25, 100, 136–37, 168, 204, 206

Gaddis, William, 130, 183
Galileo, 209–10
Garcia Marquez, Gabriel, 158
Gass, William, 166
gender, 29, 114, 140, 145, 149–50, 170, 190, 198
genetic, 17, 130, 199, 200, 208–9; art, 2, 3, 198, 200, 204
genre, 1–3, 16, 23, 56–59, 62, 64, 80–82, 99, 115, 134, 145–46, 158, 161, 197, 202
geography, 38, 56, 216
geology, 130, 164
Ghost Dance (Maso), 114, 128
Gillis, Steve, 167
Girl Imagined by Chance (Olsen), 3, 160, 163, 176–77, 180, 181, 215
Gladman, Renee, 1, 3, 70–79, 215–18
Gluck, Robert, 82
Glyph (Everett), 42, 53
God's Country (Everett), 52, 53
Godard, 194, 201
Goldsmith, Kenneth, 88
grammar, 11, 13, 25, 32, 81, 182

Grand Canyon, Inc. (Everett), 54
graphics, 100, 122–23, 177, 197
Gravity's Rainbow (Pynchon), 170
Greenaway, Peter, 195
Grenzsituationen, 174
Grisham, John, 167
Grusin, Richard, 99

Half an Inch of Water (Everett), 54
Handke, Peter, 64
Haraway, Donna, 93, 140
Hawkes, John, 148, 188
Hayles, Katherine N., 178, 213
Head in Flames (Olsen), 161, 172, 175–77, 180, 215
Hearne, Vicki, 67
Hegel, 14
Heidegger, Martin, 14, 172
Hellman, Lillian, 34
Hermes, 111
Hideous Beauties (Olsen), 181
Hind's Kidnap: A Pastoral on Familiar Airs (McElroy), 130, 132–33, 139, 142
history, 2, 4, 20, 25, 29, 53, 57–64, 66, 84, 85, 87, 93, 97, 121, 123, 130, 132–33, 139–40, 162, 164–65, 173, 179, 184, 190, 197–99, 204, 211, 216
History of the African-American People (Proposed) by Strom Thurmond, A (Everett), 53
Hitler, 97, 207–8
Holland, Noy, 168
hollywood, 84, 194
Holocaust, 114
Homberger, Dominique G., 169
Hope, Bob, 108
Howe, Susan, 169
How to Unfeel the Dead: New & Selected Fictions (Olsen), 181
Huckleberry Finn (Twain), 53
Humanimal: A Project for Future Children (Kapil), 80, 82, 90, 92, 95
humanity, 16, 34, 90, 182, 198
humor, 6, 15, 20, 24, 42, 52–53, 65, 98, 131, 141, 145, 148, 154, 183, 186
Hunt, Laird, 178
Hutcheon, Linda, 166

hybridity, 57, 64, 67, 70, 80–81, 90, 94, 197, 216
hypermedia, 160, 169, 181. See also hypertext
hypertext, 1, 24. See also hypermedia

I Am Not Sidney Poitier (Everett), 41, 42, 53
identity, 41, 45, 57, 61, 64, 109, 115, 127, 131, 145–46, 150, 153, 161–62, 174, 182, 184, 190
illusion, 31, 42, 145, 153–54, 165, 178–79
illustration, 31, 37, 57, 59, 178, 215
image, 10, 25, 26, 28, 36–39, 47–48, 84, 86, 88, 117, 120, 126–27, 148, 163, 165, 175, 176, 178, 182, 184, 198, 202–3, 215–16
imagination, 20, 30, 62, 64, 65, 67, 86, 117, 131, 139, 145, 147, 152–54, 163, 165, 171, 176, 189, 193
immediacy, 99
improvisation, 3, 179, 184, 186, 188
IN & OZ (Tomasula), 197, 201, 210, 211, 212
Incarnate: Story Material (Field), 56, 57, 59, 60, 63, 68
Incubation: A Space for Monsters (Kapil), 80, 81, 92, 95
index, 107
influence, 1, 2, 12, 18, 29, 34, 46, 48, 110, 115–16, 119, 123, 124, 148–49, 176, 177, 190
innovation, 2, 3, 7, 20, 24, 41, 100, 146, 160, 168, 170, 173, 183, 216
Inquisitor's Tongue, The (Singer), 182, 183–86, 190, 193, 195
inspiration, 116–17
interdisciplinary, 2, 58, 60, 80
internet, 48, 107, 171
intertextuality, 123
interview, 1–4, 7, 19, 24, 26, 42, 48, 80, 82, 96–98, 103, 106, 110, 115, 124, 131, 145, 160–61, 179, 183, 197–98, 215, 217–18
intimacy, 1, 2, 67, 75, 77, 131, 133, 136, 141
Iphigenia, 165
Iraq, 8, 114, 140, 210
Irigaray, Luce, 149
italics, 100

Jackson, Shelley, 28, 60, 150, 156, 171, 214
Jaded Ibis Productions, 3, 23, 26, 30, 40
Jaffe, Harold, 168
James, Henry, 133, 183
Jameson, Fredric, 175, 180
Jasper, Karl, 174

Jealousy (Robbe-Grillet), 153, 175
Jetty, Spiral, 164
Jewett, Jamie, 56
Jirí Chronicles and Other Fictions, The (Di Blasi), 23, 24, 29, 30, 33, 37, 40
Jones, Stephen Graham, 168
Joyce, James, 14, 18, 20, 64, 100, 157, 171
Joyce, Michael, 28, 175
Juice (Gladman), 70, 72, 78
Jung, Carl, 137

Kafka, 161, 164
Kahlo, Frida, 115
Kandinsky, 66
Kapil, Bhanu, 1, 3, 60, 80–95, 215–18
Katz, Steve, 168
Kierkegaard, 14
Kincaid, James, 53, 55
King, Stephen, 171
King Lear (Shakespeare), 13
knowledge, 5, 16, 18, 21, 33, 63, 66, 115, 133, 188, 190, 192, 208
Kristeva, Julia, 124, 128
Kuhn, Thomas, 209
Kundera, Milan, 62
Kuppers, Petra, 89

landscape, 29, 49, 62, 97, 154
Lang, Abigail, 56, 60
language, 5–7, 10–13, 16, 18, 20, 25–26, 29, 32, 37, 41–42, 46, 49, 50–52, 56, 59–62, 65, 67, 70–78, 81, 83, 87–90, 96, 106–7, 109, 111, 114–17, 119–20, 122, 124–25, 135, 138–39, 145–51, 154–58, 162, 173–74, 182, 185, 199, 201–3, 205, 207, 216–17
layout, 37, 178, 202
LeCompte, Liz, 59
Leonardo's Horse (Berry), 5, 6, 11, 21
Leon Works, 3, 70, 95
letter, 4, 6, 30, 73, 92, 94, 96, 104–6, 109, 131, 134–36, 140, 147
Letter Left to Me, The (McElroy), 131, 134–36, 142
Levine, Peter, 84, 89
Lévi-Strauss, Claude, 164
Leyner, Mark, 158

limit, 12, 18, 24, 42, 90, 96, 98, 145, 147, 155, 162, 168, 173–74, 182–84, 187, 192, 216–18; text, 174
linearity, 28, 56–57, 71, 119, 130, 150, 203, 216
Lispector, Clarice, 150, 154–55
literature, 1–7, 9, 10, 12, 16, 18–20, 23, 25–26, 28–30, 33–34, 39, 41–42, 56–57, 61, 64, 66–67, 76, 85, 88–90, 97–99, 110, 114, 116, 121, 126, 145, 155, 157–58, 160–62, 167–70, 176, 183, 192, 194, 197–98, 205, 210–11, 215–18
litotes, 13
Live from Earth (Olsen), 175, 181
Lolita: A Janus Text (Olsen), 181
Lookout Cartridge (McElroy), 130, 133, 139, 140, 142
Lowe, Marc, 26, 40
Lutz, Gary, 169
Lyotard, Jean-François, 14, 164, 180, 191
lyrical, 115, 176

machine, 11, 48, 62, 100, 105, 107, 110, 180, 207, 210, 217
magazine, 31, 58, 110
Major, Clarence, 168
Malick, Terrence, 194
Mallarmé, Stéphane, 57
Malraux, André, 47
manipulation, 26–29, 34, 35, 37, 57, 101, 146, 178, 182
manuscript, 57, 80, 83, 84, 100, 216
Marble House Project, 144
Marcus, Ben, 22, 157, 171, 174
market, 58, 121, 140, 166–68, 193, 194; and marketing, 26, 39
Martone, Michael, 1, 3, 96–113, 168, 215–18
Maso, Carole, 1, 3, 114–29, 150, 171, 177, 203, 215–18
materiality, 4, 9, 10–12, 70, 71, 78, 97, 101, 107, 120, 161, 176–77, 198, 202, 213, 215–16
mathematics, 56, 115, 122, 201
Matisse, Henri, 20
Mazza, Cris, 168
McBurney, Simon, 59
McCarthy, Cormac, 188
McElroy, Joseph, 1, 130–43, 188, 215–18
McHale, Brian, 18, 21, 214
Medea, 190

media, 1, 3, 4, 10, 23, 25, 26, 29, 31, 35, 38, 48, 57, 58, 90, 96–101, 103, 110, 156, 166, 171, 178, 198, 216; literary, 2–4, 9–10, 21, 24, 37, 86–87, 96, 98, 99, 110, 136, 145, 178, 201, 204, 215–16

Medusa, 204

memoir, 82, 150–51, 156, 165, 179

memory, 25, 34, 75, 82, 84, 92, 114, 118, 153–54, 161, 172, 201

Memory Wax (Singer), 182–83, 190, 195

Mendieta, Ana, 86

metafiction, 77, 166

metamorphosis, 164, 188

Metamorphosis (Kafka), 161, 164

metaphor, 85, 132, 137–38, 163, 165, 177, 198, 202, 206, 210

Metaphorics of Fiction: Discontinuity and Discourse in the Modern Novel, A (Singer), 182, 183, 195

MFA, 80, 96, 172, 193

Michael Martone (Martone), 96, 97, 107, 112

Middle Mind, The (White), 171

midwest, 96–97

migration, 85, 87–89, 93

military, 8, 28, 62, 156, 211

Milletti, Christina, 2, 144–59, 215–18

Mitchell, David, 166

mixed-media, 31. *See also* multimodal

modernism, 7, 8, 18, 157

monster, 81, 93, 94, 204

Moore, Michael, 176

Morrison, Bill, 56–57

Morrison, Toni, 174

mother, 81, 87, 90, 91, 94, 111, 126–27, 135, 139, 140, 144, 148, 150–51, 208, 210

Mother and Child (Maso), 114–15, 126–28

Moulthrop, Stuart, 175

movie, 31, 47, 99, 131, 170–71, 194, 201, 212. *See also* film

multimedia, 3, 29, 32, 38, 56–57, 195, 198. *See also* mixed-media; multimodal

multimodal, 3, 4, 24. *See also* mixed-media; multimedia

music, 2, 20, 23, 24–25, 30, 33, 38, 39, 60, 66–86, 111, 116, 119, 162, 165, 175, 177, 198, 201, 202; and song, 31, 32, 98, 201

My Dates with Franz (Olsen), 181

myth, 15, 41, 57, 61, 97, 131, 145, 180, 190–91, 198

Nabokov, 138, 146, 158, 172, 179

narrative, 2, 4, 6, 9, 13, 14, 18, 23, 25–29, 31, 37–38, 47, 50, 56–57, 59, 62, 67, 70–71, 73–74, 78, 80–85, 89, 92–93, 98–99, 100, 114–15, 118–23, 127, 130, 132–34, 137, 140–41, 150, 153–56, 162–65, 171–73, 178, 182–83, 187, 188, 199, 201–7, 211, 216. *See also* narrator

narrator, 1, 6–7, 9–11, 15, 34, 45, 61 73, 74, 75, 76, 81, 126, 130, 132, 144, 151–53, 156, 163, 183, 187, 188, 203–7. *See also* narrative

Nashe, Thomas, 183

National Endowment for the Arts (NEA), 170

Native American, 52

naturalism, 46, 67, 155

nature, 13, 15, 131, 147, 172, 209–10; human, 34, 38, 186

negation, 13, 15, 25, 28, 64, 72, 81, 88, 152, 164

Newcomer Can't Swim (Gladman), 79

New Criticism, 171

New Directions, 39, 58, 68

new media, 4, 23, 48, 99, 110, 178, 194, 198, 216. *See also* new technology

new technology, 48, 194. *See also* new media

Nietzsche, 161, 164, 172

Nietzsche's Kisses (Olsen), 160, 161, 180

Night Soul and Other Stories (McElroy), 130, 131, 138, 139, 142

Nightwood (Barnes), 188

Nin, Anaïs, 150

Nixon, 35

Nobel Prize, 208

Not Normal, Illinois (Martone), 112

Not Right Now (Gladman), 79

novel, 5, 6–9, 12, 18–20, 23–27, 41, 45–48, 50–52, 58–59, 66, 72–73, 76, 78, 89, 90–91, 94, 114–15, 120–21, 126–27, 130–36, 138–41, 146, 148, 150–53, 155, 156, 158, 160–61, 163–65, 167, 169–70, 172, 174–77, 180, 182–87, 189–91, 194, 197–202, 204–7, 211, 216

novella, 23, 37, 131, 164

O'Connor, Flannery, 26

Ogden, Pat, 84

Oliver, Akilah, 60

Olsen, Andi, 3, 175, 176, 178, 179

Olsen, Lance, 1, 2, 3, 160–81, 215–18

Olson, Toby, 168
Once Human: Stories (Tomasula), 197, 198, 203, 209, 211, 212
One that Got Away, The (Everett), 54
opera, 59, 68, 200
orality, 76
originality, 4, 24, 26, 98, 108, 188, 217
Orlan, 201
Orwell, George, 206
Osman, Jena, 60
Otherwise (Di Blasi), 32
Oulipo, 147, 157
Ourednik, Patrik, 169

pagination, 1, 7, 11, 175, 198, 207
painting, 11, 20, 25, 27, 39, 49, 50, 99, 109, 110, 122, 153, 178, 191, 194, 195, 198, 199, 201, 207
paradox, 20, 61, 66, 70, 105, 133, 145, 147, 148, 158, 184, 188
parody, 6, 42, 44, 52
Pascal, 139
pastoral, 132
patriarchy, 3, 114
Pavic, Milorad, 169
Pelton, Ted, 167
Pensées: the Thoughts of Dan Quayle (Martone), 112
Percival Everett by Virgil Russell (Everett), 54
Perec, Georges, 147
performance, 56, 59, 60, 64, 76, 80, 83, 86, 87, 89, 94, 105
Perloff, Marjorie, 174
Philosophical Investigations (Wittgenstein), 12
philosophy, 2, 4, 7, 14, 31, 45, 65, 98, 136, 172, 205
photography, 3, 25, 86, 92, 99, 106, 111, 160, 163, 164, 176–78, 198, 199, 205
physical, 7, 10, 11, 23, 26, 27, 28, 46, 48, 56, 57, 66, 70, 71, 76, 82, 96, 100, 101, 111, 115, 116, 117, 119, 138, 140, 145–46, 163, 182, 184, 185, 198, 208, 216
Picasso, 125, 176
Picture Feeling, A (Gladman), 79
Piscator, Erwin, 65
Place, Vanessa, 78, 168
Place of Sense: Essays in Search of the Midwest, A (Martone), 112

plagiarism, 98, 107
Plane Geometry and Other Affairs of the Heart (Berry), 5, 6, 11, 22
plot, 1, 6, 13, 119, 120, 133, 144, 145, 150, 152, 154, 157, 163, 165, 168, 175, 178, 179, 190, 203, 204, 212
Plus (McElroy), 130, 131–35, 138–40, 142, 143, 217
Poe, Edgar Allan, 66
poetry, 20, 24, 30, 32, 50, 56, 57, 64, 70, 71, 73, 74, 80, 81, 84, 89, 98, 106–7, 114–16, 119, 120, 139, 145, 150, 160, 163, 169–71, 182, 199, 201, 202, 211
Point and Line (Field), 56, 58, 59, 60, 63, 65, 66, 68, 69, 215
politics, 1, 2, 7, 19, 24, 25, 34, 35, 41, 42, 46, 52, 53, 57, 62, 84, 86, 87, 101, 121, 139, 140, 145, 146, 155–57, 161–63, 167, 170–75, 183, 192, 198–99, 207–9, 217–18
portrait, 61, 82, 87, 154, 199, 203, 215
postcard, 4, 96, 101–4
postmodernism, 2, 14, 18, 147–48, 155, 160, 162, 164, 166, 198, 206, 207
power, 26, 67, 86, 133, 136, 138, 145, 146, 147, 150, 155, 157, 160, 169, 187, 193, 198, 209
Prayers of an Accidental Nature (Di Blasi), 23, 24, 34, 37, 40
pregnancy, 91, 114, 125, 203
Preparations for Search (McElroy), 131, 142
Prince, Daisy, 66
print, 1, 9, 11, 23, 28, 37–39, 58, 100, 107, 108, 132, 135, 167
prison, 35, 60, 115, 121, 194
process, 1, 4, 6, 14, 17, 18, 24–26, 28, 29, 34, 50, 53, 57, 61, 66, 77, 80, 81, 83, 85, 88, 90, 94, 96, 98, 115–16, 120, 130, 133, 139, 142, 148, 158, 161, 164, 166, 174, 176–78, 179, 182, 186–87, 215–16
prose, 3, 24, 42, 58, 64, 70–74, 80, 84–85, 90, 115, 131, 146–47, 150, 155, 157, 162, 163, 165, 175, 183, 187, 215, 216
Proust, 138
publishing, 3, 4, 5, 7, 19, 20, 23, 24, 26, 28, 30, 33, 34, 39, 41, 47, 51, 68, 70, 80, 91, 92, 97, 98, 100, 101, 107, 108, 125, 136, 161, 162, 166–68, 170, 180, 182, 185, 193–94, 202, 217
Pynchon, Thomas, 130, 166

Queneau, Raymond, 158

race, 41, 45, 52, 83, 93, 208; and racism, 83, 87, 89, 93, 206
Racing in Place (Martone), 112
Rae Thon, Melanie, 168
Rather, Dan, 165
Ravicka, 71, 75, 76, 78
Ravickians, The (Gladman), 70, 71, 74–79
re: f (gesture) (Everett), 50, 54
Reagan Library (Moulthrop, Stuart), 175
realism, 6, 72, 98–100, 110, 116, 134, 136, 145, 153–57, 168, 172, 178, 192, 203
reality, 4, 7, 10, 11, 19, 35, 41, 90, 100, 127, 128, 140, 145, 149, 152, 154–57, 161, 163, 172, 179, 194, 216
Rebel Yell: Writing Fiction (Olsen), 181
Reed, Ishmael, 166
religion, 13, 38, 173, 198, 218
Religious and Other Fictions, The (Milletti), 144–45, 152, 159
remediation, 99
repetition, 29, 80, 146, 186
representation, 2, 3, 10, 12, 14, 46, 49, 50, 52, 61, 74, 99, 146, 150, 160, 161, 162, 163, 197–99, 201, 203
research, 2–4, 23–25, 29, 32, 83, 85, 91, 93, 94, 115, 120, 131, 156, 164, 182, 183, 189–91, 197–200, 215–16
resistance, 42, 47, 56, 58, 61, 88, 140, 146, 147, 157–58, 167, 172–73
Reynolds, Susan Salter, 48, 54
rhetoric, 25, 38, 62, 108, 136, 149, 211
Rice, Doug, 168
Rilke, Rainer Maria, 136
Robbe-Grillet, Alain, 153–54, 175
Room Lit by Roses: A Journal of Pregnancy and Birth, The (Maso), 129
Rossi, Aldo, 72
Rothschild, Babette, 84
Rules of Thumb (Martone), 112

Safety Patrol (Martone), 112
Saramago, José, 166
Sarraute, Nathalie, 58, 150
Sartre, Jean-Paul, 147
Saruya, Toshiro, 60
satire, 16, 41, 103
Scalapino, Leslie, 168
Scherzi, I Believe (Olsen), 181

Schizophrene (Kapil), 80, 81, 85, 87, 88, 93, 94, 95
schizophrenia, 80, 87, 88, 93
Schmidt, Arno, 158
Schneiderman, Davis, 23
science, 2, 17, 25, 62, 64, 67, 68, 122, 130, 131, 134, 136, 138, 201, 205, 216
Sedlack, Robert, 204, 212
Seeing Eye (Martone), 112
Self-Deceiving Muse: Notice and Knowledge in the Work of Art, The (Singer), 182, 183, 185, 195
self-deception, 10, 34–35, 152, 183, 185, 188, 194. *See also* deception
self-reflective, 162, 169, 187
semiotic, 49, 51, 202
setting, 39, 51, 82, 91, 132, 144, 189
Sewing Shut My Eyes (Olsen), 181
Shakespeare, 119
Shaw, George Bernard, 87
Shelley, Mary, 6, 13, 81
Shepard, Sam, 34
Shklovsky, Viktor, 65–66, 172
Shneiderman, Davis, 23
short story, 19, 31, 155, 160, 167, 177, 200
silence, 71, 81, 86, 115, 119, 125, 177, 179
Singer, Alan, 2, 182–96, 215–18
Singh, (Reverend) Joseph, 82, 91
Skin of the Sun: New Writing (Di Blasi), 23, 37–40, 215
slavery, 53, 174, 204–5, 210–11
Smith, Patti, 25
Smithson, Robert, 164
Smuggler's Bible, A (McElroy), 130, 132, 141, 142
Sorrentino, Gilbert, 137
sous-rature, 14–15
Spahr, Juliana, 85
spatial, 27–28, 35, 57–58, 70, 81, 116, 118–20, 122, 177
Spector, Phil, 38
Spielberg, Peter, 168
Spinoza, 184–85, 188, 195
Spitz, Mark, 108
Spooky, DJ, 23
stage, 57, 59, 62, 103, 179
Steel, Danielle, 167

Stein, Gertrude, 6, 14, 20, 62, 146, 150
stereotype, 29, 31, 46, 58
Sterne, Laurence, 62, 183
Stevens, Wallace, 171
storytelling, 2–3, 20, 23, 42, 62, 63, 64, 90, 147, 165, 186, 191
Stranahan, Abbot, 56
Stravinsky, Igor, 20
Strickland, Stephanie, 169
Subject as Action: Transformation and Totality in Narrative Aesthetics, The (Singer), 182, 183, 195
Suder (Everett), 54
Sukenick, Ronald, 168
Swimming Swimmers Swimming (Everett), 54
syntax, 32, 81, 82, 85, 87, 130, 150, 175, 177, 185
system, 26, 65, 67, 73, 75, 76, 94, 105, 111, 121, 131, 138, 139, 140, 147, 171, 200, 206, 208; nervous, 28, 84, 89, 90; theory, 29
S/Z (Barthes), 44

table of contents, 107–8
taboo, 183
Tarkovsky, Andrei, 123
teaching, 26, 73, 92, 98, 99, 100, 122, 124, 154, 157, 167, 168, 169, 171, 180, 192, 197, 211
technology, 2, 4, 9, 23, 24, 28, 39, 48, 56, 89, 111, 130, 131, 136, 138, 194, 198–99, 201, 216
territory, 27, 60, 64, 81, 85, 107
Thanatos, 25, 27
theater, 44, 56, 58, 99, 184, 187
Theories of Forgetting (Olsen), 181
theory, 3, 4, 27, 29, 32, 81, 94, 109, 116, 117, 131, 136, 146, 149, 150, 162, 163, 164, 169, 171, 172, 183, 184, 188, 189, 191, 194, 201, 203; chaos, 130; critical, 1; field, 130; French, 43–44; literary, 33, 43, 183, 190
Thon, Melanie Rae, 168
Time Famine (Olsen), 181
To after That (Toaf) (Gladman), 79
TOC: A New-Media Novel (Tomasula), 197, 198, 202, 203, 211, 212, 213, 215, 216
Tomasula, Steve, 2, 3, 168, 169, 175, 178, 197–214, 215–18

Tonguing the Zeitgeist (Olsen), 175, 180
Townships: Pieces of the Midwest (Martone), 96, 112
translation, 13, 15, 71, 74–75, 165, 175, 201
trauma, 63, 84, 89, 90, 93, 206
travel, 28, 71, 73, 81, 82, 88, 114, 124, 133, 165, 176
Tree of Life (Malick), 194
truth, 6, 12, 13, 35–37, 44, 57, 64, 97, 127, 128, 135, 137, 145–46, 149, 151–52, 156–57, 172, 182–83, 198, 205, 207, 216
Trying Fiction (Martone), 113
Tulli, Magdalena, 74
Turin, Luca, 27
Twain, Mark, 53
twitter, 4, 96, 98, 105, 110
typewriter, 10, 48, 99, 100, 176

ULULU: Clown Shrapnel (Field), 56, 57, 58, 62, 65, 66, 68
Unconventions (Martone), 98, 113
university, 5, 13, 32, 41, 42, 56, 70, 80, 82, 83, 85, 89, 92, 96, 100, 102, 114, 130, 144, 160, 168, 169, 171, 182, 192, 197
Unnamable, The (Beckett), 170, 177
unwriting, 6, 13–15, 87–88, 161
Updike, John, 178

van Gogh, Vincent, 161, 164, 173, 176
VAS: An Opera in Flatland (Tomasula), 3, 22, 175, 197–203, 205–7, 209–15
Velázquez, Diego, 204, 207
Vertical Interrogation of Strangers, The (Kapil), 81, 95
Vogel, Danielle, 73
voice, 19, 30, 44–47, 58, 60, 62, 66, 77, 81, 82, 87, 108, 123, 126, 133, 134, 137, 138, 141, 151, 153, 161, 166, 169, 172, 175, 177, 179, 183, 187–88
voyeur, 84, 149

Wagner, Richard, 161
Walk Me to the Distance (Everett), 54
war, 8, 25, 35, 38, 46, 87, 88, 89, 90, 93, 120, 123, 127, 206, 210–12, 217
Water Cure, The (Everett), 41, 46, 47, 50, 54, 215–17
Watershed (Everett), 45, 51, 54

Weather and Women Treat Me Fair, The (Everett), 54
Wenderoth, Joe, 174
West, Paul, 158, 159
western, 41, 47, 49, 52, 176, 204
What the Body Requires (Di Blasi), 24, 40
White, Curtis, 168, 171–72, 180
White, Hayden, 165
White, Susan, 23
white space, 11–12, 31–32, 49, 58, 70, 80, 115, 118–20, 157, 176–77, 215
Wilde, Oscar, 66
Wiley, David, 60
William Gibson (Olsen), 181
Williams, Tennessee, 34
Winesburg, Indiana (Martone), 113

Wittgenstein, 5, 12–14, 18–19, 43, 149, 163
Women and Men (McElroy), 130, 131, 134, 136–37, 140–42
Woolf, Virginia, 62, 100, 150, 155, 157
wordplay, 7, 120
Workshop, 25, 33, 100, 102, 136, 168–69, 193
Worstward Ho (Beckett), 168, 180
Wounded (Everett), 45–46, 54
writing program, 80, 99, 168–69

Yuknavitch, Lidia, 167, 168
Yuskavage, Lisa, 184

Zingg, Robert, 91
Zola, Emile, 62
Zulus (Everett), 51, 54